Sanctuary is not simply a physical place of safety. It is a state of mind. Since its foundation in 1970, the Arbours Association has been providing sanctuary for people in great emotional turmoil, without their having to be seen, called or treated as 'mentally ill'. It has grown to include three residential communities, a crisis centre, a psychotherapy service and a psychotherapy training programme. This collection commemorates 25 years of work of the Arbours. It includes historical accounts and reflections by therapists, students and residents about this highly original approach to providing refuge within specialised therapeutic communities for people in severe distress.

The Arbours has often intervened on behalf of the most disturbed, the most chaotic, the most self-destructive individuals. They are often labelled 'borderline' or 'psychotic' in conventional psychiatric classifications, people whom other psychotherapists and facilities would not approach psychotherapeutically. One of the most striking features of this book is the detailed descriptions of the individual, group and institutional dynamics that provide the foundation of the Arbours' practical and theoretical accomplishments.

The distinguished psychoanalyst, Dr Nina Coltart, who contributes the concluding chapter, has written, 'I continue to observe the growth of Arbours with great admiration. They built a thorough analytic training for their students, created a low fee clinic for patients, established and nurtured their community houses, ran the Crisis Centre and earned themselves a unique and respected place on the London therapy scene.'

SANCTUARY

THE ARBOURS EXPERIENCE OF ALTERNATIVE COMMUNITY CARE

Edited by JOSEPH H. BERKE, CHANDRA MASOLIVER
and THOMAS J. RYAN

Process Press 'only purity of means can justify the ends'

London 1995

Published in Great Britain in 1995 by
Process Press Ltd
26 Freegrove Road
London N7 9RQ

A CIP record for this book is available from the British Library

The publication of this book was made possible by generous contributions by the
Planned Environment Therapy Trust.

ISBN 1-899209-01-8

Printed in the EC

*To everyone who has been, is or will be
involved with the Arbours, and to all who have
been touched or helped by our work*

CONTENTS

ACKNOWLEDGEMENTS

We would like to express our appreciation of the Planned Environment Therapy Trust (PETT) for covering the production costs of this book. This is one of many grants that PETT has provided to the Arbours Crisis Centre and communities over several years. The Arbours is very grateful for their support.

We also thank the Lord Ashdown Trust, which for several years has been providing two bursaries annually to cover the fees of promising students who are keen to train but in need of financial support.

And with thanks to Ann Scott for her calm and clear editorial overview and guidance in preparation of the manuscript.

The following chapters in this book have appeared, in some cases in slightly different form, in four issues of the *International Journal of Therapeutic Communities*: in vol. 10 no. 1 (1989) – Chapter 4 (as 'A year in the life of a therapeutic community: some considerations'); in vol. 11 no. 4 (1990) – Chapter 1 (as 'Twenty years on'), Chapters 3, 5, 7, 11, 14 (as 'The placement: my training ground'); in vol. 15 no. 1 (as *Therapeutic Communities: The International Journal of Therapeutic and Supportive Organizations*) – Chapter 8, Chapter 9 (as 'Personal reflections on being a resident therapist'); in vol. 15 no. 2 – Chapter 2, Chapter 6. Chapter 12 was first published in the *British Journal of Psychotherapy*, vol. 10 no. 3 (1994), and Chapter 17 in the *British Journal of Psychotherapy*, vol. 7 no. 2 (1990).

We thank Dame Iris Murdoch, Chatto & Windus, Ed Victor Ltd and Viking Penguin, a division of Penguin Books USA Inc., for kind permission to quote from the novel *The Black Prince*, © 1973.

NOTES ON CONTRIBUTORS

Joseph H. Berke has lived and worked in London since 1965. After completing his medical training in New York, he came to London to work with Dr R.D. Laing to advance his studies of the origin and treatment of psychosis, and he was one of the first residents of the Kingsley Hall community. In 1970 he became the co-founder and director of the Arbours Association, and in 1973 the founder and director of the Arbours Crisis Centre. Dr Berke has written many professional articles and books, including *Mary Barnes: Two Accounts of a Journey through Madness* (co-authored with Mary Barnes) and *The Tyranny of Malice: Exploring the Dark Side of Character and Culture*.

Ruth Cigman is a writer and philosopher who was a trainee therapist with Arbours.

Nina Coltart has been a psychoanalyst for over 30 years. The most enjoyable job she did within the British Psycho-Analytical Society was to be Director of the London Clinic of Psycho-Analysis from 1972–1982. Her first book, *Slouching Towards Bethlehem*, a collection of her papers, appeared in 1992, and her second, *How to Survive as a Psychotherapist*, in 1993. She is retiring from practice at Christmas 1994, 'to make room for all the other things I want to do before I'm too old, stiff or demented!'

Alexandra Fanning trained as a psychoanalytic psychotherapist with the Arbours Association. She was the first Chair of the Arbours Association of Psychotherapists and is currently Director of the Training Programme. She was a member of the Working Party of the original Rugby Psychotherapy Conference and is a delegate to the United Kingdom Conference for Psychotherapy. She is in full-time private practice as a psychoanalytic psychotherapist with a special interest in conjoint marital psychotherapy.

John Greenwood trained in counselling at Westminster Pastoral Foundation and in analytical psychotherapy with the Arbours, after a career as an international civil servant. He was a resident therapist for two years at the Arbours Crisis Centre. He is now counselling co-ordinator at Croydon Pastoral Foundation, teaches at Westminster Pastoral Foundation and Kingston College and has a private counselling and psychotherapy practice. He is a Diploma Member of the Institute of Psychotherapy and Counselling (WPF).

Peter Hudson worked for 20 years as a community development worker in Cardiff, Stoke-on-Trent and London. For 13 years he was Director of the Blackfriars Settlement, a multi-project youth, community and social work agency in the inner city. Since leaving the Arbours community in Crouch End, north London, in 1991 he has worked as a counsellor, trainer and organizational consultant and is currently Director of the Sutton Pastoral Foundation.

Julian Ibanez is a psychoanalytic psychotherapist who trained at Arbours and was a resident therapist at the Arbours Crisis Centre. He now lives in Bilbao, Spain, and works in private practice and provides training for health care professionals.

Saeunn Kjartansdottir was a nurse before training with the Arbours Association. She is a psychotherapist in private practice in Reykjavik, Iceland. She also works as a group therapist and a supervisor in a psychiatric hospital.

Ron Lacey has written and broadcast extensively on mental health and human rights issues. He was formerly Campaigns Director at Mind, and now works as a freelance writer and lecturer. He trained and practised as a social worker and as a psychotherapist but now regards himself as an informed layman and commentator. He lives in London.

Chandra Masoliver began her training as an analytic psychotherapist with Arbours in 1974. She is now a house co-ordinator and a member of the Training Committee. She also has a private practice and has published widely in the Arbours *Journal*. In the 1960s and 1970s her poetry was published as part of the 'Seven Women' group, and in *One Foot on the Mountain*, a feminist anthology. She has two children and a grand-daughter. She has recently written a cookbook with her partner, David Marsh. She enjoys writing, pottery and travelling.

'Matilda' is a resident of an Arbours community, having previously experienced in-patient and out-patient therapy on the NHS. She is now doing a degree in psychology as well as working in a voluntary capacity with children.

Trinidad Navarro gained an honours degree in psychology as a mature student. She has worked within mental health for 10 years, most recently leading an innovative outreach team working in Haringey, north London, with homeless people experiencing profound mental distress. During this time she completed her psychotherapy training with Arbours. She is currently Assistant Director for Care Practice in Tulip (Haringey Mental Health Group), and also sees patients privately.

Stella Pierides is a psychoanalytic psychotherapist in private practice and team leader at the Arbours Crisis Centre. She lives in London.

Sally Rose is a psychoanalytic psychotherapist who trained at Arbours. She worked both as a resident therapist and as a team leader at the Arbours Crisis Centre. She now lives in Leeds and works at the Women's Counselling and Therapy Service and in private practice.

Thomas J. Ryan is an American psychotherapist living in London who has been involved with the Arbours Association for the past 25 years. In addition to his work as Community Co-ordinator, he divides his time between teaching, various clinical and administrative tasks within the Arbours, and a psychotherapy practice.

Andrea Sabbadini is a chartered psychologist, a psychotherapist and a psychoanalyst living in London. He was director of the Arbours Training Programme from 1977 to 1992. Alongside his analytic practice, he supervises and teaches for various psychotherapy organizations. He has published extensively in the professional journals.

Irene Bruna Seu trained with the Arbours from a background in philosophy and psychology, and now teaches on the training programme. She works part-time as a psychoanalytic psychotherapist in private practice, and lectures for the Centre for Extra-Mural Studies at Birkbeck College, London, in psychology, counselling and women's studies. She is a research fellow at University College London and is currently writing a PhD thesis on 'Shame in women' from a psychoanalytic and feminist perspective.

Alasdair Stokeld was a resident therapist at the Arbours Crisis Centre from 1986 to 1988. He is presently an adult psychotherapist with the NHS in Manchester and in independent practice, teaching and supervision in Leeds.

EDITORS' NOTE

We have changed the names of all guests and residents. Pseudonyms are indicated by a first name in quotation marks on first usage.

INTRODUCTION

JOSEPH H. BERKE, CHANDRA MASOLIVER and THOMAS J. RYAN

Since 1970, Arbours has meant sanctuary, asylum and refuge for a large variety of people. Some may have never previously needed help, while others may have spent a decade or more in a mental hospital. All brought an equally varied array of difficulties, from fragmented selves to frozen hearts. Therefore we have chosen to call this book *Sanctuary*, to indicate what we have done and what we are still trying to do. We intend that this book should give clear, direct, accessible accounts of our communities, Crisis Centre and Training Programme from many perspectives – those of our therapists and students, as well as the residents of our communities and guests at the Crisis Centre.

The Arbours was founded by Drs Joseph Berke and Morton Schatzman. The name Arbours comes from the temporary dwelling places in which the Israelites lived in the wilderness after the Exodus from Egypt. Similarly, the Arbours was established to provide places of shade or shelter, sanctuaries, if you will, for people passing through chaos and confusion, a psychic wilderness, until such time as they could discard their emotional servitude and achieve a more fruitful life.

The first Arbours community came about when Morton Schatzman and Vivian Millet decided to share their home with people diagnosed, or diagnosable, as schizophrenic. In the ensuing two years, the Arbours made several attempts to found a more structured community. All were scuppered by alarmed neighbours. One example, in particular, shows the extent to which the fears of violence and bizarre behaviour attributed to the 'mentally ill' may be projections of one's own inner turmoil. Late in 1972 we were told that we could rent an unused church hall to establish a new community, the forerunner of the Crisis Centre. Yet no sooner than the word got out than we were ferociously obstructed by a hastily organized group of local residents. At a public meeting held between members of the Arbours and the neighbours, their concerns were vociferously voiced by one man. The audience applauded as he shouted that the women and children of the neighbourhood would not be safe to walk the streets if Arbours had use of the hall. He was convinced that there would be violence, rape, perhaps even murder, perpetrated by the residents of our proposed community. Needless to say, his speech carried the vote.

Months later this man came to our attention again, when he was referred to us by his lover. He was found with a shotgun in his car outside her flat. He thought she was seeing another man and out of jealous rage seemed intent on committing a crime of passion. Fortunately, no one came to any harm. He willingly saw one of our therapists for a short time until the crisis abated. But the incident does demonstrate how private passions become projections that can affect public policy.

About the same time that Morty and Vivian opened their house, we found a large house in the tranquil suburb of Norbury, south-west London, to establish a second community. In many ways it was more like a commune than a traditional therapeutic community. There were no fixed rules for people, some of whom came as helpers, eventually realizing that what they really needed was help. Some came in a very shaky state but, through the strength they gained from the setting, became insightful and sensitive helpers. Others became involved in a messianic mission and left, taking a resident or two with them. This was the atmosphere of the Sixties and early Seventies.

This early community was loosely based on Kingsley Hall, an experimental therapeutic community established in east London in 1965 by Dr R.D. Laing and his colleagues. In part, it was founded on the premise that psychosis is a journey that could prove to be self-healing, if individuals were allowed to regress, and if intervention could be kept at a minimum. But our experiences in these first communities demonstrated that there is a need for more rather than less intervention, when people regress or fragment. Subsequently, we have come to believe that a person in inner chaos needs a stable, supportive, external environment, rather than just a mirror of their internal state.

Nonetheless, we found that some people did not receive enough support and attention to feel contained within the independent ambience of the community. They became too entangled in their relationships, and their distress was too distressing to other residents. This stimulated us to start a new community where responsibility for providing care was clearly delineated in the form of resident therapists. This became our Crisis Centre. Tom Ryan and Sally Berry, who were the first residents to emerge as solid helpers at Norbury, contributed to founding the Centre. They moved into a quiet residential house in north London and invited three or four guests to live with them. Sometimes a whole family or a couple would move in. Mostly, people stayed for a short period of time, thus making it a crisis intervention centre. Occasionally someone would stay longer when they needed more sustained support.

Now the Arbours has developed into an interconnected network comprising long-stay communities in Crouch End, Brondesbury, and Muswell Hill (previously Norbury), the Crisis Centre in north London, a psychotherapy training programme, a psychotherapy service and the Association of Arbours Psychotherapists. Throughout these years of expansion our primary aim – of offering people in distress a psychodynamic therapeutic experience in a safe milieu, in other words a sanctuary – has remained the same. Some people come to us on medication; most eventually come off it, since it is no panacea. We never try to force the issue; however, with discussion by everyone involved, we do hope to provide a safe enough setting to enable most people to do without it in the long run.

The present Crisis Centre is now located in a much larger house. It can take up to six guests and the resident therapists have increased from two to three. The Centre still retains the feel of a home. Each guest has his/her own team, which consists of a resident therapist, a team leader and, when suitable, an Arbours trainee or other professional doing a placement at the Centre. After the initial consultation the team may continue to offer further consultations, make a referral to other agencies or offer a place at the Centre. The aim of the Centre is not simply to stop bizarre or disruptive experience or behaviour, but to contain it and make sense of it. Both the building and the therapists of the Centre provide this help by serving as temporary containers for intolerable rage, confusion and criticism.

Another change in the communities has been that the loosely defined role of helper has been formalized through the creation of the Training Programme. We have an Associates Year for people who would like to train with us; it also stands on its own, with a diploma given on satisfactory completion. This year provides the opportunity for us to know our students and for them to know us. At some time during their training students do a placement in one of the communities and in the Crisis Centre. Sometimes they live in, sometimes they visit; they become part of our support network. This is an absolutely invaluable learning experience, about both self and others, and is unique in British psychotherapy training. After about three years of training, students can start working as trainee psychoanalytic psychotherapists under close supervision. It is here that our Psychotherapy Service is of great value. It operates on a sliding scale, and it provides our students with their first patients. This also implements our belief that therapy should ideally be available to anyone, however low their income.

Over the last decade our communities have become registered care homes and the Crisis Centre is now registered as a nursing home. This has enabled us to continue to offer a high standard of housing and intensive therapeutic services to all who come to Arbours. It is important to us to maintain the status as registered care homes in order to finance people's stays in the communities and the Crisis Centre. It also means we can offer help to people lost in the system of Care in the Community, where they may otherwise land in unsuitable hotel-like accommodation, or on the streets. Paradoxically, our ability to provide help is now being jeopardized by the implementation in April 1993 of the government's White Paper on Care in the Community, 'The health of the nation' (1992), with its infinite ramifications of across the nation rules and provisos.

Our first meetings with Borough Registration Officers for Care in the Community felt ominous. The Borough, in compliance with the Registered Homes Act (1984), informed us that: 'There must be at least two members of care staff permanently on duty in the home throughout the waking day. For some residents it may well be that they do not need this level of staffing, but in such circumstances the establishment will not fall within the provisions of the Act and should deregister' (Haringey Social Services, 1987, p. 24). This was a Catch 22 problem: how to explain that 24-hour care was not always about physical presence, but psychological need.

Moreover, the language used was an anathema to us. We had to call ourselves 'Care Homes' and prominently display a notice in each community stating that 'We provide board and care for 8 people of either sex with a mental disorder other than mental handicap past or present'. The co-ordinators are here named 'joint officers in charge'. We were to 'run' our houses with 'user participation'. We were to have a 'core mission'. The Crisis Centre was to be an 'acute care service'; the Consultation Service an 'assessment facility'. People out there became a 'target population'. We were to have 'market-orientated projects', 'care plans', 'complaints procedures' and typed menus.

All of this goes directly against our fundamental aims and philosophy of providing home-like, non-institutional settings where emotionally distressed individuals can feel safe and contained enough to gather themselves together. We are not against being held accountable and responsible for what we do, indeed we welcome it. But the insistence of the present bureaucratic reforms can only have the undesirable effect of jeopardizing our carefully considered work. The present registration requirements do not differentiate between specific client groups. All the rules and regulations for residential care are based on the most dependent groups, the elderly and the mentally handicapped. However, the wholesale application of these regulations to our communities necessarily interferes with our therapeutic aim of helping our residents towards greater independence by actually fostering dependency.

In an early brochure we wrote:

> We feel it is more helpful and humane to give persons who have been or could become mental patients a chance not to be seen as mentally ill, called mentally ill, or treated as mentally ill. There are important reasons for this approach. The 'mentally ill' person tends to take on others' unsympathetic attitudes and abdicate responsibility for his life to outside authorities or institutions, all to his detriment. He may become typecast and see no possibility for himself other than to embark on a long-term career as a mental patient.

> We are aware that certain experiences and behaviour may be unusual. However, what is regarded as odd or bothersome in some social circles may not be seen that way in others. Many people who might otherwise be trapped within an ill identity need the opportunity and encouragement to come to terms with their problems. We intend that the Arbours should be a place where they may encounter selves long distorted and forgotten, where they can contain and regain their experiences, and achieve a sense of integrity and autonomy. In other words our task is to enable them to perceive and apperceive reality and to dream the dreams which are truly their own.

The book is in four sections. The table of contents reflects our practical emphasis. Since they were our first project, Part One focuses on our communities. We present the differing perspectives of the community co-ordinators, students and residents. Part Two concerns the Crisis Centre, so unique in helping individuals and families in distress. Then we describe the Training Programme and the Psychotherapy Service. Finally we explore the philosophical, sociological and psychological themes that underlie the Arbours experience.

The Communities section begins with 'Twenty-five years on'. Tom Ryan contrasts our original communal intentions and practices with those that have evolved over many years of working with severely disturbed men and women. Tom and his companion Sally Berry lived in our Norbury community for 18 months in the role of helpers, and then became the first resident therapists at the Crisis Centre. Both are now co-ordinators for our Crouch End community. Next, 'Confessions of a misfit' by 'Matilda' tells us what it is like to live in Arbours, from a young resident's point of view. She has been with us for some years and changed greatly during that time. In the words of the editor of *Therapeutic Communities*, the paper is a remarkable account of one young woman's painful and hazardous journey through the health system until reaching a therapeutic community where she could feel safe enough for long enough to embark on the inner journey she needed to take. There are lessons for the professionals here too, reminding us what it is like to be terrified, mystified, speechless, and quite excrutiatingly self-conscious, in the kinds of encounters we tend to take for granted. It is surprising how few first-hand accounts of their therapeutic community experience by residents have appeared in print. (Kennard, 1994, p. 76)

In 'A holding environment' Trinidad Navarro writes candidly about her experiences as a student on placement. She describes how she formed relationships with the group, and the battles she fought with parts of herself and the individuals in the community. She pays tribute to their bravery. Irene Bruna Seu was also a student when she wrote 'Rites of passage'. She tellingly addresses the problems created by lack of structure and definite roles and boundaries, and how she managed to find her own identity and space, and a way of being helpful. She found her preconceived ideas of being in the 'helping profession' were challenged.

Chandra Masoliver trained as a psychologist and then became fed up with the academic world. She was one of the first Arbours trainees, lived in Norbury with her children, and eventually became a co-ordinator in the same community. 'Learning co-ordination' describes the day-to-day realities of life in our Muswell Hill community and her role as co-ordinator. This paper, and those by Trinidad Navarro and 'Matilda' all complement each other by providing varying perspectives of the same community.

Closing this section is Saeunn Kjartansdottir's 'A community in crisis: a view from the kitchen', a dramatic and sensitive account of what happened when a new resident joined the Crouch End community and later killed himself. This had a devastating effect on the group and on each individual, and it was a very difficult experience for her.

Part Two opens with Joseph H. Berke describing the use of several therapists in a single therapeutic intervention. In 'Conjoint therapy within a therapeutic milieu: the crisis team' we see how it is possible for several therapists to work together on a shared or highly structured basis. Stella Pierides' poignant chapter, 'A savage sadness: journeys into space', focuses on how the Centre's human and physical resources provided 'Matthew' with a therapeutic space from where he could become involved in therapeutic work. Then, in 'On being a resident therapist at the Arbours Crisis Centre', John Greenwood, Julian Ibanez and Sally Rose examine the role of resident therapists. There are interesting descriptions of actions, behaviours and forms of verbal communication. The context ranges from team meetings to impromptu night-time gatherings.

Al Stokeld highlights links between the psychological and material aspects of containment in an unusual way in 'Building on metaphors'. While living in the Crisis Centre the physical environment can be seen as a psychic extension of the self, and a therapeutic atmosphere can be created and maintained. 'We never promised you a rose garden' was written by Peter Hudson when he suffered a breakdown after the break-up of his marriage and the loss of his job. After three months in a psychiatric hospital he stayed at the Crisis Centre for six weeks and then moved in to the Crouch End community. He came without hope, and slowly and painfully explored his feelings in the attempt to find some inner peace and the ability to rebuild his life. His chapter has the urgency of a lived experience.

The section closes with Joseph H. Berke's account of 'Psychotic interventions'. It is painful to see these circumstances when the designated patient and the therapist(s) treating the person may both revert to a psychotic state of thinking and action. Joe shows that a therapeutic milieu can allow people to regress and then reconstitute themselves.

Andrea Sabbadini was director of the Arbours Training Programme from 1977 to 1992. In Part Three his 'Subjective account' gives a frank historical review of the training's theoretical, ideological and institutional development, providing details of its structure and requirements. Alexandra Fanning, the present director of the Training Programme, then gives a lively personal account of the role of the placement in the training of the psychotherapist in 'Psychic muscles'. She feels the placement makes our training programme unique and stimulates the development of these 'psychic muscles', so important in her practice as a psychotherapist. The placement is also invaluable as a means of assessing trainees from diverse backgrounds, who might not be acceptable to a conventional training course.

Part Four opens with a chapter by a freelance writer specializing in mental health and related issues. Formerly Ron Lacey was Campaigns Director of Mind, the mental health charity, and he is the current Chairperson of Mind in Haringey, north London. He is an old friend of Arbours and a member of its Professional Advisory Committee. Ron's chapter describes the Arbours from its emergence as a pioneering service in the wake of anti-psychiatry in the Sixties to its current position as a radical alternative to mainstream psychiatric services.

Next, Ruth Cigman's chapter, 'Schizophrenia and the freedom to be irresponsible', poses the important question of whether so-called schizophrenics are responsible for their actions. She distinguishes between two meanings of the word 'responsible'. There are unconscious motives, intentions and fantasies behind an 'irresponsible' action. People given freedom in a safe context respond well to this understanding approach.

The final section closes with Dr Nina Coltart's warm account of her relationship with Arbours. She was a member of the Training Committee and the referral consultant for the Arbours' trainees for many years. Dr Coltart wrote her paper for our Twentieth Anniversary. 'Attention' centres on the Buddhist concept of bare attention and Bhavara, the cultivation of the mind, which aims to relieve suffering. So too do psychoanalysis and psychotherapy, where neutral attention to the immediate present is 'the sharpest and most reliable therapeutic tool'. Her criticism of clichés such as 'attention-seeking' and 'being manipulative' and her plea for courtesy and enjoyment are inspiring.

At times, however, even after 25 years, we feel like we are back to square one, having to fight battles that we thought were long won. At the moment we are trying to decide the best way to survive without losing sight of our fundamental aims and philosophy. Registration, with its demands for inspections and impersonal bureaucracy, inevitably impinges on our well-established ethos. Deregistration, on the other hand, brings financial insecurity. The proverbial double bind. How we proceed will depend on what best enables us to continue our work. This being said let us share with you what we have accomplished and what we are still in the process of trying to accomplish.

PART I

COMMUNITIES

1   TWENTY-FIVE YEARS ON

THOMAS J. RYAN

In the beginning, as the Introduction has said, the Arbours was influenced by the work of R.D. Laing, the Kingsley Hall community and the humanitarian ideals of the 'anti-psychiatry' movement. By the late 1960s, a growing number of professionals were voicing their objections to the inhumane and wasteful practices of the existing services, including the excessive use of psychotropic drugs and ECT. They were particularly alarmed about the harmful effects of hospitalization. It had become clear that the process of institutionalization itself damaged patients by stripping them of their rights, identity and autonomy.

These concerns provided the impetus for founding the Arbours, and for establishing the first household. In 1970 our second, larger project followed with the creation of the Norbury community in south-west London, loosely modelled, as the Introduction has said, on Kingsley Hall. Kingsley Hall had already demonstrated the possibility of an alternative approach, offering people who might have otherwise gone to hospital asylum in a communal setting that was respectful of their rights and needs.

The Norbury community was organized on a democratic basis with all residents having equal say in the daily management of the household. There were no staff and the firm lines between helper and helped typically found in more traditional settings were discouraged. This enabled residents to adopt different roles at different times according to their needs and the needs of the community. Therefore, they could avoid being typecast through the diagnostic labelling process. There were weekly house meetings convened by a non-resident therapist and residents were encouraged to be in individual psychotherapy. No limit was set on the length of stay; it was determined by the residents themselves.

I was one of the first members of the Norbury community, which to me always had the feel of an alternative commune rather than a traditional therapeutic community. In those early pioneer years the community attracted a broad mix of residents. They ranged from people with more of an intellectual and professional interest in our work to casualties of the existing psychiatric services. Whatever the interest or degree of distress, we all believed that we were participating in an important and unique experiment. The structure of Norbury, though, seemed to suit individuals who were not so acutely or severely troubled. The supportive yet liberal approach combined with their therapy enabled them to make real changes in their lives.

Yet Norbury prided itself on its capacity to accommodate a wide range of disturbed and oftentimes bizzare behaviour. I especially remember one young resident, 'John', who had spent a large portion of his life in hospitals. He was continuously plagued by hallucinations, and he always looked tense and troubled. Going places with John was always an event, as he would usually cause some minor disruption with his strange but often comical behaviour. He frequently engaged in the unusual habit of entering and leaving the house via the drainpipe, and, on occasion, to the great annoyance of the neighbours, he used to urinate from his bedroom window into the garden. Although he never truly participated in the daily life of the community, always positioning himself just on the fringe of the group, John was accepted by the other residents for over a year. Through living in the community, the quality of his life had been enhanced, but in the end his particular needs exhausted the emotional resources of the community and he had to leave.

During my 18-month stay at Norbury, there were several people like John who required active care and attention from the group. These residents did benefit from living in a supportive, non-institutional setting, but the community lacked the type of intervention necessary to be of any immediate therapeutic assistance to them.

This became painfully evident with the arrival of 'Ann', a young American woman, whose career as a mental patient spanned many years. She came with the definitive plan that she needed to regress and she set about trying to persuade the other residents to become caretakers in her elaborate self-devised programme. Essentially, she wanted the whole community to organize itself around her and her needs. Her lobbying did find some supporters, but a split soon occurred between them and those who were opposed to using the community in this manner. Collusions and alliances developed, creating an atmosphere of resentment and suspicion, which eventually led to an irreparable division within the community. Various members of the group attempted to bring these matters into the open, but it was insufficient to heal the existing tensions and rifts. As she became more frantic, Ann finally exploded, thus ending her short stay with a dramatic exit. Two other residents followed her, leaving the community both devastated and depleted.

These experiences demonstrated the need for more rather than less intervention. If the community was to be at all therapeutically viable for acutely distressed individuals, then we had to re-evaluate our basic premises without losing sight of the original aims and philosophy. From this the idea arose to found the Arbours Crisis Centre, which would offer 24-hour cover in a non-institutional setting. Sally Berry, my partner who had lived with me at Norbury, and I were the first resident therapists for this new project. We tried to provide a home-like setting where people in acute need would be invited as guests. Unlike the residents in the community, the guests were not expected to participate in the daily management of the centre; they were to be looked after and cared for. The introduction of a team approach provided the necessary structure to hold individuals in crisis. It also permitted a level of intervention that encouraged understanding and awareness. Over the years, both the number of resident therapists and guests have increased. But the primary aim, to provide a psychodynamic therapeutic approach in a safe and secure milieu, remains the same.

Eventually, we realized that the internal structure of the long-stay communities had to be reorganized, but we did not want to lose sight of our fundamental principles. The structure of the community required more supportive intervention without imposing a restrictive hierarchical regime. To achieve this the role of the visiting therapist was expanded to that of a co-ordinator. Instead of having a minimal say about the running of the community, the co-ordinator would have overall responsibility for its functioning. Furthermore, we decided there would be two co-ordinators, male and female, for each of the communities. In conjunction with the residents, they help to facilitate the domestic, financial and therapeutic aspects of the community. Each co-ordinator conducts one of the two house meetings per week, when individual and interpersonal issues are discussed. In this respect, the therapeutic function of the co-ordinator is similar to that of a family therapist who must constantly be aware of and responsive to the various dynamics and levels of interaction within a group.

There was an additional transformation with the introduction of a more precisely defined role of helper. Initially it was expected that the residents themselves would freely move between positions of helper and helped, according to their needs. However, this did not always prove effective in practice. For many residents, who were emotionally withdrawn for long periods, it was impossible for them to reach out or be available when needed. Of course, residents do benefit from being with each other, but the presence of a helper allows for a much-needed figure of stability, someone who can be available to intervene and become involved without becoming detrimentally entangled. This is an unpaid but supervised position, filled either by our own psychotherapy trainees or volunteers for a period between six and 12 months.

We have always viewed the quality of the physical environment as an integral part of our therapeutic approach. It has been important that the residents experience the community not as an institution, but as a home. Unless basic needs are met, it is almost impossible to address emotional and psychological problems effectively. Comfortable and aesthetically pleasing surroundings, in conjunction with the provision of good food, give the necessary basic security from which any change can take place. Also, residents have their own rooms, which ensures their entitlement to determine their use of time, space and privacy. Moreover, the community tries to enhance self-respect and a sense of autonomy by encouraging a sharing of responsibility for the domestic chores and management of the household.

A major therapeutic aim of the community is to help the residents to accept more responsibility, not just in the practical sense of learning to take care of themselves, but also emotionally, that is, to own or acknowledge thoughts, feelings or behaviour that may be experienced as alien to their definition of themselves. For example, 'Mary', a young resident of many years ago, used to cut herself or take an overdose whenever she was angry. Although her rage was apparent to everyone, Mary denied any such feelings and attributed blame for the resulting self-affliction to her voices, which continually instructed and persecuted her. An ongoing function of the community was to help Mary acknowledge these feelings and to integrate them into her sense of self. To varying degrees this is a task facing all of the residents. However, because they wish to avoid painful realizations or the confrontation of difficult conflicts, they sometimes resist accepting this responsibility through continuing to maintain a definition of themselves as ill.

If such a 'career' is to change at all, it will be through the rich web of interconnected levels of relating that is continuously present in the daily life of the community. Through awareness and understanding, residents may begin to disentangle themselves from what can be very constraining and distorted ways of perceiving and conducting relationships. The twice-weekly house meetings, which are conducted in a non-directive, psychodynamic manner, provide a structured setting where these and other issues can be discussed. The co-ordinators wear different hats at different times. Sometimes they help residents with actual problems, while at other times they help them to explore their fantasies. But they always need to keep abreast of the complex connection between the residents' internal world and the various levels of interaction and communication within the group.

While working within a therapeutic community, it is important not to lose sight of the practical and reality aspects of the group. Change cannot be effected by analytic interpretation alone. Of course, it is always a therapeutic prerequisite that meaning and significance should be identified and understood, but this task must always be tempered by good common sense. The uniqueness of the Arbours exists in the provision of a dynamic marriage between the psychological aspects of the individual residents and the more practical side of their lives.

The success of the therapeutic intervention within the community is dependent on its capacity to contain or to hold individuals while distraught. I have been increasingly impressed with the high level of acceptance that the residents have towards disturbing and sometimes unconventional behaviour. Even when emotionally encumbered, they still have the capacity to support and offer understanding to each other. During crisis periods residents and helpers contribute more time and attention to the disturbed resident by setting up rotas. Usually, this proves successful and the crisis subsides. Even though each community establishes a high degree of tolerance, there are times when limits are breached and the troubled resident may be asked to leave. Sometimes, depending on the nature of the difficulty, they may spend a short time in the Crisis Centre or, as is occasionally necessary, hospital. If the crisis extends over too long a period of time, or if the break between the community and the resident is irreparable, then he/she may be asked to move out of the community.

Until recently there has been an open-ended policy about the length of stay in the communities. This followed from our original ideas when our households were more like an alternative commune or family. People could stay as long as they liked and we considered them to be the best judge of when to leave. But we realized that since many of them were seriously damaged they would require a long time to resolve their difficulties.

Experience has demonstrated that for some residents an indefinite stay reinforces feelings of dependency and contributes to a general sense of inertia. However, after much deliberation, we have decided against establishing a fixed leaving date. We think that residents should fully participate in, and take responsibility for, these matters that crucially affect their lives. By initiating individual reviews, where residents can regularly consider what they want from the community and to think about their future plans, the question of leaving has become more of an integral part of their overall stay. This enables them to use the community more fruitfully, while providing sufficient time to work through their emotional problems.

Understandably, leaving the community may induce a crisis for many of the residents because of their fears and uncertainty about independence. This, combined with the real problem of finding appropriate and comfortable accommodation with little financial assistance in a large city plagued by housing shortages, greatly increases the level of anxiety. After living in a sympathetic, communal and somewhat sheltered environment, many of the residents cannot conceive of being on their own, especially if they have little contact with friends or family. Recently, a leavers group, open to the residents of the three communities, has been organized by two Arbours therapists to help with these issues. We have also taken steps to help the residents to find suitable housing. Moreover, the Arbours makes funds available for the continuation of the individual therapy for a six-month period subsequent to leaving. Residents are free to keep in touch with the community and other parts of the Arbours network, if they wish.

Over the years the changes and developments within the Arbours' long-stay communities have strengthened and improved their therapeutic effectiveness. This has not been without our making mistakes nor without our resources being tested to their limit; but, throughout, we have maintained our fundamental aim of providing an alternative therapeutic approach.

2   Confessions of a Misfit

'MATILDA'

I expect you might be wondering how I came to be living in a therapeutic community. To talk to and look at I seem pretty normal. I can't really tell you about the family problems I had, mostly because you would have heard it all before, and also my parents would just freak if they knew I had aired the family's dirty laundry in such a public way. All I can say is, in a nutshell, when you are a kid living in a misfit family you turn into a misfit to fit in and survive, and when you get out into the world you don't fit any more, so . . . well, you know the rest if you are the kind of person to be reading this!

I first came into the world of therapy when I was 17 and had just started boarding school. I was lonely and depressed, I guess, so I skived off my lessons and went to bed to try to escape. When the teachers discovered me in bed I took to sleeping under the bed! Many a time I heard the dormitory door squeak open, then heavy footsteps on the polished wooden floor, coming closer:

'Matilda? Are you in here? You should be in geography!'

I could just see the feet from under my bed . . . just the feet. They'd stop at my bed and look under the covers – I, of course, under my bed, would be praying my stomach didn't gurgle and betray me.

A teacher once asked me why I didn't work and I told her it was because I couldn't concentrate. She asked me if everything was all right at home, and I said yes. The most horrifying thing was I thought everyone's home must be like mine (and therefore 'All right') and they didn't seem unable to concentrate, so it just must have been something wrong in me – I must really be a nutcase.

After my first term I couldn't stand the place any longer, and I made an appointment with my old GP (against school rules) who referred me to a National Health Service out-patient psychiatric clinic for young people, and said he'd write to the school to let them know. When I got back to school I was immediately gated (not allowed off school grounds), and on the verge of being expelled. It turned out they thought I was pregnant!

I was a bit scared when I got to the clinic – I thought it would be all padded cells, straitjackets and injections – so it was a shock when I got there to find the waiting room with a fish tank in it, toys, and children's paintings on the wall. Eventually a grey-haired man appeared and gawped at me, you know the way psychiatrists do? Their eyes sort of stick out of their heads like you've just come rocketing down from Mars or something.

In the consulting room he took out a letter from the educational psychologist. 'It says here Matilda seems extremely immature for her age, giving the appearance of being only 12 or 13. What do you think about that?' What did I *think*? What was I supposed to say to that? I mean, I guess it was true enough I was somewhat emotionally behind the times, but I wasn't about to admit it to some stranger. Then I got the 'Tell me your history' bit, and 'How do you get on at school?' You know, the usual stuff. All the time he was gawping at me like he was expecting me to suddenly leap up and start swinging from the lampshade. It's enough to *make* you act mad, so I started answering in 'We're OK' rather than 'I'm OK'.

Anyway, he obviously thought I was enough of a case to come back again – it was the 'we' bit that probably did it. I didn't come again for a few months, then I came weekly to see this American lady which was great because it meant an afternoon away from school. I wasn't exactly articulate, and I guess my vocabulary was a bit backward, through not talking to adults much, I guess. I felt pretty grim but I could not show it. I'd just sit their smiling, swinging on the two back legs of my chair, not knowing what to say.

I did make a bit of progress, but not much, because people didn't want to be seen with me because they were worried what other people would say. It wasn't until I'd been there a year and some new girls joined the school that things changed.

Although I became less isolated at school I still couldn't work. I was under an enormous amount of pressure from home and I'd be up half the night trying to work. I'd get to a lesson tired out of my brains and sit down, my feet and hands like ice-blocks, and my head feeling like a boiled lobster. Someone would be picked to read. I'd try to follow but I just forgot. I'd have a countdown of how many minutes until the bell, and how many weeks until the end of term and pray the teacher wouldn't ask me to read. Then it would be 'Right . . . Who shall we have now? . . .

er . . . '. I could feel her eyes skimming the room, and I'd be thinking 'If I don't look at her maybe she won't see me . . . '.

'Er . . . Matilda.'

I'd look round the room hoping desperately I'd misheard, and to find out which page we were on.

'One hundred and seventy-five', she says tiredly. '*Do* try and keep up.'

I take a big breath. Maybe if I read fast enough I'll get to the end of my stint before I get a blank patch in my brain. I don't know what I'm reading. All my concentration is put into making the words come out as they should.

'Slow down, girl! It's not a race!'

Giggles from the others. Where's the lunch bell? I start up again like an old car . . . stutter, and come to a halt. The air is heavy waiting for me to go on, my heart is practically pounding out of my chest.

'Go on! You haven't finished yet.'

Pause.

'Cat got your tongue? I said carry on.'

I can't. It's no good. I just . . . Who are all these people staring at me? I look down at the page bewildered. I know I have to read but I just, well, have forgotten how to . . . A blank patch.

The pressure from home seemed to make me even worse. I took some of my mum's sleeping tablets, not realizing they'd make my speech go funny. I had a cutting problem by then as well. It was of course the most enormous embarrassing sign I was mad, so I told no one, and dreaded anyone finding out. Anyway, I went up to san and went berserk, so they called the doctor who could find nothing wrong with me. I could hardly say, 'I've just taken an overdose', or I'd have been expelled. The nurse told him what I'd done, that I'd acted a bit wound up, so what did he do? He gave me . . . wait for it . . . a sleeping tablet!

The next day I went to the clinic. I was dead scared someone would find out about my cutting myself and I'd get locked away for a hundred years. I was so desperate. I just couldn't for the life of me get it across. The session came to an end and it was just too much, realizing my only chance of being helped was over, so I walked out of the clinic, feeling unable to just go back to school. I mustered all the guts I had and found half a brick. I knew I had to do what I did next as if my life depended on it – I threw it at her window. The noise was a hell of a shock, so I ran off as fast as possible expecting the police to be after me. My therapy got better after that.

In the end I confessed about the cutting. She said if I did that I would not be allowed to see her and I was supposed to phone her up and she would cancel the session. Needless to say it just meant I had to keep this side to myself – and I wasn't getting any better.

Next I got 'asked to leave' school. This is so they don't have to write expulsion on their books or something. They were worried about me killing myself on school grounds. If they were that worried about it why they didn't contact the clinic I don't know.

I went to the careers office who suggested I went on a YTS (Youth Training Scheme) for learning-disabled people. Now I know I wasn't the academic pride and joy of my school, but I wasn't learning-disabled either. I went on the YTS and soon got bored, until we went on the work placements, where I didn't go. I was just so scared of all those adults, I just hadn't much experience of adults being civilized so I just couldn't go where there were large concentrations of them so I left the YTS.

I was getting more and more self-destructive and although the clinic said they wouldn't discharge me until I was ready they changed their minds.

My last meeting there was horrible. The consultant was there (the gawpy one I mentioned earlier) and my therapist. I kept my eyes on my therapist's boots – I had asked them if they would refer me to an in-patient adolescent unit I'd heard of. Well it was 'No way José' so what was the point of saying anything? They'd already decided my future and therapy wasn't going to be part of it. Eventually the consultant said 'You're discharged'. Just like that. It felt like the bottom of the earth had fallen out. Why wouldn't they listen to me?

My therapist said 'Goodbye Matilda'. I didn't say 'Goodbye' back because I didn't want it to be the end and I wanted to see her again. I never did, and now having *not* said goodbye I haven't resolved the ending, so I regret it now. It still gets to me that people who come to mean so much to you just march out of your life because you're just part of 'the job'.

Somehow I went back on YTS and promptly went berserk in college, so I got a counsellor who phoned up one day: 'We know somewhere that might help you . . . you spend five days a week and you sleep there. They help young people with their problems. We've made an appointment for you.' This, to them, was a tactful way of telling a young person they're going to an in-patient psychiatric unit, so we don't say 'I'm not a fucking loony, so piss off!' and slam the phone down.

I kept this secret from everyone. I knew I needed help, but it wasn't something I was about to advertise. If you say the word 'psychiatry' to some people they picture incoherent people with long collars and flares shuffling along totally out of their tree. When you're young nothing could be more untrendy than being different. You're desperately trying to fit in with the same clothes, slang, etc., and living in a psychiatric unit is just not part of it.

Ten weeks later I got admitted. The clinic had a 9–5 programme five days a week. We had a community meeting every morning, usually where the staff would bring up stuff that had happened the day before. If you were going to do something wrong it was a good idea to try to restrain yourself till after Tuesday's meeting cos they were notorious for putting you on the rack because the 'hardest' staff went then. We then had OT, individual therapy, sports, art therapy, or education, so it was all very structured.

Everyone new has to stay in the clinic for their first weekend. It was so boring, you weren't allowed out and all the other patients had gone home. I was bored out of my brains the first weekend, and on finding a plank of wood I managed to amuse myself by climbing on the roof. (Well, I had to do something.) I couldn't work out why the staff freaked out so much. I mean I wasn't going to jump! I was just bored.

That wasn't the last time I went on the roof. To my surprise after that other people came up with me. I was quite chuffed about that cos I hadn't considered myself a great one for influencing people before. One night this boy asked me if I wanted to go on the roof so we could watch the sun come up. We thought we'd better ask some of the others too, in case it came up in 'community' and we'd be accused of not keeping our hands to ourselves.

That night, the majority of the clinic got on to the roof. The night staff didn't notice, because we left the clinic in small numbers. When the staff *did* notice we couldn't come down as 'Emma' thought the director would be called out. One of the night staff had clambered on to the roof at this point, while one of the boys was throwing duvets out of the window for us behind him. The night staff went away again. By 2 am everyone was feeling the cold and decided to climb down. I decided to stay, after I'd gone through all that trouble. It was a cold night and the moon was up. I felt like the only person alive on earth as I looked up at the stars, wrapped in my duvet. When the sun melted away the night and glowed yellow across the sleeping city it was worth all the trouble, more so because I was the only person to see it.

When I peered over the roof later I saw the director arrive. On seeing me he shouted 'Matilda, get down from there *now!*' I thought 'No way José', I mean the guy was seriously pissed off, and I was temporarily safe from him on the roof. All I could think of was to wave at him!

From what I gather it was good not to have gone to community as the staff were throwing wobblies. I decided to come down after community, after the staff had got it all out of their system, but horrors! Someone had taken the plank away! How was I going to get down? Then I saw my therapist standing below, saying (how embarrassing) that they'd sent for a ladder from Barnet; now I'm no weed, I could have got down using the plank, thank you very much.

When I came down I had an emergency management team meeting and they all had a go at me for influencing the others, etc. I wasn't listening because the patients were mega-pleased I'd managed to last the whole night! That pissed the staff off even more, but it felt good that the patients were on my side.

Individual therapy, I suppose, was confrontative, which means having a go at you a lot of the time. But I guess in the NHS there isn't the time and money to get too analytical. Management teams were like that too, and you knew you were in deep shit if your admitting doctor ever turned up. Fortunately she wore these high heels, which worked for me as an early warning system, as you'd hear her – 'squeak' . . . (the door opening in the corridor), then the clickety-click clickety-click of her shoes, and then I knew it would be a good time to make myself scarce. She was nice too, I mean she did admit me to the place, didn't she?

I suppose being in such a structured programme with its funny rules, etc., gave you external boundaries. I guess a lot of the patients didn't have many boundaries inside. Well, I don't think I did, so it gave me some external reality to test myself against. I managed to leave a lot better able to contain myself self-destruction-wise.

Every three months or so the patients had a review. This was a meeting where the staff would have a meeting to discuss what to do with you. They decided my fate should be the therapeutic community at Peper Harow, or Arbours. I wanted to go to Peper Harow. I didn't want to be sent to Arbours and get stuck with a load of old fuddie-duddies, did I? I ended up going to Arbours because they thought I might get institution-alized at Peper Harow, and anyway I couldn't get the funding off social services.

So off I went to be interviewed at the Arbours Crisis Centre. I think I went twice and they decided I should go there for six months. I didn't mind too much as I thought it would be a stage between the clinic and an Arbours community. It's not, but never mind, I couldn't even get the consultation fee paid for by the social services, let alone a six-month stay. It was decided I should apply to live in an Arbours community, as it didn't need social service funding.

I applied to the Crouch End community for an interview and had to see Tom Ryan, the house co-ordinator, first. He had these big, black Mastermind chairs and X-ray eyes that look into you. When I arrived I had my interview round the kitchen table. Someone gave me a cup of coffee and I was so busy talking that I forgot about it, so I drank it cold in case it would go against me if I left it. Anyway, I didn't get in – they wanted a man.

Next I tried the Muswell Hill community. I didn't like it as much as the Crouch End one. Maybe this was because the interview was in a big front room instead of a cosy kitchen, and everyone looked mega-depressed. 'Roger' (a resident) gave me the house co-ordinators' names and telephone numbers as I'd have to see them too. I phoned Mike first. 'Use the basement entrance', he said to me on the phone. I thought he was a bit weird (me not knowing about 'consulting rooms' in therapists' houses then). What was wrong with the front door?

The interview was all right – I don't remember much about it. I was too busy wondering about things. He had babygros on the washing line and shelves of Freud books behind him in his consulting room. But what was that mattress thing for on the floor? Maybe this was his spare bedroom.

Muswell Hill hadn't got any vacancies, but someone was about to leave, and the clinic said I would just have to go home (my family) and wait from there. I could just see it, being sent home, once the clinic had washed their hands of me I'd be there for ever! No one seemed to be listening to how I felt at all. I decided the only way I could deal with the situation was to bump myself off. I looked it all up in the BNF (British National Formulary), how much and what to take for a symptomless painless way to go, but it didn't work out as I'd planned.

The following week I had my interview with the second house co-ordinator, Chandra. She was a horrible one to be interviewed by. It was all the usual questions about my family, etc., but she left these sort of silent spaces after my answers, and it was all I could do not to lose control of my emotions in them. However, at least I didn't let on about the OD the previous week, which is quite good when you realize how psychic therapists can be.

I'd already had a McDonald's before my interview at the community to stop my stomach from gurgling, and then I got invited to stay for supper! Well I couldn't exactly say 'no' could I? We had fish and peas, and I spilled my peas on the floor; as no one seemed to notice I kicked them over to someone else so no one would think it was me, because they hadn't accepted me yet!

They did accept me eventually, and I just had to wait for someone to move out. I decided to go to another type of therapeutic community while I was waiting – a dreadful mistake. It was a house of about 20 residents and four staff, and you were interviewed by the whole group. 'Tell us about yourself', one said. Now we're talking of 24 people looking at you. They sent me away for 10 minutes while they took a vote. They called me back in, 48 eyeballs on me. 'We've accepted you', said someone. Thank God. Can you imagine if they'd said 'We don't want you?' What could you say to that? 'Uh, well, bye then.'

I don't know why I was thanking God, if only I knew what I was walking into. Just before I moved in someone had hung themselves, and another person had jumped out of an upstairs window, breaking a leg. I was a bit worried about it but the staff assured the clinic this was all over with. It turned out the staff ran the place like a borstal. I guess because there was so much acting-out and disturbance and so few staff, they hadn't got time to give people the amount of support they needed.

At night I'd try to go to sleep, then I'd hear the smash of a window. I'd lie there waiting for something to happen – at least I was safe in my bed. Then someone would start screaming or I'd hear 'thud, thud, thud', and I knew someone was banging their head, so I'd hide under my covers and switch on my Walkman to make it not be real . . . I left three weeks later after I got physically attacked by one of the staff (that particular house has closed down now).

I moved back home for six weeks before finally moving into Arbours. Soon after I moved in we went on a house holiday to Wales, and I was really struck by how silent everyone was on the minibus. All the minibus trips I had been on before had been dead noisy with the radio blasting, everyone chatting, arguing, even fighting. Here was the dead silence you get in a dentist's waiting room. Talk about living in a morgue, but at least I was finally in Arbours. I didn't really feel part of the group until the holiday, I was as green as the grass then and hadn't sussed out any group dynamics, who were the bullies and what boundaries I couldn't cross as regards people guarding their hang-ups. All I saw was this quiet anticipation.

Anyway I went to go and get a Hobnob biscuit, and oh, what? Sitting on the top Hobnob was a worm of fag ash. It could only be 'Josephine', so I said to her something like 'Can you not put fag ash in the Hobnobs?' She replied, 'How dare you say that to me you haven't been here long enough to know how things happen in this group, so piss off!' Then I replied, and she got out of her chair and started pushing, hitting, pinching, etc., and finally threw a World War Two shell case at me! (It was polished up and was being used as a bin or something.) Now I wasn't going to sit back and take all this so I sunk my nails into her and she stormed out.

All this happened in front of most of the other residents, and I asked if it was normal to be in a fight and the others said no, but I'd just broken an unwritten rule of Josephine's, which was no one should challenge her. Josephine kept storming in and out, so I went up to my room and 'Maria' was there. Josephine was talking to one of the students downstairs, and Maria and I were on the landing, ears flapping. Maria and I had to keep rushing back into the bedroom to burst into fits of laughter. It wasn't really funny but it relieved the tension.

From that point on I was part of the group, which was a group that was united together against Josephine, who was making everyone's life difficult. This is when it all becomes confusing as she wasn't going to take any responsibility for constantly bullying people, and everyone found it very difficult to confront her, so people would moan to each other. Because it was so bad people forgot about the difficulties they had with each other, and the focus became Josephine. The house felt unsupported because the co-ordinators kept focusing on 'scapegoating'. This meant Josephine had licence to carry on as she was, people felt powerless and became more united against her and the situation went on for another year or so, until she left.

When I first moved here my transition from my clinic therapist to an Arbours one was not easy. I did not want another therapist, I was happy with the one I'd got, thank you very much. You can guess what this new one asked me within the first five minutes of being in the room. 'Tell me about your life.' Well she could just get stuffed. How many times had I told my story to this Arbours bunch?

Poor woman. I don't know how she survived those early days. Co-operation was not my strong point, I just wanted my old therapist back. Who was this woman anyway? How many people do I get attached to who then let me down? Another therapist? No thanks. So I was no angel to start with.

The couch made me laugh. Another one of those mattress jobs, you know. All of a sudden in my life I was encountering these therapists with beds in the room. Weird or what? I thought all that stuff went out when Ziggy Freud kicked his clogs. There was no way I could lie on one of those like Count Dracula flat on my back and keep a straight face.

I guess the main thing in Arbours is there isn't this time pressure to leave, so my therapist didn't have to put the thumb-screws on me as far as my life history was concerned. Therapy became a space for me to say what I liked when I liked, so it was difficult for me to do battle with her. I couldn't cope without what I thought were boundaries either, so if she wasn't going to get in to a battle over my last therapist then I'd have to get her to have spasms some other way, by walking round the room and fiddling with the plants.

I know I just said in Arbours there isn't this time pressure. What I meant is that you could be in the community until you're drawing your pension if you like, but come 50 minutes in therapy and that's it. I'm usually working up to the juicier bits of my life in the last five minutes, or I am coming out with some confession and she says 'Well, it is time'.

Have you noticed how therapists wear their watches? Loosely, with the watch face on the inside of their wrist. It's so they can look at their watch without making it too obvious, so when they are bored out of their brains with your ramblings they can check how long they have to last.

Another thing that seems universal among Arbours therapists and co-ordinators is that they seem to think that the world revolves around them come holiday breaks. If you are having spasms because you are overdrawn at the bank, they think it means you are having spasms because they are (a) about to go on holiday, (b) have been on holiday. Try telling them otherwise.

There are two house meetings a week. These are stomach-churning affairs generally. People sit round in silence not even looking at each other, it's really peculiar. We used to have to really battle a lot to bring things up about Josephine. It was so dreadful because you did not think you would get the support of the co-ordinators, and there would be no guarantee that other residents would have the guts to back you up. Sometimes your heart would be just about to explode out of your body and you'd be about to say what you felt about the jar of piccalilli that went flying and Josephine would say, 'I just want to say I'm having a difficult time in therapy at the moment, and I just want to be left alone'.

After Josephine left we weren't out of the nightmare. Mike and Chandra were worried someone else would get scapegoated. Most people could see this was a problem by now. After a couple of months 'Mac' jumped in to take the role, which is ironic when you consider how much he battled to get Josephine to leave. Well maybe it's understandable, because when Josephine was in the house he even contacted social services to get her to leave, and when it came to a vote whether she should stay or go *he was the only one that wanted her to stay* (e.g. to continue the conflict).

After she left he tried to create conflict with other people in the house, picking on each person individually. When he had done the rounds most of us wised up to the fact that he actually wanted us to be provoked, so what did we do? Ignored him. He got more provocative, so we ignored it further (even by limiting how much house meeting time we spent on him). We all had to make a very conscious effort that if he wound us up in the house we would not talk about it (other than in meetings) because people would be likely to get mixed up in other people's anger towards him and he would become larger than life!

Eventually after stealing from the food tin and making off with five weeks' rent he left of his own accord. This has been the pattern in the group for the past four years. I think it's been a problem from my point of view because the co-ordinators seemed blind to the effects of Josephine or Mac on the house, and it felt like only the group was being seen as bad. There was just no room for manoeuvre. I don't think anyone wants someone to jump in there and be a focus for conflict in the house, but it's a hell of a problem, cos when someone does the rest of the house gets the blame.

I don't think this particular dynamic has solved itself; it's just no one has moved into that position yet! Looking back on it I think maybe it would be better if the co-ordinators met with the person that seems to be making trouble for themselves to see if there was a way to bridge the gap before it got irreparable. This is because they probably feel too threatened by the group to think about why they are behaving in such a way as to invite anger, and the group feels too threatened by the person's behaviour, so the house meetings do not provide the space for a shift on either side.

About two years ago I went into the Crisis Centre. It was after the Christmas break and I was feeling self-destructive, so Chandra and my therapist agreed I should go there. My first consultation at the Crisis Centre was dreadful, because you have two therapists scrutinizing you, trying to work out if you are a desperate enough case. What did they say? 'Come back in a week.' I had enough trouble getting through the next five minutes, let alone a week! (To cut a long story short I did get in.)

The team meetings (individual therapy with two therapists) are dead weird if you don't know what to expect. You are sat thinking, 'What am I supposed to do in team meetings anyway? Why are they sitting there in silence? Am I supposed to initiate something?' While these two strangers are peering at you.

I didn't sleep the first night due to no locks being on the doors, and on the second night I did something with the handle mechanism so no one could get in, which is just as well as one of the men came to my door at 3 am. I was having spasms! After that I stopped feeling self-destructive, as I saw the attack coming from outside myself now. The Crisis Centre became this dreadful place that could not feel more unsafe, and the community a paradise. However, despite the horrors of the Crisis Centre it did give me space from all the entanglements and invisible dramas of living in the community.

My opinion of the psychotherapy students we get on placement has changed a lot. I guess in the world of work they have a specific role, and the people they work with might appear less together than the residents at Muswell Hill, so there is less of a distinction between their normality and others' abnormality. They also don't have a specific role in the house. Some cope by getting involved as little as possible, doing the placement because they have to (it shows!). Some jump in there and make a bit of a mess (but they'll probably make the better therapists if they are able to *listen* to what the residents say), and some seem to strike some kind of balance.

I have now started a degree course. It's only 10 hours a week (although it's called 'full-time') and I've found I can do the work during my better days as at the moment I only have to hand in two essays a semester. However, the Department of Social Security (DSS) are saying if I am capable of doing the course I am capable of not living in what they term 'residential care'. There seems to be no room in DSS regulations for me to go through a transitional phase in the house. They are going to write to me any day to find out how well I've been doing – I am very worried my funding for living in Arbours could be cut off. I could try and do really badly in my exams so I sink to a satisfactory level for the DSS, but it seems so crazy. It is an uphill struggle trying to fit in at university as it is, and I don't need this hanging over my head.

I am very lucky to have a place in what the government terms 'Care in the Community'. However, unless I have the same rights that other people in society have, there is little point in such a policy. Currently, every intelligent person has, in theory, a right to higher education. I do not, simply because of where I need to live.

What has worked for me in Arbours is living with other people and struggling with the difficulties I've had with them, and them with me. The meetings provide the space, in that it's hard not to say something about a conflict if you are forced to be in the same room as someone for two hours. The individual therapy provides the space to help me reflect on difficulties in a disentangling way. The space Arbours provides is experienced as supportive and fruitful, persecutory and negative at different times. If I had known how hard I was going to have to struggle I wouldn't have come, but now I'm here there's no going back: I can't lose the resources I have built up internally while being here, and I'm glad it wasn't the rosy picture I thought it would be before I came. If it was I might never have begun to discover myself.

3   A HOLDING ENVIRONMENT

TRINIDAD NAVARRO

? Refer too for proper

A major decision in my life was to embark on a psychotherapy training course with the Arbours. This requires commitment and sincerity, to a degree of which I could only become aware through regular experience of my own difficulties in these areas. I had a powerful experience of this during my six-month live-in placement in the Muswell Hill community. I would not have allowed myself to work with these issues had it not been for the challenge provided by the residents. It was principally the sense of holding from that environment and within myself that made this a positive experience.

I had previously worked in a therapeutic community, the Northgate Clinic in north-west London. This provides residential care for adolescents and intense individual and group therapies staffed by a large multi-disciplinary team ranging from nursing staff through to psychologists, social workers and consultant psychiatrists. As a nursing assistant I spent much of my time in the milieu as well as receiving extensive daily individual and group supervision. This gave me some confidence in my ability to cope with being in another therapeutic community. At the same time I had a niggling awareness that the Arbours was different. There would be only three formal groups a week in the community, I would have no peer group to relate to and above all I would have no professional status or role within it. This knowledge disturbed my arrogance and caused me anxiety. I wondered how it would work with such little professional input and structure. In response I thought that I would be left to fill inadequately all the other spaces.

My relationship with the residents at Muswell Hill began when I was interviewed by them for the placement. There were three men and five women living there whom I will call 'Ralph', 'Steve', 'Nigel', 'Patricia', 'Linda', 'Elisabeth', 'Janet' and 'Susan'. This was an intense interaction between myself and the house which set some ground rules around what was expected of me. The main issue that was stated clearly by Steve, Susan, Patricia and Elisabeth, with nods of agreement from the others, was that they were unhappy about aspects of the relationships they had made with previous students. From this came the imperative that I was not to form special relationships with individuals but to relate to the group as a whole. They told me that it was painful for the individuals who were left out, and it caused in-fighting and rivalry among them. Patricia told me that they did not want a student living with them at all but that they had little choice. Ralph and Nigel asked me about my work and the impact it would have on my time commitment to the house. Patricia expressed relief that I would be out during the day and Susan said, 'Good, you shouldn't become too dependent on us'. They asked me to expand on my experience of working with groups. In reply to my information Patricia said that I might not be too bad as I wasn't completely green. Nigel asked me a number of times exactly what I expected to gain from the placement, I answered that I didn't know exactly but that I hoped it would become clear as I lived there. The interview ended with Elisabeth saying that I appeared to be all right but that she was sure I would make some mistakes and I said that I was sure that I would step on somebody's toes. Nigel said that he would phone the following week to let me know if I was accepted. Instead I suggested that I would phone the household.

I felt and thought so many things when I left the interview. I had been given a role of relating to the group which was reassuring, but also sensed that maintaining it would be difficult and challenged. This excited me. The group, although made up of very different people, presented itself as united against the idea of an incompetent student. I was faced with uncomfortable feelings: being given a role fed the part of me which was an aspiring professional; on the other hand I was not dealing with 'patients' but, instead, eight extremely articulate people who in relation to my role were much more experienced and knowledgeable about the pitfalls. They dictated the terms – not me. And there was not even a 'job description'. I was conscious of the fact that I had been unable to give a satisfactory answer to Nigel's question about what I expected to gain. In part this was due to not knowing and not wanting to be bullied into saying something false, but it was also a defence against a sense of vulnerability suggested by the idea that I might gain something. Equally, I was aware that I had started the process of attempting to maintain the boundaries they had set me, by not allowing Nigel the task of monitoring my placement. I phoned the house a week later, and was told by Ralph that they had decided that I could come and live there.

The first few weeks were incredibly painful. I felt tearful, lost and depressed. I was estranged from my loved ones and my familiar world, and did not belong to this new one. I experienced fear in leaving the house and found myself scuttling to the shops and back as quickly as I could. Coming back to the house from work was probably the most difficult physical act I had to perform during the day. I wondered if I was experiencing some of the group's feelings towards me. The tension I felt was like that between fear of leaving the mother whose holding did not feel firm enough to make it safe to venture forth, and fury at having to return and be dependent. Perhaps my resentment would keep us apart, and maybe we all wanted that rather than negotiate a true relationship. As I tried to find a united group to relate to, I was confronted with the reality that it was, in fact, quite fragmented. This was evidenced largely through behaviour I witnessed in the evenings. Now let me cite a typical example.

> I come into the lounge where Linda, Elisabeth and Patricia are sitting. Elisabeth asks me about my day; Janet comes in and sits near me. Linda leaves almost immediately, Patricia fiddles with the TV channels. Janet complains to me about how much the TV is on and then asks me why Linda has left. Steve comes in and makes jokes. Patricia tells him not to be silly. Elisabeth goes quiet and Steve leaves the room to have a cigarette. Nigel is not around but I hear him upstairs. Janet tries to start a conversation with me, and then Elisabeth gets up and leaves. Elisabeth comes back shortly after, and then Janet leaves. Ralph is in and out, complaining a lot about how useless psychoanalytic therapy is. Elisabeth argues with him about this. I can only see Susan going into the kitchen from her room.

I had to acknowledge that I was stuck, without the familiar backing of a professional status and a peer group with whom to share my difficulties, but most of all with the knowledge that 'the group' would not be over soon and I would not be going home. Besides a massive desire in me to pair up or join a subgroup I did not know what to do with myself. I felt deskilled, and had not grasped the reality that this was part of the learning process, wherein I could not apply unfelt skills. I shared these pains in supervision, and was not told off but encouraged to reflect and not avoid. I was concerned about how to break out of being a petrified spectator and start taking an active part in the life of the house.

The opportunity for me to break out of this state was provided by Janet at 8 am on the third Saturday of my living there. I was dressed and having coffee in the kitchen when she joined me. I had been to see my nephew the night before and this triggered a conversation about our families. As the conversation progressed I felt increasingly frustrated and unclear about what was happening. She appeared not to be listening to what I said; I felt she had a different agenda and by the tone of her voice that she was angry. Elisabeth came in and entered the discussion. Within a couple of minutes, Janet announced that she was unhappy with the conversation. When I asked her why, she replied 'It doesn't matter'. I had a choice of pursuing this but I felt unable to deal with it particularly as I was half asleep and had a feeling that Elisabeth would be excluded. Elisabeth continued talking and very quickly Janet jumped up screaming at us that she was very upset, and left the kitchen slamming doors and proceeded to smash things in her room.

I was furious at her violence, and her attempt to control brought about a desire in me to respond in kind. People started coming out of their rooms, looking bewildered. Patricia asked me what we should do, Elisabeth was very angry and dismissive of Janet's behaviour. Steve asked if Janet was all right. I realized that I was frightened but was unsure if it was of her rage, my rage or the rage of the house. I thought about what to do, and became confused about whether I should call the co-ordinators, or if I could contain it, or if I had the right to take on the responsibility which was being given to me by the group. I decided that I was strong enough in my belief that it should be stopped and then hopefully discussed in the group.

I approached Janet's door, knocked on it and asked her firmly to stop. She told me to go away, it was her room and she could do whatever she wanted. I heard another smash. I repeated my request and added that what she was doing in her room was affecting everyone else in the house. She said 'Go away'. I offered her the opportunity to talk with me as part of the group downstairs. People gathered in the living room, and not long after Janet came in. It took quite a while for her to move from a position of denial, where it had nothing to do with anyone, to one where she could hear other people's comments about how it made them feel. Indeed, it took effort on my part to get the group to admit that they were affected, and for some it made them conscious of how close they were to this type of expression. I also shared my feeling about how angry and frightened it had made me. An hour later we were able to have breakfast and I went shopping with Patricia and Steve for the night's dinner.

I was exhausted, but was also left with a sense of achievement. Scapegoating of Janet had been prevented, because she had come to talk to the group, but the group were not silenced, and Janet had had the opportunity to say sorry. I first became aware that this was not simply a challenge to me from Janet, but from the whole house, when I went to her door and sensed myself being watched. Was I going to tell her off, go into her room and give her special attention leaving them behind, or perhaps I would do something they felt unsure about? This made it clear to me that Janet was in a sense acting on behalf of the whole group.

I experienced being pulled in different directions. Reasons for this became clearer at the art group later that morning. Julia, the art therapist, asked if something had happened in the house. Janet answered 'No' and everyone else remained silent. The atmosphere felt tense and Julia commented on it. This gave me the confidence to say that I thought that we should tell her what had happened, and started to outline the morning's incident. Janet told me to shut up, that it was none of Julia's business. The others colluded with this by remaining silent and someone soon changed the subject. I felt that although I had fulfilled the role which the group had asked of me, bringing that experience forward in another context was something they did not like.

I was relating to the group in sorting out the row, but bringing it forward in the art session put me outside the group. By breaking an unspoken agreement to keep the incident a secret I had established my independence, but was left to face the anger aroused by my breach of consensus. This incident had demonstrated that I would address the group as a whole, but this meant that the individuals were forced to acknowledge each other.

Before this incident I had experienced fear, a sense of aloneness and a desire to act this out and pair up. Meeting my own confusion and chaos face-on that morning, but countering it, left me feeling that I could be unique while at the same time belong to the group. By my not pairing with Janet or with the rest of the house against her we discovered a new space. We held on to the tremendous anxiety caused by the contradictions in motivation for this challenge. This enabled me to stay within the mandate they had set me during my interview. Within this space there were many tugs of war between me, the individuals and the group. At times people tried to get me to form exclusive relationships with them. Different people appealed to me with a similar message, e.g. they would talk to me alone about how awful it had been for the group when students formed special relationships and then add that they had suffered the most because they had not been the favourite, and that perhaps they would be my favourite. When I did spend time alone with someone, I was accused of breaking the rules. Sometimes the person I had been with would say that this happened by complete accident. But the group usually won, because these accusations and denials could be discussed and disputed by everyone.

It was clear that despite themselves, the residents were gradually relating to me and each other more and more. They felt safer to express hateful feelings and to show affection for each other. They also expressed a lot of care for me through loving gestures. They saw that love as well as hate could exist between individuals and myself without damaging group solidarity. Therefore, they began to take more risks among themselves, to speak, to feel, to be. I soon realized that we had all moved from a position of group rigidity and individual isolation to something approaching shared intimacy.

Initially I had many unfocused doubts about my role as a student. But from this point I really accepted my dependence on the community for my continued training. I acknowledged the frustration and anger and pain involved, and learned to hold on to these feelings. I also appreciated that the residents had given me the space 'to be', and had accepted that I had something worthwhile to give to them.

Through all these experiences in the house, all the interactions among them and me, them and themselves, and between different parts of myself, a new attitude had evolved. I have stopped worrying so much about presenting a smooth professional exterior. More importantly, I have realized that therapy is not something you do to another, or for another, but with another. I feel the aspiring therapist in me has grown and gained confidence to continue the course I have chosen.

4   RITES OF PASSAGE

IRENE BRUNA SEU

Rites are a complex of material and symbolic actions operative at different
levels of experience.

(Fabietti, 1982)

PART 1

Generally speaking I think it is possible to identify two specific levels
always present in any rite: the psychological and the sociological. This is
particularly apparent in rites of passage where the individual emerges
'changed' both psychologically as well as in his or her social status. Very
often the change in status is the more visible and recognizable but, although
the two are intrinsically linked, it is the internal, psychological change that
is ultimately the more dramatic and long-lasting. Some anthropologists
consider this as an 'ontological change in the existential regime'.

Very few initiation rites are especially enjoyable; on the contrary, more
often than not they are extremely painful and testing. Mythologically they
involve metamorphosis, doing battle with monsters, visits to the under-
world, etc. Above all there is the recurring theme of dying in order to be
reborn. This is the essential function of the rite of passage: to enable the
'novice' to die as the person they were and to be reborn as the new one.
This applies as much to puberty as to the initiation into a social group.

But the rite has another function. Apart from simply affecting this 'before
and after' change, the visions, dreams and thoughts the novice has *during*
the rite are conveyed back to the 'medicine-man/woman', the 'shaman'
performing the rite. These 'experiences' then become the basis of
accumulated knowledge on which the shaman will build and will refer
back to over and over again. It is in this respect that my placement served

as a 'rite of passage' for me, as I believe it has for many other students. Alexandra Fanning, writing about her placement (1990; and see below, p. 134), says: 'I still remember walking through the front door of the community and the strong sense I had of leaving one world and entering another. In crossing that threshold, I left behind me theories and ideas and entered the world of "being".' She also stresses how, when reading other students' reports on their placements, she frequently found reference to the phrase 'having to survive'.

This sensation is perhaps evident in the second part of this chapter, which was written straight after the placement. The experience is described in a fragmented and sometimes chaotic way. It is the distillation of hundreds of frenetically written pages attempting to make sense of and to record what was happening inside and outside me.

The essential role of the placement was that it forced me to think and make decisions about two particular issues which are crucial in becoming a psychotherapist: *'how' to be a therapist* and *'what' being a therapist entails*. *'How' to be a therapist* is, I believe, inextricably linked to one's own philosophical/ethical stance, which of course needs to be explored in regard to the interpersonal aspect of any profession. But I feel it is especially important for any 'helping' profession, particularly around issues of power and responsibility.

We are, as psychotherapists, in a position of power; a power arising from the subtle and delicate nature of the relationship. We also have responsibilities; responsibility to help our patients, while at the same time maintaining respect for their integrity as individuals. I start from the assumption that every human being has the right to choose and to be respected in his/her choices. When does help become infantilizing? Where are the boundaries between respect and responsibility when confronted with very harmful and self-destructive behaviour? A full examination of these questions is out of the scope of this chapter but hopefully by the end of the training one will have thought about these issues and made a conscious or preconscious decision which will shape one's work.

I feel very strongly that these issues are not talked about enough and are too easily summarily resolved through the fixed division of roles within the therapeutic interaction. One unique aspect of a placement in the community is the upsetting of this balance of power. Although I was a 'helper' and a 'trainee', I was ultimately a guest. My uncomfortable privilege was to be allowed to witness the therapeutic process from the other side and without any fixed roles to protect me.

In the community one was faced with the dilemmas of responsibility,

not in a sterile, academic environment, but with the terrifying immediacy
of physically and emotionally self-destructive behaviour. Directly linked
to this experience of crisis management and crucial to 'how to be a
therapist' is the issue of technique. The privilege of being a witness
allowed me to see the effect that therapy has on people. We don't normally
see how our patients carry our interpretations into their daily lives. Living
in the community gave me the opportunity to observe and to reflect on
this, as well as noting how and when interpretations were delivered, the
tone of voice, the choice of words, etc.

As for 'what being a therapist entails', I am not referring here to what
the therapeutic process means in terms of theory and technique and our
role within that process. I am referring to the experience of sitting in a
room, day after day, for an indefinite period of time, with people who in
varying degree and intensity attack and reject one's best efforts to help.
Therapy is a long and difficult journey and it requires endurance and
strength; we all know this from having been patients ourselves. My
question is: how can a trainee know how it feels to be on the other side?
And without this knowledge can anyone realistically decide to become a
psychotherapist? No theoretical training, or even one's own therapy, can
prepare a trainee for the power of the emotions one has to cope with
when you are at the receiving end.

The placement helped me to discover that the human process of
healing, likewise that of development and living, is not smooth, linear and
predictable. In spite of the illusion conveyed by some literature and the
neatness of theory, a therapeutic process does not follow charts nor
develop in clearly defined phases. My initial reaction to this was a sense
that 'Theory' was not only useless, but had betrayed me. Later I realized
that I was going through my first real encounter with how theories are or
should be formed; by real, un-sanitized, close-up experience of the issues
and problems we are dealing with. From this point of view, I feel that the
placement, with all its difficulties, was the only possible and 'realistic'
introduction to the incredibly ambitious task of helping people to heal, to
take control of their own lives and empower them to change.

PART 2

I believe that my experience in the community was not unique, and that
the difficulties I experienced are shared by others involved in therapeutic
communities. Deeply influenced by R.D. Laing's work, I had expected to

find a large degree of 'solidarity and shared experience' among the residents in the community. I thought that through madness people would be freed of the ties that stopped them from sharing deep experiences. Better able to communicate, I thought they would be able to 'read' each other, to understand the stages they were going through and therefore help each other. My staying in the community brushed away all these ideals and I now wonder whether they share any more than their pain and desperation. It seems that one of their major problems is, in fact, isolation and difficulties in communication.

I was struck by their fear of sharing with others and their unwillingness so to share. I felt great frustration in seeing people so blocked in themselves, still living in their islands of pain, anger and resentment, while having so much to share and confront. I hope I will be able to show how my views and ideals had to change, how I became aware of other underlying dynamics and how, eventually, I was left feeling incapable of helping any longer. I desperately wanted to get inside the community as quickly as possible while unaware of how terrified I was of doing so. It was only when the full explosion of feelings, sensations and reactions hit me that I realized that I was truly immersed in a therapeutic community.

It may be impossible to describe fully what it meant for me seeing people creep like shadows against those yellow walls, the smell, the dirt and the depression everywhere. I was all the time aware of people alone in their rooms, fighting with their ghosts, unable to fall asleep, going thousands of times over their problems and their past while the world slept. It was painful to find some residents awake at eight in the morning after a night with no sleep.

Sometimes it felt as if everything was pulling so strongly in different directions that the situation was going to break into pieces. One of the attempts to contain and negotiate these differences was through the house meetings. These were among the few structured and regularly held events, together with the network meetings, art therapy, yoga and, more recently, movement therapy. There are two house meetings a week, each chaired by one of the co-ordinators. The official meetings last for one-and-a-half hours and start after the evening meal; these were followed by unofficial meetings carried out in different parts of the house by various residents.

Residents used the house meetings in different ways. Some wanted them to be informal and relaxed; others took them as a duty to be performed to keep a place in the community, or to please the co-ordinators. Others would have liked the co-ordinators to be more directive and ask questions, rather than leaving the task of raising important issues to the residents' initiative. Other more long-term residents who had already been to hundreds of meetings simply felt they were a waste of time.

Generally speaking, the residents' expectations of these meetings were very high and yet the majority were spent in intense silence. The atmosphere was dense with frustration and anxiety. When I was not completely immersed in these same feelings I often resented the residents for being so nice during the meetings, then saying such terrible things afterwards. They seemed reluctant to accept any responsibility for the success of the meetings and needed to blame someone else for a situation they were partially responsible for. As far as my position in the house meetings was concerned, I never understood completely what was expected of me by the residents. Something was clear: it was very difficult to do the right thing. Very often their confusion and ambivalence affected me so deeply that I felt paralysed, torn between doing what I thought was right, what they expected of me and the desire to avoid hurting anybody.

One source of great controversy was the issue of confidentiality. The unwritten rule was that if a student was told something confidential s/he wasn't supposed to repeat it in the house meeting unless the person concerned started talking about it. I found this quite reasonable at the beginning, but soon became aware that residents often used this rule destructively to control and sabotage the meeting. Silence and paralysis were the result. The alternative was to dare to break this pattern, which I and other students attempted a few times with disastrous results: fury and rage from the confidant, explosion of persecutory feelings, accusation of using confidential information by the 'vicious' student against the 'harmless' resident in public, and temporary withdrawal of information. At least one could see the community united in a common goal against the scapegoat.

I felt very strongly about the way both individual and group supervision were handled. My opinion is that residents should be told clearly that these mysterious events actually happen. It is then up to the student to decide how much s/he wants to reveal. In my view continuity and firmness are the only things that could decrease the paranoia. All this information should be passed on to the new students. In fact, although it is true that the residents feel persecuted, talked about and spied on, it is also very reassuring for them to know that the students are professionally supervised. Because I do not think matters like these have been taken seriously enough until now, I can partly understand the shared feeling in the community that decisions are taken elsewhere. To label the residents' confusion as paranoia is a very effective way to get rid of our responsibilities and deny the confusion we help to create.

My first contact with therapeutic communities had been through a thesis I wrote for my studies in Italy. I wanted to live in a community to gain some clinical experience and hopefully to help. I believed that I could learn more by sharing the experience than by observing it and judging it from the outside. The fact that my involvement with the community was not part of my training had made my position even less clear than that of the other students. Where did I belong? I was not a resident, nor was I in the Training Programme. Sometimes it seemed that I was there to fit in with all the residents' fantasies. They saw me as a wonderful person who was not going to use them as guinea pigs for the Training Programme. I had come because I was interested in them. However, had I not done so by then, I disappointed them deeply when, after six months, I joined the Associate Programme.

Anxious to be helpful, I was trying from the beginning to find out what a helper was expected to do. This proved to be a very difficult task as the following quotes from the residents show, illustrating their ambivalence: 'We need at least two or three students to provide enough support for everybody.' 'It is impossible to cope with more than one student. They are different and things get confused.' 'The students should not have problems. If they do, I get involved and I did not come to an Arbours community to help a student.' 'I don't want a superhuman student who does not change mood or has no problems. It is reassuring to see feelings and weakness in a student.' 'They should care more about us; they close the door behind our problems, go home and forget about us.' 'They should not chase people around and follow them everywhere they go – even in the garden we cannot get rid of them.' These contradictory messages left the question about who I was for them and what they wanted from me still unanswered. Perhaps the famous Phoenix capable of rising from its own ashes would have been the prototype of the perfect student.

I was certainly a parental figure. I was expected to feed them, not to be fed by them. There was competition for my attention and a constant attempt to draw me out of the group and into their own rooms. There they could be reassured that I was really there for them and that I liked them; they could confess that they were angry with me only because they would have liked to have me completely for themselves. For some residents, little by little, the time we spent in their rooms became a sort of ritual which took place with a certain regularity. That reminded me of feeding time and of a child holding on to the image of the mother until the next feeding session. It reminded me of Winnicott's remark about the child adjusting his needs to the mother's, and waiting patiently without pushing too much. For some residents it meant gradually establishing a relationship.

I do not know whether it was human vanity or omnipotent ideas, but I felt that had I been able to give them all my time they would have felt safe. Or was this just my anxiety about the helplessness of their situations? For a while I actually thought it would have been a solution. But it was not. Not only because the residents wanted more and more, but also because another role I played for them was to be the envied object. In fact retrospectively I think that one of the main contributions a student can give is to provide an example of 'normal' life, to have varied interests, to bring life into the community but to be deeply hated and envied for the same reason. Due to projections and identifications, the same situation could be experienced in two different ways. For example with regard to my going out to work, to 'Carla' I represented her independent and strong part, getting on with life and not getting stuck at home as a housewife. For 'Sarah', however, my going to work brought up her anger at having to cook for me, because she experienced me as the husband who goes to work while the wife stays at home.

What I found disquieting was that a student is not only a giver of love and attention, but also a container of anger and depression. The residents desperately need someone whom they may perceive to be bad, be persecuted by and to blame. At the beginning I felt persecuted by this and only later did I realize that this was an important function. By accepting the polarities of the role I could offer an integration they did not yet have. For example, one of the residents woke me up in the middle of the night to tell me how much he hated me: 'Why do you think I should be your friend?' He told me: 'I have been officially unemployed for 10 years, to find a job is so difficult for me and you come, foreign to my country and get a job. You complain about something it would be so important for me to have. Besides you came to spy on me; I have been hating you since you walked through the front door. You said you wanted to be friends, no way, you are a student, even more dangerous because of this.'

The situation changed drastically when he worked for a while, coming back at 5 pm and receiving the anger and envy from other residents. He experienced feelings of rejection at being cut off from what had been happening in the house during his absence. At least with me they did not pretend to have had an interesting and exciting day, as they did with him. They knew perfectly well that it was much more effective with me to highlight the fact that I had left them to their despair and depression. At the same time, I felt that people were testing the outside world through me: the external world and the routine were not so threatening if I was not destroyed by them.

I soon came to realize that the residents had been acting on the inner part of myself. I started to feel very angry and yet I could not understand where the anger came from. Was it coming from the realization that my identity and personality did not matter that much and that the space in which I could act beyond their projection and investment was rather narrow and limited? Was it because I had identified with these projections and unwillingly colluded with their repeated patterns when I could have been more confrontative? Or was it because I realized how much the residents had been able to touch hidden parts in me, sometimes hidden also to myself?

I had very strange feelings going into Carla's room. It was like a cave of darkness. She used to sit with just a candle in front of her, smoking. She curled up on the floor which made her look even smaller. I used to feel a cold shiver going through me; basically I did not like being there, but somehow I felt it was worthwhile. In fact only when we were there was she able to show me all her 'madness'. She felt secure enough to let go of all her anger without caring about the reactions her words might have caused. She could let go of the 'dark' side of herself and be suspicious, mischievous, ruthless and hard toward others, and terribly destructive.

But only when she calmed down did things become difficult. At the beginning it was almost devastating. It seemed that only after the rage was there space for her tormented self, for the pain and desperation; then she could show her fear of being hurt, together with the need to be accepted and loved. Sometimes I just could not follow her: I could gather, from the way she was presenting facts, the existence of a preconceived reality so powerful that everything was coloured by it. My knowledge of the external reality made it easier for me to realize that, in her perception, there was something which did not belong to the 'here and now' of the situation; it came from within, so strongly that it left very little space for the facts themselves.

She was starting from an internal reality which had stayed untouched for all this time and from which she could not detach herself; this 'something' cemented inside of her was becoming 'the world' and I could see the pain when she could not understand or be understood. Little by little the single individuals for Carla had started to lose their boundaries, the differentiation between one another becoming a tormenting mass with a thousand faces, a persecuting mish-mash she could not escape. Concepts like time and space, cause and effect were totally suspended; she could jump from a person in her past to one in the present with no distinction, and episodes in her life seemed to be happening at the same time.

The contrast between the two images of Carla was really striking: she was incredibly alive, humorous and articulate; she appeared to be the most open person in the community, open to dialogue, openly self-centred and petulant, but surely very capable of making contact with and relating to people. The person I encountered one-to-one in her room was the most isolated of all. I could not say what the most difficult part of it was for me; the pain of being the helpless audience of her suffering, or the anger at her destructiveness and her seeming resistance to change.

Winnicott (1975) said that feeling real was more than existing; it was having a Self into which to retreat for relaxation. Carla did not have this; rather her Self was a prison and like a blind bird she was bumping painfully against the walls. I felt terribly helpless and powerless and sometimes it was very difficult not to impose my reality on hers. Only by setting my boundaries was I able to listen to Carla's reality and to respect it without feeling I had to destroy it to be safe. It is relatively easy theoretically to accept the existence of realities different from one's own, but very difficult not to feel confused and threatened by them. The fact that there was no point in arguing which was more valid, and the fear of losing her confidence, in a sense pushed me to collude with her. Keeping her hatred in her own dark room, she could save her image in relationships outside; a nice split to protect her ambivalence. I often felt helpless and impotent and I was constantly confronted with my limitations. On the other hand I was not a therapist and her pathology was a solid wall in front of me. Still I felt I was somehow helping her. If nothing else, I hope I was able to show that being close to her had not destroyed me and if that was possible she could take the risk of being herself with someone who was capable not only of listening but also of helping.

To accept the limitations of my role in the community helped me to appreciate the value of listening and paying attention to people. The starting-point is still to respect the dignity of people without dismissing what someone is experiencing as just 'madness'. Both interpretations and immediate experience are important, and will co-exist in a properly functioning community. For instance, Sarah's recognition of the fact that she was angry with me because I represented her husband did not eliminate other elements of the relationship between herself and myself as Irene. The fact that she could be angry with me as though I were her husband, and yet see me as Irene and not her husband, was a step towards integration of all the conflicting feelings she had towards me, and hopefully between all her different realities.

I think the element of freshness and actuality in the community is as important as the analytical one. The 'here and now' of each situation has to be respected without trying to interpret every single breath. This respect means the possibility of people having space as real people capable of being angry or happy about something happening now. If we do not leave this space, we sentence people to be only ghosts of their past, without any real existence in the present. We prevent them from integrating these two parts of themselves. The uniqueness of a therapeutic community lies in the fact that projections and identifications are continually discussed in a context of genuine human interactions. Along with the richness of being able to recognize a projection, people are continually confronted with external reality, with real people day after day, and not merely left with their thoughts and their ghosts. The student offers a special sort of zone in which these interactions and confrontations can be worked out relatively safely. This, at least, is how I came to see my role, and to understand my usefulness in that therapeutic community. To return to the 'rite of passage' model. My change of status at the end of the placement was obvious: I became a trainee psychotherapist. Still today, after many years, the internal change in my psychological, ontological state is much more difficult to describe, but finds expression in my day-to-day work with patients.

5   LEARNING CO-ORDINATION

CHANDRA MASOLIVER

I joined the Arbours as a student in 1974, the first year of the Training Programme. Six months later I moved into the Norbury community as the first student doing what is now called a placement. My two children came with me, and they loved the suburban house with its seven unusual men and women. They slept on a mattress on the floor in the same room as me, and we travelled up to their school by train each morning.

All my previous work had been in the academic field. While doing a PhD in psychology I became increasingly dissatisfied with the questions I was asking, and statistical analysis seemed a gross way of finding answers. I began to work on magazines with nefarious titles like *Rat, Myth and Magic, Humpty Dumpty*, and *Red Rat*. We dedicated a whole issue of the last to alternatives to psychiatric hospitals – or bins, as I think we called them. I went off to investigate the Arbours and decided I would like to work there.

My training in Arbours felt like an eye-opening magical crash course in bewilderment, excitement and survival. Four years later I became a co-ordinator of the same house in Norbury. That was in 1979. The Norbury community eventually moved to Muswell Hill, where they live in a beautiful Edwardian house. Although there have been many changes, the old spirit of independence has remained. This is symbolized by the cat they took with them; they always have a cat.

In her chapter in this book (see below, p. 157) Dr Nina Coltart has stressed the importance of attention in our work as therapists. I think our communities change as we learn to listen better – to what is most helpful in creating a sanctuary and a place of growth for people in distress. Sometimes therapists working in other therapeutic settings criticize Arbours for combining individual and group therapy. We have found people need a private place in individual therapy, and a group where they can talk and learn about their relationships. These two enhance each other and help to make the Arbours communities what they are. We call ourselves a network, but we are a family: for some the Arbours is the only home they feel they have. People also bring their own internal families with them, and residents may become entangled in each other's dramas, past and present.

When 'Simon' moved into the community his first friendship was with 'Bill'. They made an unusual pair, for Simon was short, fair and strongly built, while Bill was tall and fragile. Then they started to wrangle for position in the house. When one was 'in' the group, the other was 'out', and vice-versa. The other residents felt drawn into this, yet silenced.

Meeting after meeting was taken up with them in centre stage. Simon felt Bill gave him no space: whenever he made a coffee, Bill would be at his elbow, needling to get his cup there first. If Simon was talking with someone, Bill butted in and took over. They almost came to blows, which Bill dreaded. Simon threatened him and said he must never even say hello; they were to live as total strangers.

It seemed impossible to form a bridge between them. Each demanded total understanding, which meant that one or the other constantly felt their reality denied. My colleague Michael Kelly (Mike) and I decided to meet with both of them. They needed to understand why they reacted to each other as they did.

It emerged that they came from radically different backgrounds. Bill was the middle child of a family of nine. Everyone jostled for dominance among constantly changing alliances, and he never received individual attention. Simon was an only child, his father was psychotic and his mother permanently depressed. He grew up in isolation and had to care for his parents from an early age.

In our meeting they slowly began to understand why they were not able to communicate. Simon felt hassled by Bill's intrusiveness, while Bill had no conception of giving someone space. Back in the house meeting they were able to express some sympathy for each other's predicament. In fact, they had a lot in common, for neither of them had felt listened to or heard; nor did they know how to listen to others. They were engulfed in their inner family dramas.

As co-ordinators, we reached out further by questioning the function of their impasse to the group. What feelings had they been carrying for the others? This freed the atmosphere for people to share their own experiences of feeling caught up in a vacuum, of never receiving the right kind of attention.

The concept of 'space' is very important in Arbours. At times my function is to make room for changes to take place. This means helping to create a containing space, where people can share. This is different from 'leaving people space', in the mistaken sense of letting people become increasingly isolated and alienated.

It is quite rare for Mike or me to see individual residents on their own once they have moved into the community; our job is to work with the whole group. It arouses understandable jealousy if we single anyone out for special attention.

The co-ordinators of each community have evolved different ways of working. Tom Ryan and Sally Berry, the co-ordinators of the Crouch End community, will see residents on their own more frequently than Mike and I. One of them may see a resident in therapy for a short time if there is the need to bridge a gap. This then would be a private relationship.

When the whole group recognizes that someone is in crisis, it is the task of the co-ordinators to help decide what to do about it. If we think it is necessary, we may call together all the relevant people, including the person's psychotherapist. Any private meetings are referred, with the resident's permission, back to the group for general discussion. In this way we often manage to contain the situation and help the person to survive the group.

People in our communities tolerate an enormous amount of disturbing behaviour from each other; but when it all goes on for too long, they become exhausted. The communities, which are people's homes, have their limitations, and it is important to realize this. We do not give round-the-clock help for long periods of time. The group as a whole cannot be sacrificed and allowed to become a one-person-saviour band. Occasionally someone needs to leave the community for a while so that everyone can have a rest, and the feeling of being a group can be reconsolidated.

It is on these occasions that the Crisis Centre plays a vital role. Since it is a central part of Arbours, a resident does not feel so threatened about going there, rather than to hospital or somewhere outside Arbours. The Crisis Centre offers them more intensive attention on a short-term basis. The co-ordinators and the person's individual therapist can become involved in some of the meetings. During this time understanding can be gained as to the cause of the problem, and its effect on the community the person has been living in.

At this moment the co-ordinators are buffers and interpreters between the person and the other residents. The (temporarily) 'ex-resident' has to renegotiate acceptance into the group, and new terms of contract may be drawn up. This happens during the house meetings, which the 'ex-resident' continues to attend.

'Don' had been living in the community for two years when he decided, with everyone's knowledge, slowly to decrease his medication. If all went well, he would stop taking it. Don felt particularly nervous about this, since a misguided psychiatrist had once told him that if he ever stopped taking his anti-psychotic drugs he would become quite mad and never get better again. Every so often he reduced the amount he took, monitoring himself carefully, and checking out how the group felt about him. Unfortunately, in August, when many therapists take their holiday, he suddenly decided to stop his medication entirely. This was bad timing since there were not enough people around to be of much help to him.

Mike and I returned to find him in full-blown psychosis, thoroughly frightened and, I must say, occasionally frightening. Don was a very large man with pale staring eyes; he would thrust his face right up to mine and hurl threats of violence at me, so neither he nor I quite knew if he would carry them out. At such moments faith and stubbornness carry me through.

Once, when he was yelling at me with his nose practically touching mine, he suddenly stopped and said: 'It's funny, I only get like this when I'm wearing a brown sweater; if I was wearing a yellow one I'd be much calmer'. With no thought of making an analytical interpretation at this tense moment I said: 'Well, for heaven's sake go and put on a yellow one then!' I was acknowledging that I too had had enough; off he went, and did indeed return much calmer in a yellow sweater, and then we could talk.

The residents, who had to put up with such treatment frequently, not just once a week, became fed up with him. Don went to the Crisis Centre, but with no guarantee that the community would want him back again. First, it was necessary for him to understand what had caused his behaviour. Here, the Crisis Centre was of great help to him. He then needed to explain himself to the residents, enough to repair his tattered relationships with them. It was Mike's and my task as co-ordinators to create a situation where this could happen.

On his request, we met with him and his psychotherapist. With her help he told us of the horrific sexual abuse he had suffered from his father as a child. The memory of this was what had come exploding up for him in full force without the barrier of medication. This caused him to become aggressive with the male members of the community. He was enraged with the women too, for standing helplessly by, without protecting him, just as his mother had done. No one had known about this, so his behaviour had been inexplicable, and therefore doubly frightening.

Mike and I were present at the next meeting. Usually this only happens once a month, but in emergencies we sometimes go together. At first Don was silent and glowering, but he knew that he wanted to return to the community. With tears streaming down his face, he bravely told people what had happened to him in his childhood. He managed to explain to people why it had made him so aggressive. It became clear that he was now managing to distinguish between them – innocent participants in his drama – and the terrible events of his childhood.

Next, Mike and I met with him and his Crisis Centre team. We discussed the conditions he would have to fulfil if he returned to the community. We had to create a realistic structure within which he could go back to the house. He could no longer take over the community and the house meetings. He needed to return as a participating member of the group. We also suggested the added support of therapy five times a week for a while.

In the final house meeting, where the community would decide if it would have him back, Mike and I were sympathetic, but the decision lay with the residents, who would have to live with him. Don did manage to listen enough to understand and accept the terms, and he was accepted back.

At the request of the community we decided to review his situation regularly; people wanted to feel that Don's state would continue to be contained. We agreed to meet with him in a month's time. Also, in the house meetings the residents would tell him how they experienced him. Don was glad, and agreed to discuss how he was feeling on a regular basis. This has become part of our way of working in a crisis, so as not to let things get out of hand. Sometimes a person can be too afraid of accepting the next step, or too angry. Maybe they are not yet ready, or simply it can be too much for them. The co-ordinators cannot make everything all right, neither should they.

One of the tricky aspects of being a co-ordinator is keeping the right balance between openness and confidentiality. It is our role to be a pivot, feeding in observations which prevent rigid closures of group behaviour, thus creating space for change. When I am told something privately, by phone or letter, I try to understand what it has to do with the person's involvement with the group. Sometimes, however, it is a personal problem which is difficult to talk about openly, as with 'Christine'.

Christine was in many ways the leader in the group; she was quiet and pleasant, and would sometimes wonder if she really needed to be in a community. She was already talking of getting a job and leaving, when I got a letter from her pouring out torrents of anguish about another part of herself, whom she called 'Becky'. Becky was dirty and smelly and destructive. Becky hated Christine, and kept tripping her up and saying horrible things to her, even suggesting that Christine would be better off dead.

So far, Christine had dealt with Becky by trying to ignore her existence. As the time to leave the community approached, Becky stepped up her demands. Christine was terrified she would spoil her re-entry into the world outside Arbours. In her letter Christine begged me not to tell anyone about Becky, and yet why else should she have told me?

I decided that I would bring up the fact that she had written me a letter, without mentioning the contents. After a lot of silence and much encouragement from the others, she told them about Becky. People were very sympathetic, suggesting she should let this side of herself out before she left the community. Then everyone began to talk about parts of themselves that they too tried to disown. It turned into a very open and insightful meeting.

The best meetings are when everyone joins in and I take a back seat. It is natural for residents to want special attention from the co-ordinators, but that is not what we are there for. One meeting started with an extra long silence; people hardly moved, no one looked at anyone, and I felt outrageously bored. 'Hugh' then burst out with 'Well, Chandra, what are you going to say?' I said that they seemed to want me to begin the meeting, but nothing more.

When they started talking among themselves, it emerged that they were very angry with 'Kate'. They hated her being so depressed; it oozed all over the house. She wanted too much from them, and anything they said was rubbished by her. If they asked her to do something, she smashed plates. She destroyed and stole things, she was always the same, and they wished she would go. My only comment was that it seemed they despaired of her ever changing; but was it only Kate's despair of change? People talked quietly together about their feelings of hopelessness, how difficult it was to change; they even listened to Kate! At this point the atmosphere altered and it became more hopeful, and so did they. There was no need for me to intervene beyond having helped them to clear their boundaries with Kate. People can get very muddled about what belongs to themselves, and what to others.

The Arbours communities are basically for people who want to work

to gain understanding and to change. The role of the co-ordinator is not
to dominate the group. Most of the time the residents are alone with each
other, and it would be destructive and persecutory to swan in once a week
and take over. Occasionally, when the group is extremely fragmented and
in crisis, I will hold forth. Then I insist on certain events being discussed
by everyone, or particular people talking together. It is as if I then stand
for a reality that is being swept under the carpet. The first time I did this
I was surprised at how glad people were. They said it made them feel
safe, and even asked me to do it more often. I understood this as their
asking me to help them to reconsolidate themselves as a group. The
following night 'Judy' had a dream that I went round the room and kissed
everyone goodnight before I left.

I will sometimes turn to a person sitting in a corner, or behind a sofa,
and ask them directly what they feel about whatever is being discussed.
Or I may challenge the person who is monopolizing the meeting in order
to prevent uncomfortable issues coming up. Soon after, others in the group
take over this function for me, and once again I have a less dominant role.
As the years go by, I am constantly learning more about when to intervene,
and when not to. A single comment that shifts the emphasis of their
discussion can be enough.

Recently, 'Rose' said very forcefully, and clearly, that group meetings
must not be for people to speak of their individual problems: they have
their own therapy for that. Neither, she said, is it enough for people to
make supportive or challenging comments to a focal person. She said she
felt everyone must learn to take things further, and talk about their own
experiences regarding whatever is being discussed. Everyone agreed, and
I was asked to help facilitate this. So, I think another role of the
co-ordinator is to become more active (if asked) when the group is trying
to evolve one step further, until the group can take that function upon
itself.

When there is a general issue to discuss, like where to go on holiday,
or what sort of sofa to buy, it is easy for all to participate. So too when
everyone is angry with a particular resident. The real work of the
co-ordinator is to allow what is going on in the group to emerge.

Meetings often start with a rather heavy silence and a few disparate
comments. In one meeting 'Lily' eventually said someone had phoned her
and the message about it had been rubbed off the board: who had done
it? How, if this sort of thing happened, could she have any chance of a
social life outside the community? Rose then said that she wanted to miss
next week's house meeting because she had the chance to go to a party

and she had little enough contact with the outside world. Then 'Barry' broke in saying the old cat was really too much and should be put down; she was making a mess all over the house.

I thought they were being a bit precipitate; I asked what the old cat might represent, that they were so keen to get rid of her. There was a chorus of how easy it was for me to say it, I didn't have to live with her; I lived in my nice flat with my family and had an exciting life. They were stuck in a community with a dirty old cat.

It emerged that everything said so far – the phone message erased, the party that might be missed, the decrepit cat – was a way of giving voice to a general feeling in the group at that moment. They felt they were rotting away in a backwater without contact with the world. They wanted to kill off the part of themselves that was like the old cat. Then, like the Phoenix, they could miraculously transform themselves into the young tomcat they had in fact recently acquired, with all life before them.

Of course it was important to talk about who had rubbed Lily's phone message off the board, whether Rose would go to the party, and what should be done about the cat. Eventually we got round to these practical discussions. But it was more important for them all to be able to voice their despair about how hard it was to change, how time was passing, and how sometimes they felt that being in a community just wasn't enough. There was also their anger with, and envy of, me for breezing in with my interpretations about young and old cats, while having my own life outside.

Cats have played an important part in voicing feelings in the community. There is the sad story of the death of the same young tomcat, which they called Greedy. Shortly after the old queen had to be put down, he too became ill. Sometimes 'Diana' took him to the vet, sometimes 'Ron'. The men and the women were fiercely divided about the best way to cure him. The women wanted to pamper him and give him bread and milk; the men thought he should be toughened up, put outside, and fed on raw liver. They were avoiding the fact that he was dying by quarrelling among themselves.

As co-ordinators, we look for the fantasy which may be behind an action or an argument. At the same time, when people live together, there is also a lot of reality that must be addressed. It is our task to try and get the balance right, with a specific point given due weight, and the fantasy involved fished out.

When 'Betty' threw a milk bottle through a window, narrowly (and intentionally) missing 'Hugh', it was not appropriate merely to peer verbally at why she did this. She had broken the rule of no violence, and everyone said how furious they were with her. It was necessary to find out what feelings had driven her to do it, and what was going on for her as a member of the group.

During the same week someone had also broken Hugh's favourite mug, and he accused Betty of doing it. There was a certain eagerness in the way everyone in the house was sure it was Betty. Throwing the milk bottle was her way of saying 'OK, you think I'm violent, well look at this then'. She chose an empty milk bottle because she felt that she had no place in the community, and that she was receiving no love or care from it. The houses are for people who can control their violence enough not to act it out, but to find words instead. I had to help Betty to try to explain herself, so that others could take their share of responsibility in it.

If a resident is made into a scapegoat, there is usually a reason for it. Betty was being destructive. Nevertheless, she was embodying everyone else's destructiveness too. There was a general feeling in the group that if only she would leave, everyone else could live in a friendly and civilized way. In fact, Betty had not broken Hugh's mug, someone else had. By throwing the milk bottle she was also expressing a current running through the group, a general fantasy. People were feeling unloved, and they angrily wanted to smash their way into being held and contained. They felt there were no limits, no one cared for them, and they were not getting 'enough'.

Violence in a community is rare, but occasionally limits have to be set. I am sure it is very unpleasant to live with a physically abusive person. When I did my placement as a student this problem did not arise; however, recently something did happen to me in a meeting. People had been afraid of 'Simon', whom I spoke of earlier, for some time, and Mike and I were criticized for our laidback attitudes. One week he attacked an unprovocative new member of the community. I was just agreeing that the time really had come when, for a number of reasons, we would have to ask him to leave. Suddenly a door slammed. Simon was in the house. There was a panic-stricken silence and everyone held their breath. I called out to him and asked him to come into the meeting. When he was confronted, his fury filled the air. He whipped out of the room into the kitchen and we could here him rattling around with the cutlery. I felt I was his target. I had a clear image of the sharp, glinting knife they had recently bought. I sat still, wondering what would happen next. Simon came silently into the room and stood behind me, so that I could not see him. There was a rustle, and I was showered with thousands of little tea leaves. My relief was stronger than any feeling of looking ridiculous! I had taken part in the group's fantasy of violence.

The whole group often participates in acting out a feeling. In the Muswell Hill community Mike and I take turns to have a meal before the evening meeting, so I share their supper once a fortnight. Usually the food is delicious and the co-ordinator brings a bottle of wine. We feel the meal is important, as well as pleasant, because it gives us the chance to be convivial together.

One year, after the August break, both Mike and I had a couple of unavoidable commitments outside the house. For the next two or three weeks the schedule became rather messy. We had to swap round our meetings, or go on a different night altogether. Then one of us was ill, and there was only one house meeting that week. I arrived for my meal, with a bottle of wine, after a long day's work. I had eaten very little that day, and I found there was no food. I felt a furious disappointment and asked for some bread and cheese, whatever they might have, and a cup of coffee. Keeping my bottle of wine firmly unopened, I went straight into the meeting. This time it was I who had to keep a check on my feelings. I had to wait until an appropriate moment in the meeting to understand what the whole group was expressing by not feeding me.

The room was looking unusually scruffy and disordered; people were nonchalant about taking any trouble to create the atmosphere of a meeting. After some time, I realized that it was up to me to comment on their way of telling me how uncared for they felt: how scruffy and disordered Mike and I were in the irregularity of the house meetings. When I raised this, they certainly responded, firing out their anger that we had been so neglectful. Why should they be expected to attend house meetings regularly when we were being so irregular?

However disparate or ungroup-like a community may seem at any point in time, it is always a whole. As in the old morality plays, people may get labelled – Mr Open and Honest, or Mr Do Nothing, Miss Keep It All Nice, or Mrs Nothing's Right. It is important that people understand why they find themselves in a particular situation, and that it gets talked about. Here, the way the co-ordinators intervene is crucial. We have to be a mirror, reflecting back the hidden fantasies which underlie the casting of people in specific roles.

When Hugh first came to the community he found any decision extremely hard to make; he had wavered about accepting the place offered to him for so long that he nearly lost it. He even found the decision to speak difficult. He had a quality of slumbering anger, and even before he moved in people were saying they would like locks on their doors. A group fantasy had emerged about him which we co-ordinators had to try to shift.

In fact, Hugh never was violent; all his efforts went into trying to learn to make decisions. When he found his voice, it sounded wooden and stern. He began to be seen as a dictatorial father, and people objected to any of his suggestions on principle. Since Hugh had never lived with his father, it was painful for him to realize that other people were seeing him as their own bad fathers.

Some of the residents had been abused by their fathers; others had fathers who had never been there in any real sense. They had plenty of anger, fear and resentment to heap upon him. In the face of this he retreated into his previous indecisiveness, and his inability to communicate increased his problems with the group. Mike and I struggled to disentangle this. At first we were seen as siding with Hugh, which did not help him. Then we became – combined in one person, as it were – the bad, aggressive father; their anger was siphoned off Hugh on to us. As he then began to feel more secure he relaxed, and finally became a member of the community in his own right again.

It is important for the co-ordinators to tolerate being seen as bad; students often have trouble with this at first. Residents have so much to work through, including letting out angry feelings; understanding that the co-ordinators can survive without becoming antagonistic is a helpful experience.

A lot of the work in the community is about residents catching up with the present, thus gaining increasing clarity. Otherwise they use each other as flints, off which to spark their problems from the past. This is one of the most difficult but fascinating tasks of the co-ordinator: to facilitate their living with each other now, rather than seeing people obfuscated by beings from the past.

An individual resident's feelings about either or both co-ordinator(s) may be a reflection of how that person is using the community. Lily did not feel liked by either co-ordinator when she was participating in the community as little as possible. When she became able to talk in my meetings she felt anxious lest I should single her out as favourite, and then she would have to deal with the other residents' jealousy.

In a way, the co-ordinators are a symbol of the group, for it is in their presence that everyone meets together regularly. So, feelings towards the co-ordinators can be a reflection of the group's feelings about itself. The arrivals and departures of particular residents affect the group's character, but the group has a growth pattern of its own, even regardless of who is living there. People join an evolving group culture.

When the men and women form separate subgroups the women may turn towards me and close off from Mike, while the male residents will seem insubstantial in my meetings. However much I interpret this, time will have to pass before there is any breakthrough in this pattern of house relationships. Then there is an atmosphere of female intimacy, and I am seen as the mother the women wish they had had. The women are very involved with me in the work they do in my house meetings. Good meals are cooked, a scarf of mine left in the hall with my coat may go missing. Once two residents knitted themselves sweaters in the same kind of wool I had used for one myself. Any of these actions can lead to fruitful discussions with interesting resolutions.

Alternatively, the men may feel more able to be open in my meetings, tentatively expressing their feelings about me as a warm and nurturing mother. They explore the female side of themselves, encouraging each other with great honesty. I can feel bowled over by the things people say about themselves and to each other.

At other times Mike will be seen in a more lively way and people trudge through my meetings. The men see him as someone whom they can trust to protect them, and to enhance their fragile manhood. Or the women come forth shyly and flirtatiously in his meetings, exploring the possibility of a relationship with a kindly father. Then the women may cast me as a disapproving mother who is unfair and forbidding. Or the men may see me as a dangerous woman who can in no way be depended upon.

This is only one kaleidoscopic image of the infinite possibility of groupings that appear between residents and co-ordinators. Sometimes I am mother, sometimes father. So too with Mike. On other occasions we are a couple, or even the dreaded 'combined parent'. Often we are none of these, and the group works within its own boundaries. It is always essential that we explore as clearly as possible both the reality and the fantasy in what is said. Mike and I have worked together as co-ordinators since 1981; we too are part of the developments that have taken place. The best changes that have come about are in the direction of a closer interrelationship, fewer secrets and more communication between every-one involved in our network.

6 A COMMUNITY IN CRISIS: A VIEW FROM THE KITCHEN

SAEUNN KJARTANSDOTTIR

When I took on the role of a visiting student in an Arbours community, I felt like an apprehensive little girl who was going to school for the first time. Although I hoped my previous experience as a psychiatric nurse in Iceland would be a valuable provision for my new venture, I felt uncomfortably aware of its limitations. I had become increasingly critical of psychiatric practices and treatments in conventional hospitals, which I saw as mechanical and void of introspective thinking. I wanted to expel my rigidity and myths about mentally ill people and simultaneously open my mind to new perceptions and dimensions.

In this complex and continual process my self-confidence has been shattered and my professional identity perished. This was partly a relief, and partly a loss. Relief came from no longer being a figure of authority; a nurse, the responsible one, the mother who knows best. The feeling of panic and loss was: if I am not the mother, who am I then? In this frame of mind I launched into my placement in the early days of my training.

My first visit to the Crouch End community took me pleasantly by surprise, but also added to my confusion. Having worked with very disturbed people, this was an unexpected contrast. The community was a group of highly articulate and intellectual people, who seemed willing to share the responsibility of shopping, cooking and cleaning the house. They were required to attend two weekly house meetings, and to be in individual therapy at least twice a week. They were all friendly and considerate and seemed enthusiastic about me coming there. This felt comforting, considering my own doubts about my merit in this new role.

However, my initial doubts returned when I started my thrice-weekly visits and found no trace of the enthusiasm expressed on my first encounter with the residents. I usually arrived around midday to find that no one was there; the house seemed either dead or fast asleep. I wondered whether it was because of me or in spite of me. I made myself as comfortable as I could and waited for some signs of life. Sitting in the kitchen I wondered: where was everybody? What were they up to all day? What was I doing there?

As daylight dwindled the house slowly revived. People came from their mysterious hideouts for their essence of life: tea. The kettle seemed to have a magnetic attraction, being a bountiful source of warm, filling and satiating comfort.

As we all tried to get used to my being there, the focus was directed on the highlight of the day; the evening meal. One of the residents would go out into the winter darkness and bring home a selection of fresh vegetables. Preparing the meal took on a different meaning at different times. Having to cook was sometimes a drudgery, while at other times the preparation was an impressive creation. Then the whole afternoon would be spent on choosing recipes, and then chopping, grinding and marinating various ingredients. The residents had strong views on what was acceptable to eat and, especially, what they would never eat. One of them didn't like fish, another hated carrots and onions, and yet another one never ate peppers, or was it maybe leeks. Most of them never ate meat, which they equated with eating a corpse. All feared eggs and cheese as a potential source of contamination and there were even some reservations about vegetables and fruit. It was assumed they were sprayed with pesticides that might lead to cancer. All these different needs were patiently taken into consideration. Finally, in a kitchen covered with cigarette smoke, a meal would emerge, usually plentiful and often delicious. This was the time of the day when they all came together and shared the goodness of life. While some ate from bare necessity, others had generous helpings and seemed to enjoy every bite.

Visiting the house was in many ways like coming to an island, a different world, where people's predominant concern was their therapy, their feelings, their moods, their lives – little outside this house seemed to be of much importance. The general fantasy of the outside world was that it was bad; it was polluted, cruel, frustrating and very demanding. The house was their shelter, where they hoped to find nourishment and care.

My greatest anxiety during the first weeks was finding a place in the community. Feeling ignored as I often did, it puzzled me that they wanted me to come. I searched them for hostility, but found what seemed more like benevolent indifference. My experience seemed to be so different from most other students. The stories I had heard were that the residents were unbearably needy, that they fought for our time and attention, and drained us with intolerable demands. In contrast I felt like an abandoned old grandmother as I sat on my own in the kitchen with my knitting. At first I would leave in the evenings feeling lonely and out of place. Then my car took on new dimensions; it was my getaway and my refuge. But as weeks became months I gradually felt more at home and the residents found their way back into the kitchen.

My greatest difficulty was in coping with the residents' rejection. In spite of my conscious effort, I found it very hard to dissociate myself as a person from the role I was in. Even though I understood intellectually that a student is a target for various projections, I feared that their rejection really had to do with me. I wasn't sharp enough, my grasp of English wasn't up to their standard or they couldn't bear my insecurity. These fears gradually wore off, as did my awe of their proficient and clever conversation. It was a relief to realize that what they were looking for in me was not a bright therapist who could interpret everything they said, but rather someone who took an interest in them and was willing to listen and share their experiences. When I felt confident in that role, I could more easily accept my limitations; I was not a therapist, but I still had something to offer.

During my first weeks in the community, 'David', a man who sat silently around the dinner table and seemed less than keen to make my acquaintance, was often my only companion. David was 39 years old and had been living in the house for six months when I started my placement. Usually David got up in the afternoon and, in time, came down for a cup of tea. Then we would both wait for him to show some further signs of being awake. After some silence and many sighs he told me that he really should not be there. His only problem was being too lazy to get a proper job and he hated living on his own. He had been feeling pretty low when he first came, but it was different now. He thought it was embarrassing and humiliating to be on benefits when in fact he could be supporting himself. David felt he was forced to have therapy through no will of his own and he thought the house was useless. It didn't give him what he needed, which was encouragement and support. He said he felt sorry for me spending my days there and was convinced I hated it.

What I soon noticed about David was the way he related to me. He would talk about various things, but I had the uneasy feeling that he wasn't aware of my presence at all. I feared it was my fault that we could not establish a fruitful relationship in the long afternoons we spent together – that I didn't have anything interesting enough to say. But whatever I would contribute to our 'conversation', he would look at me, listen patiently to what I said, comment on it briefly, and then carry on as if nothing had happened. He usually started off in a quiet way, but the contents of his monologues were invariably tuned into one of his very general themes: the inadequacy and corruption of politicians, how the school system breaks people down, how those who hold power or authority are invariably stupid, ignorant and complacent and how people in general are hypocritical, selfish and narrow-minded. All this he would present to me in a very articulate and eloquent manner, which left me feeling quite speechless and rather depressed.

After David had evacuated himself and left me feeling depressed, he sometimes found the energy to do his art work. That, however, was not done without pain, for he doubted his talent and frequently feared that inspiration and creativity had left him. He would start with his mind blank on a painting or a drawing and invariably he ended up with a man's face, a marked, grim face, in dark colours. He searched his pictures for meaning and answers and started to look at them as his salvation. Painting was his therapy, only through his creativity would he find his true inner self. Formal therapy had never helped at all; it was a dead, intellectual, grown-up people's game with words.

And that is what I believe therapy became in David's case. In order not to let any real feelings emerge, he filled the session with words. It was a desperate escape from feeling any sign of loneliness or emptiness inside himself and any hint of need or dependency.

Around Christmas David started a sexual relationship with 'Cathy'. He had spoken very contemptuously to me about women in general, whom he believed were only after great big men who could provide well. Cathy, on the other hand, was different. She was the only person he valued in the community and he admired her creativity, her independence and her status in the house. At Cathy's initiative they broke up a few weeks later, as the tension of having an intimate relationship had become unbearable. Whatever David went through, he kept it to himself. He was in a productive phase and creating things was his first and only priority. David told me that relationships come secondary to art – if he were successful in his work, problems would naturally and effortlessly solve themselves. Through the seeds of art he would harvest meaningful relationships.

During my period of initiation there was a vacancy in the house. For several months uncertainty reigned about whether a former resident would return or not. Finally, when everyone accepted he had left, a new problem arose. Choosing a new resident who would fit into this quiet and in many ways harmonious little household was not going to be easy. Whoever it

would be, he or she must not be too demanding or disturbing. He would
have to adjust to the group; the group did not want to adjust to an outsider.
After several meetings with anxious applicants the community chose a
pale, thin man who seemed to meet all these requirements; even his name
was that of a quiet stranger, 'John Brown'. We didn't learn much about
his background and he seemed eager to burn his bridges by giving up his
council flat and most of his possessions. One of the few things he said
about himself was that he had been living on his own in London for some
years and coming to the community seemed to be his last resort. He had
no contact with his family and when I asked him whether his parents were
alive, he replied, 'Well, I guess so'.

I myself made little contact with John. He spent most of his time in his
room, at mealtimes he would come down, sit on the edge of his chair and
eat what to me seemed a bird's portion. After thanking us for the meal
John used to return to his room. At times I forgot that he was in the house
at all.

I think the residents felt sorry for John and realized he needed time to
settle in, but they thought there was not much they could do to help him.
They were friendly towards him and I think they easily identified with
someone so deprived, needy and frightened of close contact. John's only
initiative was to ask time and again what was expected of him, what could
he do or not do. He seemed frightened to be in the way or to be a nuisance.
A few residents were irritated by his constant apologies and told him he
had the same rights as everyone else in the house. My attitude towards
him was the same as the residents'; to give him time.

But there wasn't much time. Five weeks after John came, he left the
house one Wednesday morning. Late that evening the police in Southend
phoned the community and said they had found John and feared he was
in danger of killing himself. Two of the residents went to fetch him. The
following evening there was a house meeting, at which people expressed
their worries and concern. John repeatedly said that he could not believe
or feel their concern. He knew that they were just saying this out of duty
and it had nothing to do with caring for him.

When I arrived at the house on Monday, there was no one there. This
was not unusual, but I had a strange sensation that all was not well. The
house seemed empty and cold and dark, in spite of its being a warm and
sunny day. I didn't give this much thought and was glad to find a note on
the table, saying that I could collect a book in the office, which is near to
the community. Only when I went there did I learn that John had

committed suicide the previous night by throwing himself under a train. He did this at a station which is practically on the community's doorstep.

My immediate reaction was to go back to the house. I started cleaning the kitchen, not just tidying up, but scrubbing the cupboards, almost frantically. Thinking back, it was like I was trying to wash John's blood off the house. This was a situation I was not prepared for. Strangely enough, my nursing textbooks don't deal with the possibility of patients succeeding in taking their lives. The case histories are about prevention and invariably have a 'happy ending'. This seemed to be reflected in my working reality, for although I had experienced a few 'unhappy endings', I did not know where to go from there. As any member of nursing staff I had learnt to 'cope', which meant basically brushing my feelings under the carpet and getting on with my work. Not so this time. Regardless of my interventions, I was faced with people who were determined to talk openly about their feelings.

They soon returned to the house. Some of them had been to a park. They had talked and cried and hugged each other for the whole day. They talked about how this tragedy had opened their eyes to what life is about, how determined they were to take care of one another from now on, that nothing else mattered, everything else was trivial. There was a sense of desperate clinging to life. In the face of death they had to put all emphasis on living and being alive. As time has passed this day has been remembered and longed for like no other day. The closeness and intimacy they conveyed then was never recaptured.

The essence in the discussion about the suicide was not John himself or his personal tragedy, but the suicide as a reflection upon the people who lived there. John's personality seemed to fade away. What remained was an idealized image of a very delicate, sensitive and unhappy man, who had considerable artistic and creative potentials. When they went through his things, they discovered his poetry, his paintings, his violin; every interest of John's was shared by someone else in the house. A representation of what they valued in themselves had been killed in a sudden and brutal way.

Some residents seemed to admire John's courage, that he actually did kill himself and ended his sufferings. They guessed how devastated he must have been since he saw no other way out. This view was fiercely rejected by others. They said that his unhappiness was no more than that of the others in the group. He just didn't have the courage to live and struggle like the rest of them. John made this choice and it was a choice none of them would make.

In the days that followed, the atmosphere of the house was coloured by one of sadness, grief, loss and intimacy. Suicide was something they were all familiar with; they knew every aspect of it, except the definite experience. But in their fantasies, the residents themselves were in control. They were the ones who left and rejected their families, the community – life itself. Instead, *they* were being abandoned and rejected. The actuality was so cruel and aroused such intense feelings that it was almost unbearable. They tried to hold and comfort one another, determined to let something good come out of this. All except 'Rosa'.

Rosa had been living in the house for about a year at the time of the suicide. She had never looked at herself as being a part of the group. She told me that she was opposed to groups in general and to this one in particular. Her attitude towards the house was cool. Staying there was something she had to endure in order to have therapy. She did what was expected of her, like cooking and coming to house meetings, but apart from that she stayed away as much as she could. Her main criticism of the group was their lack of interest or genuine care for other people. As much as she valued her therapy, Rosa said she was worried that psychotherapy made people very egoistic and self-indulgent. People in therapy were always thinking what is best for *me*, how can *I* feel better, while consideration for others vanished into thin air.

John's death seemed like a confirmation of her view. No one in the house had really cared for John, or for anyone else, come to that. She had no patience for 'those people' and she withdrew completely, blaming the house for his death. Rosa felt endless contempt and rage, not against John, but against herself, the house, the co-ordinators, John's therapist, therapy in general, everyone except John. The group was the bad, uncaring, callous monster, while John was a victim, a vulnerable, helpless, idealized child. He had come to the house and seen through their hypocrisy, and she admired his guts for rejecting them. He had acted out her revenge on them for being uncaring.

When I left in the evenings and tried to understand the complexity of my feelings, I mostly felt sad and angry. I felt sad for someone so desperately isolated, who caught a glimpse of a different world, but could not believe he would ever be a part of it. I was deeply moved by the residents' sincere and painful endeavours in dealing with their trauma. This fuelled my resentment for what I saw as John's insidiousness, giving the impression of himself as a harmless invalid and then destroying himself and the goodness he could not have: the community. I felt rejected by him for never giving me or anyone else a chance, for assuming that we were all useless, impotent.

In the first days after John's death, David contributed greatly to a feeling of closeness and intimacy in the house. But he knew no limits. He could not be seized by grief and it was as if he had at all costs to avoid feelings of being abandoned and being alone. He went into a phase of total denial. John's death was not tragic, on the contrary it was a beginning of something beautiful. It was like a floodgate had burst, but all the overwhelming and powerful feelings that suddenly erupted could only be perceived as good, loving, creative.

The group's sense of unity so prominent in the first days after John's death drastically gave way to a state of disintegration. David filled the kitchen completely with endless talking and messy creations and the residents felt they were being pushed out.

I was lost in all this. I could see that David was losing control and in the situations I had previously worked in he would have been treated with tranquillizers. But this was different. Or was it? With hindsight I can see that I was only too willing to give up my nursing uniform and too naive in my belief in omnipotent psychotherapy. I was reluctant to accept that the situation was getting beyond reasonable management as I waited for a magical breakthrough.

After several sleepless nights things went from bad to worse for David. He was extremely disruptive, and unless he changed people would not have him in the house. I stayed with him for a few hours one night, trying to help him to get some sleep. When I had put him to bed like a little boy, a very different David emerged. He accepted my restrictions, like not smoking or talking, and seemed to be relieved that someone took control of him. For the first time I had a sense of closeness, catching a glimpse of what was underneath his armour of defence. He started crying and said he didn't want to die. He felt the bed was his grave and the duvet the soil on top of him. If he were to fall asleep, that would mean death. He was afraid of the dark and several times he called out my name, just to make sure I was still with him. He finally gave in and slept for 14 hours, or until he was woken up by one of the residents for a doctor's appointment. He exploded with rage, and although his fury subsided within minutes, this was the limit. No one would tolerate him any longer and he was admitted to hospital.

In my account I have not done justice to the residents who survived this ordeal and continued to enrich their lives in the community. Instead I have focused on the two men who could not be contained there. For me this was a shattering experience, bearing in mind that when I entered the world of psychotherapy I had little doubt that I was going from a bad alternative to an ideal one. But with the recognition that therapeutic communities are not ideal, my perception of good therapy and bad medicine has lost its force. This experience has enabled me to appreciate that in the endeavour to be 'good enough', therapeutic communities are neither black nor white, but contain a wide range of colours.

PART II
CRISIS CENTRE

7 CONJOINT THERAPY WITHIN A THERAPEUTIC MILIEU: THE CRISIS TEAM

JOSEPH H. BERKE

Conjoint therapy, that is, the use of several therapists in a single therapeutic intervention, is really quite unusual. Sometimes group therapists may utilize a partner. Alternatively family therapy may be practised as part of a multi-focused intervention. In this chapter I shall describe the extended use of two or more co-therapists in the direct psychodynamic treatment of severely disturbed men and women. This work has been done at the Arbours Crisis Centre in London since 1973.

At the Centre we begin every intervention by establishing a treatment team. This 'crisis team' carries the primary responsibility of working with the individual who has come to stay at the Centre. It includes a team leader, a resident therapist and often a third member as well. The team leader is an experienced psychotherapist who co-ordinates the intervention. The resident therapist is the therapist who lives at the Centre and has the most immediate involvement with the guest. The third member is an Arbours trainee or other professional doing a placement at the Centre.

Throughout his or her stay, the guest will meet with this team three to five times per week in formal 50-minute sessions. And in the rare circumstances when a guest becomes exceptionally agitated, we may convene additional ad hoc team meetings. But besides these meetings, the guests usually have informal discussions with the resident therapist or third team member several, sometimes many times per week.

The team itself is part of a multi-system approach to working with people who can no longer cope with their lives for a variety of intrapsychic, interpersonal or situational reasons. They come to the Centre when they are depressed, withdrawn, panic-stricken and/or self-mutilating. Sometimes they are in a state of psychosis during all or part of this stay.

The diagram on the next page illustrates the Centre's three separate but

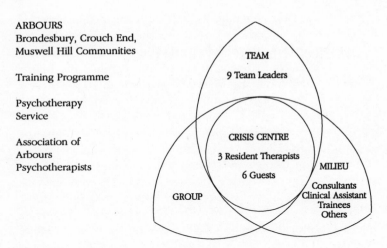

ARBOURS
Brondesbury, Crouch End,
Muswell Hill Communities

Training Programme

Psychotherapy
Service

Association of
Arbours
Psychotherapists

The Arbours Crisis Centre's three systems: the milieu, the group and the team

interrelated and interrelating systems. These are the milieu, the group and the team. The milieu is the Centre in its role as an overall therapeutic environment. The group encompasses the organized set of formal house meetings that take place three times a week. Consequently the context of the team is the group and the context of the group is the milieu. One might even point out that the context for the milieu is the whole Arbours network. As I have also demonstrated in the diagram, the Arbours network includes three long-stay therapeutic communities, the Training Programme, the Psychotherapy Service and the Association of Arbours Psychotherapists. Thus, the Arbours, as a whole, involves over 70 therapists, 50 trainees and 25 residents of our community.

Before focusing on the conjoint intervention of the team, it is important to consider the milieu and the group in greater detail. These two basic operating systems sustain and are also sustained by the work of the team.

The milieu is an active therapeutic environment. It includes the resident therapists, the guests, the team leaders, a clinical assistant, various consultants, an art therapist, a movement therapist, therapists in charge of our Follow-Up Support Programme as well as several trainees and professionals doing placements at the Centre. This intense social environment serves several purposes. It contains feelings. It sets boundaries for different and difficult behaviour. It manages the expression or nonexpression of feelings. And generally it deals with the practicalities of day-to-day living together. In other words it mediates external reality.

The group consists of all the people who live in the house: the therapists and the guests. They are the ones who attend and conduct the house meetings. The only exception is that once a week the trainees are invited to attend. Essentially the house meetings provide the opportunity for mirroring, role-playing and social feedback. It often provides the occasion for one of the older guests, an individual who has been at the Centre for weeks or months, and has begun to reconstitute himself emotionally and socially, to act as a guide, teacher and therapist for new guests. The house culture tends to be passed on during these meetings. One resident, for example, who came to the Centre because he couldn't tolerate feelings and, indeed, looked like a zombie, began to emerge from this state after six weeks. Subsequently, he took the lead in explaining to new guests at house meetings that the reason they had come was '*to learn to know what you feel*'.

The milieu and group (the house meetings) attend to external reality – what we do with each other, and to some aspects of internal reality – feelings, the emotional tides as well as the undercurrents. In contrast, the task of the team is to explore, to interpret, to pull together the feelings and phantasies that arise with a particular guest. Thus, the team mediates internal reality by focusing on the transference relationships that emerge, towards the house, the group, the therapists and towards other guests as well.

Of course there are many times when the work of the team overlaps with that of the milieu and group, but I think it functions best when the team is able to concentrate on the here and now of the team meeting, its space and its time. In this sense one of the most basic therapeutic goals of the milieu and group is to enable the guest to use the team. Often guests find this very difficult. When they first come, they may try to protect themselves against the impact of the other team members by silence, withdrawal, or by missing meetings. With these individuals you can follow the development of a therapeutic alliance by their participating in the life of the house, then in the work of the group and finally by their actively attending the team meetings.

The team is a complicated therapeutic system in its own right. First, there are three to five formal meetings per week. Second, there are a variety of informal meetings among the guests, resident therapists and trainees. These comprise a set of significant subsystems without which the formal work of the team would be relatively impoverished. Third, the therapists and trainees hold a regular discussion each week and a variety of shorter informal exchanges. Finally, the team itself links up with all the therapists at an extended clinical discussion once a fortnight. (In between, many informal discussions take place.) From this outline of extended network relations, one can glimpse the multi-levelled tiers of support that this system provides both for the guest and his therapists as well as for the Centre as a whole.

Significantly, the internal structure of the formal team meeting also varies. It functions in two different ways at different times: as a *shared team* and as a *differentiated team*. This organization and reorganization of the team is of particular relevance to our ability to work with severely disturbed individuals.

In the shared team, the members can play any part and take any role. Thus a therapist may take on the role of a guest, or a guest may take on the role of a therapist. Some members may remain as silent witnesses, others may be active interveners. The resident therapist and team leader tend to be equal partners and each feels free to make interpretive comments.

In a differentiated team one member, usually the team leader, acts as the therapist, making interpretive comments and focusing the transference onto himself. The resident therapist and trainee remain as silent witnesses, but active listeners. They take a much more direct and vital part after the formal meeting is over. Then they help the guest to digest what has occurred, what the team leader has said. Thus, in a differentiated team the resident therapist and trainees act more specifically as surrogate egos for the guests.

Interestingly, my description of these two ways of working with guests parallels current developments in family therapy. These allow for two different forms of engagement according to the clients and issues involved. They are the 'partnership model' and the 'leadership model'. The partnership mode emphasizes an egalitarian relationship. Both therapists and client explore problems together and there is plenty of room for empathy and self-disclosure by either side. On the other hand, the leadership mode emphasizes a hierarchical relationship. Here the roles of therapist and patient are clearly defined, with one giving help and the other receiving it. In either case, the work is often carried out by a team which uses and integrates both the partnership and the leadership approach at different points in the therapy (model discussed by Hoffman, 1990–1991).

When a guest comes to the Centre, the team will initially function as a shared team, that is, as a partnership. Then it may shift to a differentiated, leadership mode. When this happens depends on the degree of disturbance of the guest as well as the stage of his stay.

What do I mean by the expression 'stage of stay'? In a previous paper (Berke, 1987) I explained that all guests pass through five distinct periods or stages while they are at the Centre, regardless of their reasons for coming. These stages can be compared to five states of mind and greatly influence the feelings and actions of the guests while they are at the Centre. These stages are Arriving, Settling-In, Settling-Down, Leaving and Following-Up.

During the *Arriving* stage, the primary fears of the new arrivals have to do with leaving home, relating to a new place and new people, loss of control, regression and going mad. Whatever else, these fears have to be considered first, otherwise the new arrival will not be able to establish a therapeutic alliance with the Centre, the group or with the team.

The second stage, *Settling-In*, is marked by a decrease in arrival fears and an increasing willingness to reflect on the underlying issues that brought the guest to the Centre. It is during this stage that the framework of meetings is fully fixed. The third stage, *Settling-Down*, is the occasion for interpersonal association and intrapsychic consolidation. During this stage a lot of internal integration takes place.

The fourth stage, *Leaving*, may arouse a fresh crisis because leaving necessarily arouses ambivalence, sadness and depressive feelings which may seem too strong to bear. Therefore a wish to repeat the original breakdown may occur.

The fifth and final stage, *Following-Up*, can cover weeks and months after the guest has left and can be a period of further consolidation. The team holds two follow-up meetings at the Centre over the course of a fortnight. During this period we often arrange for a further course of individual therapy to take place, either with the person's previous therapist, or with a new therapist as needed. In addition we ask all the guests to fill out a detailed questionnaire about their stay. This is a help to us and many people find this effort has a therapeutic impact.

These stages have a separate, objective existence. This has been demonstrated by the fact that they occur in other, different facilities as well as the Centre. Most notably, this paradigm has been confirmed by colleagues at the Mount Sinai Hospital in Toronto, Canada. In a paper on the intensive treatment of borderline patients they delineate stages which are practically identical to the ones I have described (Silver, Cardish and Glassman, 1987). They describe these stages as follows: one: *Assessment* or the *Honeymoon*; two: *Therapeutic Encirclement* or *Symptomatic*; three: *Therapeutic Engagement* or *Working Through*; and four: *Discharge-Liaison* or *Separation/Re-Entry*. Although the Toronto group doesn't specify a follow-up stage, they do refer to the period 'following discharge' when patients like to return to the ward.

Having considered the stages of stay, let us return to the basic issue, how, why and when does the team differentiate, or not. As I have indicated, at the beginning of the intervention the structure of the team is always shared. This allows the team to explore the emotional range and relational capacity of the guest as well as to focus on his fears of arriving. These are usually directed to the Centre as a whole but may be displaced on to a member of the team or resident of the house. At this point we pay particular attention to the kinds and extremes of feelings aroused in the team members. I previously mentioned the post-team discussions with the guests, an essential subsystem or subcomponent of our team or conjoint approach. Equally vital are the 'post-team' discussions that the therapists have among themselves, where they can explore the tensions, associations and phantasies that develop in and among themselves. This subsystem focuses on the countertransference. Here each therapist can serve as a surrogate ego for the other and is an indispensable support in dealing with the confusing, destructive elements which the guests seek to evacuate into them.

Many guests are not in touch with their feelings. Therefore they can't talk about them. In other words they are emotionally and verbally inarticulate. Instead they dramatize or act out what is happening, or not happening (in themselves) within the team (a reflection of what happens in the house meeting and the Centre as a whole). The shared team serves as a very sensitive barometer of such issues which occur outside conscious awareness.

Let me describe one guest, a middle-aged Spanish man, who came to the Centre feeling suicidally depressed. Far from being withdrawn, he initially talked incessantly, barraging us with words, demands, questions and more demands to the point where the resident therapist felt severely under attack and wanted to scream at him, and at me for inviting him to the Centre. This went on for several days. She felt very pressured by him. I also felt pressured by him, but more so by the resident therapist who also had to put up with his difficult behaviour in the house when I wasn't there. As for the trainee, she just withered on the vine, that is, became more and more withdrawn.

In our discussions we considered a lot of these experiences, but to no avail. We seemed to get increasingly acrimonious in our relationships with each other. It was painful to attend the team meetings. Then it occurred to me that this sense of intense pressure we felt, and were inflicting on each other, had to do with the very tensions which this man was suffering. He was not able to articulate them directly, but he chose to communicate and to get rid of the pressures by arousing them in us. As far as he was concerned, they were crazy-making and non-containable. He could not think and we were in danger of becoming like him. Yet, as soon as we appreciated this, the tensions in us became manageable. We didn't need to interpret this to him. At the time he would have felt that we were shoving the experience back into him. But our realizations meant we could approach things differently. In the sessions, we became calmer and less hostile. Perhaps, most important of all, we could think again. The outcome was remarkable. Almost as soon as we accepted these pressures in ourselves, he proceeded to calm down.

When thinking about the interpersonal complexity of such a situation, it is not sufficient to say that the guest simply pushes non-containable experiences into the therapist. Rather he acts to stir up an area of disturbance which is already pre-existent in the therapist. When this happens, the therapist feels as if he or she were under attack. Invariably he will attack back by withdrawing, by making premature interpretations or by actual verbal and physical abuse. The guest, in turn, correctly perceives that he is under attack and tends to respond in kind. An escalating aggressive tension ensues. Alternatively, when the therapist understands (and thereby accepts) the disturbance in himself, he is able to be less aggressive to the guest. This person is then able to calm down, because he no longer feels under external threat, and because he is less intimidated by his own impulses.

In another intervention 'Ian', a young Scotsman, was referred to the Centre because his life had come to a standstill. He used to work and play cricket and socialize in pubs. Now he stayed at home, didn't see anyone and watched TV. He felt desperate and hopeless, but he was willing to give us a try. A month of meetings passed. He replied to almost everything we said with 'That's right', but remained impassive and blocked.

In the house he kept talking about wanting to have sex, but kept aloof from the women. They, in turn, disliked and avoided him, especially when he seemed to stare at them from the corner of his eye. We found out that his mother had thrown him and his father out of their house in order to take in a variety of lovers. As a teenager, women had found him attractive, but when a girl told him she fancied him, he went out and smashed up cars.

Finally, after two very long months at the Centre, he began to talk about feeling depressed. He said that there was pressure in his head, that he wanted to turn off the valve, let it out, but that he couldn't. In doing so he engaged me, but studiously avoided Lois, my co-therapist. There was also a distinct tinge of hostility in his voice. About two-thirds of the way through the session Lois exclaimed angrily,

'You know, I really feel left out. I feel very jealous that you two are doing all the talking. I'm a nothing, just ignored and left out.'

I hadn't appreciated this but immediately realized that I had been colluding with Ian to shut Lois out. So I turned to Lois and began to focus on her. Here was someone who felt 'bloody annoyed', and I tried to bring her jealousy, her upset back into the group. At that moment Lois was the 'guest' and Ian the observer, watching the drama of himself played out before his eyes. Eventually I turned back to Ian,

'What do you think about Lois?'

'Oh, she's just a slag!'

But Ian was engaged and the jealous anger that he had tried to bury in Lois became amenable to discussion. And as he retrieved his jealousies, a strange new current emerged in the team and in the house. The women began to like him.

These two vignettes exemplify some of the useful interventions that can be made by the shared team. With short stays or less traumatized guests the team may continue on a shared basis until the end of the stay. But with psychotic or very chaotic individuals the sooner the team shifts to a differentiated organization the better. This allows the focal therapist, usually the team leader, to direct the strong libidinal and anti-libidinal or aggressive transferences to himself and protect the resident therapist who is otherwise in continuing direct contact with these currents. It brings 'the craziness' into the team, and away from the house. It creates calm space, both within the house and within the psyche of the resident therapist. From this we can see that in order to be effective, the team leader, along with the resident therapist, has to be open to confusion, despair, fear, rage, worthlessness, fragmentation, panic and similar terrible experiences. Both need to take in, and be willing to suffer, all the intolerable feelings that perfuse the guest and from which he is desperately trying to escape by annihilating his states of mind.

I have written a paper (Berke, 1981) which illustrates the use of the differentiated team. In it I discussed a businessman called 'Paul', who was going through a psychotic breakdown. This was connected to the anniversary of the death of his brother.

We started with a shared team. During the Arriving stage Paul repeatedly tried to escape from the Centre or set fire to it. He feared being trapped inside a constricting, confining inferno, his mother. Slowly, as he settled down, the acting-out diminished. But the resident therapist and trainees were overwhelmed. They felt they were trapped inside a hell which he was orchestrating. In response, we decided to change the structure of the team, from shared to differentiated. I agreed to see Paul in a daily analytic therapy. The RT and trainee agreed to serve as witnesses.

Paul missed the first session, but then began to come regularly. These meetings were wild and chaotic, but the acting-out in the Centre tailed off dramatically. During the first week of the reorganization, he described a dream about a pyramid of bodies covered with blood. His associations led to seeing me as a bad, angry figure, like his father, like his conscience, someone who was out to decapitate and castrate him, as I put into words. Suddenly he froze and spat at my glasses. Then he cried, came over and flopped into my arms. After a couple of minutes, he got up, took my glasses and went into the kitchen of the Centre to get a rag to wipe them clean. He returned and put the glasses on a drawing done by another guest, which was a big sun with red marks on and about it. I interpreted that in attacking my glasses he was also attacking my breasts. They were covered in blood, the results of his angry, biting attacks on me. And this was another reason why he feared I would retaliate and cut off his head. Further associations and interpretations led to a great sense of relief.

Afterwards he went to his resident therapist and carefully went over what we had discussed. He feared he would lose my words, my understanding, his understanding. Other guests in similar circumstances have gone to my co-therapist and complained about me: ' *What's that crazy stuff Joe's been talking about ?*'

In all these circumstances the function of the co-therapist, the witness, is to explain carefully what I meant, and to help the guest digest what I say. However, I don't wish to suggest, nor give the impression, that the role of the co-therapist is just limited to agreeing with my interpretations and to repeating them to the guest in post-team discussions. Often the formulations made during the course of the team meetings have been arrived at after a long period of thought and discussion involving all members of the team.

In the differentiated team the resident therapist is an intermediary, a transitional figure between the team leader and the guest, between his craziness and the house culture, between inner reality and outer practicality. Then by identifying with the resident therapist, and his capacity to tolerate and assimilate my thoughts, the guest gains intermediary space within himself. The expansion of this intermediary or transitional space within his own mind gradually enables him to regain what we might call sanity.

Paul stayed at the Centre for a couple of months. This period of time is what we call a medium stay. Long stays may last for up to a year. Both medium and long stays allow for the transference to be elaborated and for the team to shift to a differentiated structure. We do have guests who come for shorter periods, a few weeks. During these interventions we usually maintain a shared team structure. However, I now think that all teams can profitably shift from a shared to differentiated structure once the guest has overcome the Arriving stage.

Leaving creates distinct problems of its own. It is frequently necessary for a differentiated team to shift back to a shared structure in order to respond to the massive outbursts of feeling that accompany leaving. At the same time the resident therapist may also undergo a shift in his mental state that complements the guest's 'leaving crisis' and may find it intolerable to remain a witness. The feelings evoked here are not simply to do with countertransference. Having lived with another human being at a very high level of emotional intensity, the resident therapist can and does feel tremendous loss, sadness and emptiness when his guest goes. As with the guest, during leaving, we need to help the resident therapist to 'assume his depression'.

The conjoint therapy I have described allows for a great flexibility in working with disturbed and disturbing individuals. It also allows us to provide crucial support for the therapists involved. Then they are able to assist each other in coping with the massive onslaught of projections that occurs during an emotional crisis, to experience and contain them. At the least this allows the guest to identify with, in transference, a containing maternal/paternal figure who has been able to modify otherwise impossible pain and despair. But the active role that the co-therapists play means that the guest, by the creation of a transitional internal space, and by identifying with the therapist as analyst and therapist as witness, is able to regain his capacity to perceive and evaluate reality.

In reality, our therapeutic goals are modest. We can't turn around a person's life in a few weeks or a few months, especially the kind of people who come to our Centre. What we can do is help guests to tolerate their underlying despair, to identify their difficulties and conflicts, and to expand in some small ways their relational capacities – to begin to feel the possibility of intimacy, empathy and trust. In order to achieve this we do not remain passive onlookers. Rather we are active participants in the experiences they try to disgorge. Sometimes it seems that the main difference between them and ourselves is that we are more able to ask for help in struggling with intolerable feelings and states of mind. In other words as therapists we can turn to each other for support, for advice, for supervision, for understanding. And if we can't get that from each other, we can, at least, turn to our colleagues, the multiplicity of healing systems, which comprise the Centre, and to other aspects of the Arbours network.

As one might expect, there remain many problems. I have not been simply describing conjoint therapy, but a co-therapy with colleagues who live in a residential milieu. They need to accept the burden of the guests' turmoil both as a member of a dynamic team and, on a continuing basis from many different angles, as a member of a dynamic household. The resident therapists can easily feel used up and burnt out, all the more because we do not depend on drugs to force guests to stop feeling or acting distraught.

Remarkably, the existence of split transferences, which we expected would present great obstacles to a therapeutic engagement, does not seem to do so. If anything the team is able to utilize the split transference, good and bad, self and other, maternal and paternal, as it emerges in and among the resident therapists and the team leaders in order to reach the inner realities of the guest more clearly. In this respect, it is worth noting that the work of the team can never entirely remove the threat of the powerful transferences that are directed to the resident therapists. But by focusing these currents on the team leader, they become less oppressive in the group and milieu and give the resident therapists more space to develop non-transferential relationships with the guests.

Whatever the difficulties, the conjoint therapy I have described has allowed us to effect significant change in severely disturbed individuals without relying on biochemical or other forms of physical restraint. We have also seen, time and time again, that a tangle of sorrows can lead to a tango of joy. Nothing is more uplifting both for the team leaders and resident therapists than to see someone who had been dismissed as a 'hopeless case' regain his hope and vitality.

Before he left, Paul rediscovered a trove of lost affection for his wife. And Ian, who 'never felt nothing about no one', exclaimed he felt better, although 'God knows why'. Ian was happy/sad. He knew that he would miss Lois. He was also pleasantly surprised. When he came he expected his lot would be bread and water (prison food, deprivation, absence). Yet, upon leaving he realized he wanted and could enjoy the roast chicken, the chicken that Lois made for him at his leaving meal, the chicken which for him and us came to symbolize our work together.

8 A SAVAGE SADNESS: JOURNEYS INTO SPACE

STELLA PIERIDES

A stay at the Crisis Centre can be seen as a journey one undertakes in the hope of arriving at a safer place within oneself. People embarking on such a journey set out with hope but also, more often than not, with great fear. The journey itself may become unbearable, at times, and for some, it may have to be interrupted. For others, however, who manage to hold on to hope and persevere, a stay at the Crisis Centre becomes an enriching experience. Even though it is not – and indeed it cannot be in such a short time – a cure, it does provide an opportunity for individuals to explore their inner space and to begin to look, with help, at the conflicts raging within themselves. Often this initial journey catalyses the long and arduous process of personal therapy. Alternately, the gain from a stay at the Centre may be sufficient in itself to enable the guest to resume his relationships, his work, his life.

Needless to say, each Odyssey is a unique experience; the blend of an individual's personal luggage, his specific history and difficulties, with his interactions with the special environment provided by the Crisis Centre. In this paper I illustrate one such person's passage, and in doing so I hope to show how the Crisis Centre team worked with him.

'Matthew' was 20 years old when he came to the Crisis Centre for a nine-month stay. He had many hospitalizations and different diagnoses. Schizophrenia was one of them. Matthew entered the Centre with a sweet smile on his face that evoked, almost automatically, a smiling response from whomever was around. It emerged that the smile served to hide his immense fears and literally disarmed anyone who came into contact with him. The idea of meeting us made him feel extremely threatened. He thought that we could hear his thoughts – after all, he spoke them aloud – although he disclaimed them as not really his own. He continued to say that he had no thoughts, feelings, desires or needs.

Having locked himself out of his sense of self by denying his own thoughts and feelings, he immediately made use of the physical space of the Centre to express his distress. Each team meeting began with his going in and out of the room, in and out of the room. These movements seemed to go on interminably. I was sure that he was driven by the need to test whether he could go out, that he was not trapped, and that he could also come back in. This behaviour became an important aspect of our work together and we spent a lot of time trying to put words to the issues around the psychic sojourns that made it necessary.

Around the Centre, outside the team meetings, Matthew expressed this particular aspect of his distress in a variety of ways. Terrified of people, and the feelings they might arouse in him, he was unable to be around the house during the day; he had to stay in his room. Terrified of the people who filled his dreams, he was unable to sleep during the night. He could not go outside the Centre except to the front garden, becoming a prisoner of the actual space of the Centre.

Matthew also used his body to express the struggles in his internal world; he had asthma and eczema. He would often break out in a rash during the meetings, scratching frantically and spraying the air with scales or he would rush out of the consulting room to breathe. At other times, he would come in 'for a breath of fresh air'. In this way, he expressed, through his actions, his fears/wishes about the therapeutic space and his attachment to it.

During the initial stage of his stay, Matthew would often miss his meetings. Unable to enter the space he had previously filled, in his phantasy, with the unwanted aspects of himself, he stayed in his room. During these times, the resident therapist in the team and myself (the team leader) would be sitting through his meeting trying to make sense of how we felt about his absence – frustrated, angry, hopeless – and the meaning(s) behind it. My co-therapist would then make contact with Matthew some time later during that day to say to him something about the missed meeting.

This was always something that we felt would convey a sense of continuity from what went on in the previous team meeting without putting any pressure on him. We came to see this contact as offering him a little concentrated food for thought, like a 'peanut' that would sustain him till the next meeting. At the same time, we were aware that this 'peanut' could very easily be turned into 'peanuts', into nothing, or into poisonous food that would turn him to 'nuts'. I found that struggling with this issue, tiptoeing along a line which seemed precarious and yet important to follow, bore fruit. Matthew would manage to let himself out of his room and into the consulting room. For this to become possible, the resident therapist had to provide the bridge between two, or indeed several, spaces, thus allowing our work to progress in a way that would not have been possible otherwise.

This bridging function allowed Matthew to come to his meetings more consistently and to bring his distress inside the consulting room. For instance, in one of the meetings he literally threw himself on to my chair, almost hitting me in the process. He refused to give up my space for a good 35 minutes, putting me on the spot. I was standing up all this time, increasingly seeing the importance of standing my ground for both of us. We came to see that his sitting in my chair meant for him that he could turn his back on both of us, and on our working together towards a common goal. Yet, at the same time, he was being a baby himself, evacuating what he called his headache, his painful thoughts and feelings, which he expected me to have. On this occasion, sitting in my chair brought the headache of his being powerless and separate to an end, because I was to carry the headache for both of us.

Later on in the meeting, when I was back in my chair, Matthew reported that the headache was back. Yet it took us weeks before we could connect the headache to his birthday, that is, the day he was physically separated from his mother. The problem was that he could not experience himself as a separate person. Any ideas, sensations or feelings that he was separate tore him apart. We had to carry them for him. In a very real sense we became the containers of his intolerable anxiety about separation. In this way the team meetings became equivalent to his mental space, but an expanded space.

The expanded space didn't last for long. The continuous comings and goings, like a bizarre mental traffic, attacked and quite often managed to splinter our thinking. The resident therapist and myself felt that our minds were under attack and that our team was in danger of falling apart. The team itself needed help. So we enlisted the help of a colleague from the team leader group, who, being outside the team, was not caught up in its internal dynamics. The extra 'holding' provided by the outside team member became particularly important when some of the forces from which Matthew had been fleeing were freed. These forces of attachment, together with his wish to annihilate them, appeared in the form of suicidal threats. It became our task to find – between ourselves – the strength to hold things together in the team and not act out our fears of disintegration by medicating or hospitalizing him. On this occasion, staying with and resolving the conflict resulted in Matthew finding 'a new lease of life' and feeling 'reborn', muttering all over the Centre: 'They have faith in me'.

This extension of the team, the drafting of an extra member who remains outside the formal team meetings, is necessary when emotional storms brew up in a guest. These occasions are intensely threatening to everyone living in the house, guests and resident therapists, and to team leaders directly involved in the team. People feel that their own psychic, if not physical, survival is at stake, while their thinking space has drastically shrank. The extra team member helps us to remain calm, re-expand our thinking boundaries and do our work.

There was another way in which Matthew experienced the Centre. Just before I was about to take a holiday break Matthew began to mumble a lot about holiday camps. Encouraged by his resident therapist – who had already heard his mumbling before the team meeting, and was also aware of certain happenings in the house that seemed to be about the break – he said that this place – the Centre – was becoming like a holiday camp. 'Someone in the house had been angry about that', he said. It thus became possible to discuss his being angry with the holidaymakers (me in this case), and also his wish to turn the house into a holiday camp. From there he would not mind my being away, while at the same time he would be keeping me there, totally identifying with me. My co-therapist's sustained encouragement of Matthew, in spite of the pressure coming from him to the contrary, made it possible for him to say that he had secretly gone to the room of a female guest and tried her skirt on. This acknowledgement enabled me to link up his identification with me as the holidaymaker and his wish to avoid separation by literally becoming me.

The understanding of the meaning of this intrusion produced further food for thought. In the context of the group of guests living at the Centre, Matthew's going into someone else's room meant the breaking of important boundaries. Our work enabled Matthew to discuss the incident in the house meeting, with all the guests present. Freed from internal pressures at work in himself, he had been helped to survive the group's anger.

In the context of the team meeting, this interaction enabled Matthew to feel some of his sadness. He showed us his foot. It hurt, an insect had bitten him. 'Is there a plaster in this house?' Becoming aware of the separation, of the impending holiday break, of his sadness about it, was experienced by him as 'being bitten'. This awareness felt like a persecutory and monstrous insect. It had been the fear of his sadness, the fear of its savage nature and overwhelming intensity, that kept Matthew outside any space, especially his own. In this instance, it had come into the consulting room in the form of an insect – which after all was small and manageable. Thus, Matthew had made the transition from the monstrous and intolerably savage, to something that was bearable and workable with.

Our work at that meeting was continued afterwards by the resident therapist who was able to think it, keep it in mind, repeat it to Matthew and also link it with issues in the house for him. In this way the team functioned as a 'differentiated team' as Joe Berke has described it in Chapter 7. The resident therapist became the bridge between the team meetings and the Centre, the inner and the outer, and helped to make the links that Matthew couldn't bear or dare to make or keep in his mind. When later on two guests were leaving the Centre, Matthew was able to tell them, within the by now safe space of the house meeting, of his own anxieties about his own leaving. Modelling himself on his resident therapist, he was also able to admit that 'I have feelings and I fear'. Matthew's increasing ability to move in the different spaces of the Centre and of himself in a more coherent way also became apparent in his art therapy when he stopped ripping apart his paintings and started allowing them the right to exist.

Matthew gradually progressed from not being able to stay in the consulting room for more than a few minutes to being able to use the couch; and he twice fell asleep on it in the conscious hope that he would dream. We came to see this as, to some extent, serving the function of helping him to leave the room in a different way, through sleep. Mainly, however, his sleeping in my presence meant that he could allow himself to feel safe in the presence of another, to experience consciously a moment of peace with another, whom he now saw as enabling him to start moving on the right path of drawing some boundary between dream and reality. In this instance, shutting his eyes occurred mainly in the hope of opening them to the expanse of the unconscious, of dreams, instead of living out his nightmares.

The struggle for a space where Matthew could feel at peace, and from where he could start to experience himself, to weave his own dreams and own his own voice, continued for a long time. The Centre as a whole living and interacting unit helped Matthew reach, like Odysseus, his own 'Ithaca' and find for himself a safe position from which he could begin to collect his thoughts, needs, wishes. His sadness, made a lot more bearable, was one of these experiences.

9   On Being a Resident Therapist at the Crisis Centre

JOHN GREENWOOD, JULIAN IBANEZ and SALLY ROSE

A combination of chance and common circumstances brought the three of us together at the Crisis Centre where we each spent two years as resident therapists, overlapping slightly, between 1990 and 1992. We came with little idea of what living and working there would really be like despite our previous involvement with Arbours and experience in other mental health settings. We have now gone our separate ways and are in a position to reflect upon our experience there and begin to reach an understanding of the complexity of being a 'resident' psychotherapist.

The role of the resident therapist at the Arbours Crisis Centre is a multi-faceted one which involves taking an active part in the treatment of the guest's difficulties, offering support, setting limits and managing the daily running of the Centre. As far as we know, the relationship between resident therapists and guests, combining psychotherapeutic treatment and living together in this way, is unique to the Crisis Centre.

The role of the resident therapists has evolved as an oral tradition passed on from one generation to another. To illustrate our role we will use typical situations drawn from our own experience, beginning with the arrival of a new guest. And even though our experience is now in the past, it has felt right to use the present tense in the main.

When new guests move in, it is the resident therapist's job to help them to settle in both to the physical and therapeutic environment. We find it useful to draw on the memory of our own fears and fantasies around moving in to the Centre. We try to strike a balance between initiating contact, offering support and giving the newcomer space to find their own way. Sometimes, as with 'Jim', we got it wrong. We had not realized just how scared he was. Jim was a young man whose vulnerability was masked by angry and anti-social behaviour. In the follow-up questionnaire sent to guests after they have left the Centre, Jim said he would have liked someone to come to his room after he had been shown around as he had felt lonely and frightened. For Jim to be able to express this to us was an illustration of the progress he made at the Centre.

The Monday afternoon house meeting is the first to be attended by a new guest. The resident therapists try to facilitate open discussion between the group living in the house of which they themselves are part. The meetings vary from lively discussions to awkward silences. At times, they are chaotic and it is difficult to understand what is happening. On other occasions, guests and therapists alike are confronted with how they affect each other.

The first meeting 'Stan' attended was dominated by the group's response to a guest getting drunk and threatening people the night before. Some were angry, some frightened and some even felt that the person involved should leave. One of us, Julian, commented to Stan that it must have been difficult hearing all this on his first day. Stan replied that he would have expected us to help people to stop such behaviour. Stan was worried about how being at the Centre would affect him. What would he discover about himself? Would he feel better or more disturbed?

The next important experience for a new guest is the evening meal. This is the one time of the day when we all get together to share food and companionship. It is a regular moment of physical and emotional nourishment. Guests often find their difficulties painfully exposed at mealtimes and many have eating problems.

One man came to his first evening meal to find 'Tom', another guest, helping himself to most of the lasagne and we had to ask him to leave some for the others. Tom regularly did this and it fitted with the understanding of his impoverished internal life that was emerging in his team meetings. For the new guest, this was a powerful introduction to the rivalry in the group at that time. New people would soon become familiar with the house and its routine, with more experienced guests and ourselves guiding them into the nuances of life at the Centre.

Each guest also has their own team leader (see Chapter 7), a non-resident psychotherapist who works closely with the guest's allocated resident therapist but does not usually meet with the guest other than during team meetings (therapy sessions). On the whole guests find it reassuring that their resident therapist is with them in their therapy and around in the house although they also find the continuity scary. It makes for an intensive therapeutic experience.

The nature of the attention given to the guests inside and outside team meetings differs. Our presence in the therapy sessions serves both as a bridge and as a boundary between the meeting and life outside. We take events in the house to the therapy and use insights from the team meetings to make sense of everyday contact. Often, a guest will mull over with us comments and interpretations made in their sessions. The negotiation of how and when this is done and balancing it with more ordinary everyday contact is a central part of our role. On the other hand our other commitments, need for time for ourselves and for sleep, might, for example, conflict with what a guest wants from us. Handled sensitively this tension proves to be a powerful learning experience for the guest and for ourselves. We seek to allow our guests to feel and express their pain and distress and to be comforted. We try to spell out our limits in a straightforward, non-judgemental way.

The evenings, nights and weekends are when resident therapists become truly resident and when the peculiarities of the job are most marked. The rituals and events surrounding bedtime and night-time often have a family flavour. They evoke the fear and pleasures of childhood. During most of the day we are busy with meetings and not generally available to the guests. As the working day draws to a close, visitors thin out and people begin to relax and feel less under scrutiny. Those for whom the Centre is home, that is just the guests and ourselves, get together.

Each of us has developed our own way of relaxing in the evening. We do not just disappear to our rooms, even though we might long to do so. Sally often sits with her knitting and is companionable; Julian tries to catch up on sport on TV, commenting in a characteristically ebullient Latin way; John is a little less available for conversation, taking his first opportunity to read the morning paper. Evenings at the Centre can be rich and enjoyable; alternately the atmosphere can be heavy and hostile. Feeling and living with the mood generated by the group is a central aspect of our job.

Any tension in the atmosphere is likely to be heightened when we go to bed. Some guests feel abandoned and left to deal with their feelings on their own. They resent being left full of tension and imagine that our nights are restful and pleasant. Some believe we spend the night together (like a parental couple) and one did room checks to satisfy his curiosity.

Crises often occur at night. One night 'Irene' got Julian up because she felt like killing herself. They talked together and Julian felt useless and sad. Before he returned to his room he said, 'I know you still feel awful. I'm going to bed now. I feel worried, but I hope to see you in the morning. If you feel unsafe again tonight, please wake me up'. Irene did not need to do so. Julian had taken some of her despair with him and she knew it. He acknowledged feeling helpless but unlike Irene he could also harbour hope for another day. What is important at such critical moments is that we take into ourselves and tolerate some of the other person's anguish.

On another occasion, however, when faced with a different guest in a similar predicament, we assessed that the risk of suicide was so great that we arranged for him to be admitted to hospital. A crucial factor in this assessment was the breakdown in the alliance between us. Our swift reaction had an important effect on him. He felt that we had appreciated the real danger he was in and to our surprise he discharged himself the next day and returned to the Centre to work on what had happened.

Like anybody else, our attitude to being woken up at night is that we would rather not be disturbed and would not go out of our way to invite it. On the other hand, it is part of the resident therapist's job to be available in an emergency and this is made clear to guests. Fortunately, night interventions are generally rewarding and make us aware of our unique position; the consolation for lost sleep is often an intimate sharing of an otherwise private world. We are not 'night staff' watching over a group of patients. The role has more in common with that of a parent and, like parents, whatever happens we have to function the next day.

One night John was woken up by a guest to be told that 'Lucy' was taking paracetamol tablets. The crisis was more than an attempted suicide. It involved three women – Lucy, 'Maggie' and 'Barbara' – who seemed to be so caught up with each other that it was difficult to know whose feelings belonged to whom.

John was infuriated by the way Lucy seemed to concentrate her energies on creating dramas and crises rather than making contact in a way which felt genuine. He thought that there was little possibility of soothing her and that the situation was far too complicated to be teased out at two o'clock in the morning. The only consolation was that physical safety seemed assured. John said that he could not magically take away Lucy's bad feelings and returned back to bed.

A couple of weeks later on a Friday evening as she left for her time off, Sally, who was the resident therapist for Maggie, warned John that Maggie was likely to feel self-destructive over the weekend because of what she had discussed in therapy that day. Sure enough, she was distressed, but managed to talk about it with John. He was moved by her state and said that she must wake him rather than cut herself.

Well into the night he was woken by a tapping at his door. To his great surprise it was not Maggie but Barbara, highly agitated, saying she just could not stand her feelings of despair. They talked downstairs for about an hour during which she calmed down sufficiently to be able to go back to bed. He had not really understood the nature of her anguish but his listening and soothing voice had an effect like a parent holding a troubled baby.

The next night he was woken again, this time by Maggie. This was the first time in her stay that she had ever woken any of us up. She had been cutting herself and was terrified that she was not going to be able to stop. It was impossible to ignore the seriousness of her crisis or the immediacy of her appeal. So again, John went downstairs and this time abandoned his sleep for a long talk until the sky lightened and the dawn chorus began.

After each of these events, Lucy, Barbara and Maggie discussed John's behaviour in their respective team meetings. Mary admitted that she had developed a negative pattern of getting attention. She remembered that she had always had to infuriate her mother in order to get any response from her. Barbara explained that, although she had found John's severity the first night with Lucy alarming, she could tell he was caring and described how on that night she had felt as if he were actually holding her. She was now able to appreciate that the team leader too, unlike her mother, could be loving rather that disapproving as she had experienced her before. For Maggie, being able to ask a man for help during the night was a milestone on her path to regaining trust after years of abuse.

The focus of the team meetings is the guests' internal world; what they bring to and make of their relationships, with the team, the Centre, their family and others. Responses to and fantasies about other guests may also be considered. Attention to the guest's intrapsychic life is the main focus in the team meetings. This frees us to direct our interventions around the house to interpersonal and reality-based issues. Through everyday contact, guests get to know us and each other. There are many opportunities to test out perceptions and to give and receive personal feedback.

In a house meeting, Tom said that everybody hated him. Sally suggested that he check this out with the others. He did this and other members of the group described their feelings towards him. Though he found it hard to accept, it challenged his inner convictions and gave others an idea of what influenced his attitude to them.

We often voice our own feelings and responses to people and situations. This can relieve guests of emotions or ideas they may have but cannot bear at the time. It provides an example of feelings being shared safely. We do this in a deliberate and courteous way and, where possible, exclude personal feelings that are not connected to life at the Centre. These are kept for our own analyses and relationships outside. Anything else is utilized in our work. Our feelings and responses are continuously checked by ourselves and by colleagues to help us assess the emotional climate in the house.

There are periods when guests are reluctant to come to house meetings and everyone seems oppressed by a dead or deadening atmosphere in the house. 'Gareth', who had previously been an active member of the group, had withdrawn to his room and was not going to his team meetings. He was approaching the end of his stay and was unable to voice his anger and disappointment with us for withdrawing the help he still needed. Other guests did not mention him and stopped talking about themselves in the house meetings. Gareth was absent from the house meeting the following day. Sally said that she was worried about him, felt a failure and feared that he might try to kill himself. Other guests were then able to say that they had felt the same but were afraid to say anything. John added that he was irritated with Gareth for withdrawing. Sally, however, who was herself approaching the end of her time as a resident therapist, said she felt anxious and sad as well as pleased to be going (this being a way in which a resident therapist can model, for the guest, the pleasure of development). Her mixed feelings often left her numb and unable to make plans.

Hearing us discuss our own feelings enabled the guests to be aware of theirs and feel safe enough to express what was disturbing them. We had managed to voice some of the anxieties which had gone underground and had resulted in a dead atmosphere in the house. The atmosphere became more alive. The guests made contact with Gareth again and eventually he became more aware and less afraid of how he felt.

Sally learnt how to use her reactions purposefully when she became tearful in team meetings with 'Michael'. She wondered why that was since she had been composed before. Rod, the team leader, thought that one of Michael's main difficulties was that he avoided sadness because it was unbearable. Rod thought that Sally might be attuned to the sadness that Michael could not bear and wanted to get rid of and that it might be helpful if she talked about her experience in the sessions. At a subsequent session Sally said, 'I feel very sad at the moment but I don't know why'. Michael asked Sally, 'Do you feel tears pressing at the back of your eyes?' She said that she did. Rod suggested that Michael understood how Sally was feeling. To which Michael replied that he had noticed tears at the back of his eyes recently and had thought it strange because he was someone who never cried. In expressing what she was feeling and allowing herself to be supported by Rod, Sally had paved the way for Michael to do the same.

The attachment guests develop for their team leader is often the focus of the analytic work in the team. It is always a turning point for the guest to realize that the team leader can be both understanding (good) as well as frustrating (bad). Our role in this model of working is to gather up and bring feelings into the team meetings that are expressed to us outside. Often a guest feels positive towards us and negative towards the team leader or vice-versa. We wonder where these feelings belong and whether a guest's attitude to us may also relate to the team leader. We do this to help the guest integrate their experience as we believe that dividing everything into good and bad is restricting. In these situations we are careful not to encourage such a split. Yet there may well be times when guests need to divide their experience of us.

Weekend absences and holiday breaks can be especially difficult for guests. 'Colin' was very positive about his team leader; he felt understood and generally good about the Centre. But, as Christmas approached and his team leader went on holiday, he became hostile towards us. Nothing we did was right. He became quite obnoxious. John, who was part of his team, bore the brunt of this. The Christmas tree was too small and the food too rich. He did not want any of it and yet kept complaining that there was not enough. Luckily our group supervisor (more will be said about supervision later) had not yet gone away.

When the RT team met with our supervisor John said that he was really fed up about the situation with Colin. It was not fair that Colin continued to hold his team leader in high esteem while he himself was derided. Our supervisor pointed out that John was resentful of the team leader for going off and leaving him with Colin. We deduced that Colin might also feel resentful but could not show it as it threatened his view of his team leader. We decided to be more open with the guests about our anger with team leaders for not being around to help us over Christmas. Unfortunately this did not seem to help Colin who needed to keep 'good' and 'bad' separate. However, understanding this helped us to bear his hostility.

Many of our guests, especially those who are confused or withdrawn, find it impossible to engage in psychotherapeutic treatment without active help from another person. The fact that we ourselves have to struggle with fears and resistance in our own therapy helps us to understand and support our guests with theirs. By going to the sessions and demonstrating a willingness to think about our relationship with the guest, we support and may even carry within ourselves their engagement in the therapy for a while. In the beginning we may remind the guest of their session times. We may bring things that have happened or been talked about in the house to the sessions and we hold on to links made in the team meetings so that they can be assimilated later and connected with other experiences. We do hope that they will begin to take on more of these functions for themselves. The team meets and thinks about what is happening with the guest even if they do not attend. We use our responses as clues about how the guest may be feeling and communicate this to them. We often have conflicting responses which we feel are more than our own differences and reflect the internal conflicts of the guest.

Another aspect of the resident therapist's role is to preserve the Centre as a safe place. Preservation of the thinking and physical spaces goes hand in hand. The therapy and supervision help thinking and understanding. Care of décor, cleanliness, warmth and privacy communicate a regard for the Centre and each other. The essence of the Crisis Centre is protected in many ways, ranging from the care and maintenance of the physical fabric of the house to helping the group set limits for acceptable behaviour or in extreme cases asking someone to leave if they become too disruptive.

'Milton' tested us to the limit. Halfway through his stay he became very agitated. He talked incessantly, in a penetrating tone, until we ceased to be able to talk or think in his presence. He would bang on Julian's and John's doors all through the night, trying to get inside, and would return again minutes after being asked to go back to bed. Gradually, we became more and more tired and tempted to retaliate. Even though we tried to use our reactions to try and make sense of his fears, his behaviour continued. We could not cope with him and were losing our therapeutic stance. We wanted to preserve something good of his stay before it was spoiled so we asked him to leave for a while. Milton left and hated us. However, something good was preserved as he came back for a second stay and was able to learn from this experience.

We had a similar problem with Tom, who got into the habit of taking possession of the consulting room by spreading his belongings all over it. We had to intervene to preserve the space for others and to show Tom the value of boundaries and respect for others. The setting of limits in this way is an essential part of our work. We try to convey that we are human with finite capacities. This is particularly helpful for guests who boost themselves up to avoid feeling vulnerable.

Supervision and the variety of formal and informal forums for discussing our own responses are crucial to us. Our weekly group supervision with an external facilitator enables us to look at the stresses and strains as they affect us and our relationships with each other. Solidarity is essential in order to survive the attempts of the guests to come between us and stop us thinking and working together. Likewise, we have to be able to air conflicts and differences between us to prevent us colluding in a pretence of solidarity which would block necessary confrontation. We make time in the working day to discuss our work informally. Furthermore, a team leader is always on call and may be consulted. We all also have our own psychoanalysis outside the Centre.

To some, the amount of time and energy put into supervision and support might seem an excessive luxury. We find it essential to our work, especially as a constraint against acting upon our feelings as opposed to thinking them through. When we do react without thinking, these forums provide a safe arena after the event to think and learn and help us keep our behaviour within reasonable limits. We aim to offer a close therapeutic relationship that is both supportive and bounded. The secure setting of the Crisis Centre and our mutual support help us to allow the guest's disturbance and pain into and through us without our collapsing under its weight.

We have tried to illustrate some of the varied aspects of our work, how we strive to combine them into an integrated intervention and how open communication between us is paramount. Numerous people have asked us how we survived such an intensive and demanding live-in job. Now that we have had time to digest and reflect upon our experiences we can see that the personal benefits compensate for times when we felt exhausted and depleted. Two things stand out as being particularly valuable. First, being part of a common effort where resources are pooled to tolerate and understand experiences which seem intolerable and incomprehensible. Second, we learnt a lot about ourselves and our individual strengths and limitations. We share a sense of pride about that time and are aware that it has shaped our personal and professional lives profoundly.

10   BUILDING ON METAPHORS

ALASDAIR STOKELD

The physical environment of a therapeutic setting is important – almost everyone involved would agree – however, it is a topic that is surprisingly absent from most therapeutic trainings and literature.

The Crisis Centre has maintained a highly containing and facilitating environment: drawing on my experience there and in other residential settings I would like to try to make explicit some links between the psychological and material aspects of its provision. The link between the psychological and the material, as with all language, is of course the function of metaphor.

In Scotland once, when I was little, I was invited to sit nearer the fire with the words 'Come into the body of the kirk (church)'. Daft as a 6-year-old, I wondered for a while about what this meant. An invitation to community, as at church perhaps, was implied by context. We would take the sacraments of tea and shortbread. But what was this body that one was being invited to join? This gave rise to some anxiety. I felt I was quite all right with my own, thank you for asking. If pressed, it would be all right to be an arm or a leg. Someone else was going to be the head (used to that from school). Was there going to be a willy in the room? Who was going to be bum? Or worse, were there going to be innards around?

Of course once one starts to think this way one's life can begin to seem littered with stray body parts; a sort of abattoir of 'dead' metaphor. Have you been 'stabbed in the back' today? Or felt 'held'?

In our analytic way, however, the 'dead' vernacular phrase 'body of the kirk' can be unpicked to demonstrate the possibility of potentially vital meanings. An associative path might progress from the cruciform shape of the church, echoing the disposition of Christ's body on the cross, to the place in the church where communion with the body of Christ is joined. From there to the sense of community, joining together and so on.

The Crisis Centre is a place where these many-levelled relationships are often explored. One young woman who arrived in a highly distressed and incoherent state spent the first few days of her stay going out of the front door, standing on the doorstep for a moment, ringing the doorbell to be readmitted, going out, standing for a moment, ringing, etc. In work with her and her family we had already seen that it seemed impossible for this young woman to feel comfortable either with or without her mother. If she was close to her mother she felt overwhelmed and trapped, exposed to malevolent attack. If she was separate she felt lost, utterly abandoned and excluded. Feeling excluded this girl made furious attacks to get inside; once inside she would have to struggle equally furiously to get out. As the hours of this demented doorstepping passed the cycle became elaborated to include setting off the fire alarm, yelling that she was being locked up to be tortured, phoning for an ambulance to take her away. On the doorstep, even after we had left the door so that it could be opened freely, she would shout loudly and ring the doorbell endlessly, saying that she had been locked out, that we had no right to do so, that she would call the police and so on.

It is obvious that the material here is a fairly direct recapitulation of the family relationship. We might also hypothesize that what are being 'acted out' are primitive and pre-verbal fears of being swallowed or eaten up by the mother. We were left wondering just where the transference relationship lay. Was it with ourselves as therapists, or was it in a rather more diffuse way with the house as an object in its own right?

It certainly seemed as if a period of direct, concrete experimentation with the door was necessary. It was not until later that our words 'You can come and go as you choose' could be heard and believed. It was later still that our interpretations (that it is scary to come to a new place, that she might be worried that we might be damaging to her) could be taken in.

One woman guest who had just arrived at the Centre very nearly left after five minutes. Why? Her room had no curtains. The curtains had been cleaned; we had forgotten to put them back up. In the several hours of reassurance and exploration of her fears of being intruded into and spied upon, we had to face the fact that the care and security which we had hoped to offer had in this case been 'not good enough'. It was very difficult, she said, to believe our words when our actions as displayed by the material facts had such a different meaning. The point here is the same as before: actual curtains: the actual door: these have to feel 'good enough' before anything more sophisticated can be taken in.

Other visitors to the house have commented on the lush and fertile garden or the high quality and expense of some of the furniture. The tone of comment varies from admiration and appreciation that so much should be provided to a feeling of guilt that may be intense. Of course these remarks can be unpicked to reveal a rich skein of lexical meanings within a frame of 'object relations'. We have found it useful to supplement this way of thinking with a consideration of relationships with actual objects.

The term 'concrete thinking', a prime feature of psychotic process, can often be a term of psychiatric abuse. The term can, however, be rehabilitated to think about just how direct perception and sensation in the physical environment underscore a therapeutic transaction.

Staff use observation of the physical community as a means of finding their bearings as to the psychological 'state of the house'. A milk jug 'poisoned' with cigarette ends; the young man who urinated daily and secretly in the same corner of his bedroom, the kitchen plundered and defiled; the gift of a growing plant to the house after a successful stay; have very obvious interpretative potential and give clues on many levels as to what might be 'going on'. In these examples themes of envious attack on the mother's body and a wish to make reparation find concrete expression in actions in (and on) the physical containment of the house. The 'reading' of them takes place in a way that is akin to a response to an expressionist painting. The mess (or order) evokes a response at a gut level, one reconstructs the angry gesture or measured action as if one's own body had carried it out. Or as if one's own body had been acted on. Resident therapists achieve a great sense of identification with the house and its functions. The effect is powerful.

I can remember being moved to near mortal anguish by a carefully stubbed-out cigarette end in the middle of a wall I had just repainted. The effect was less of anger at wasted effort (after all, the damage could be put right in a few minutes) but rather one of horror at the sheer ugliness of the act. It was as if *my* body had been attacked. I felt very depressed; how could I cope with such barbarity? As I sat with my head in my hands the perpetrator of the deed asked if I was all right. I replied that it was very sad when damaging things happened. He agreed. As we made good the damage together I realized that the war film that seemed to occupy his consciousness had stopped. He seemed to feel better for a time. Me too.

Here it seems that 'reparation' can mean concrete repair. An opportunity to repair the concrete damage can begin to symbolize a capacity for psychic reparation of damaged inner objects.

The opportunity to participate in the care for the physical 'body' of the house is a feature of the Crisis Centre that seems valued by many who stay there. There are few things so devastating as a perceived impossibility of repair. Reparation can be as simple as helping to wash up the dinner dishes as well as tidying up the ravages of an angry outburst.

The opportunity also to allow an experience of bodily well-being through aesthetic pleasure is a process that is both analogous to (and syntonic with) the business of 'talking' therapy within the milieu. The root of the term 'aesthetic' is directly and unambiguously that of 'feeling'. We can, and do, talk a lot of how we might hope to feel in the future. We do also take time to consider such questions as just how do the carpets and fabrics feel?; what is this floor like to walk on with bare feet?; is a bathroom a place where bodily functions are dispatched with a maximum of efficiency or is there room for the experience to be one of pleasure, sensuality even? Similarly, purchasing policy for household equipment, furniture, and fittings has been to buy the most pleasing that can be found. The mood or 'feel' of the environment can be more or less explicitly thought about, altered to create a desired effect (or affect!).

This is the business of creating 'mood' or atmosphere that Melvyn Rose of the Peper Harow community has discussed (1986). Messages of worth, of self-value, find powerful statement through non-verbal means. A picture speaks a thousand words . . .

Direct sensations and perceptions are 'what communicates' here; truly, 'aesthetics'. These, when it is a matter of 'interior design', are messages that are often covert. The principles of the use of such inexplicit messages have been exploited by cultures as disparate as those of the Feng Shui man[1] of Imperial China down to the deployment of 'buy-more' lighting in the local supermarket.[2] I wonder if a fairly general disregard for these matters in therapeutic community settings is a function of the sheer busy-ness of the verbal environment. However, before any of us had words we had a direct and physical interaction with our world. It is this 'facilitating environment' that I propose forms the reference point for consideration for how a useful therapeutic environment can be maintained. Winnicott (1965) suggests there is a need for the facilitating environment (The Mother) to protect against physiological insult if it is to be good enough. Similarly indicated in his work are the need for qualities such as resilience, a capacity to acknowledge reparation, and a nurturing of the senses. For the infant the provision of these qualities is direct, concrete and physical. The concrete facilitating environment or community can be usefully considered in the same way.

NOTES

1. Feng Shui practitioners were and are consulted to ensure that the orientation and disposition of buildings, furniture, colours and so on are 'in harmony' with their location on the earth and the purpose for which they are intended. Not surprisingly, good examples of this art have great aesthetic power.
2. Many retailing operations research thoroughly the effect that different sensory messages have on consumer spending. Changing a light bulb can make a difference, as might the smell of freshly baked bread.

11 'WE NEVER PROMISED YOU A ROSE GARDEN'

PETER HUDSON

I wrote the first part of this piece in 1990, after I had been living at one of the Arbours communities for four months. Before that I spent six weeks at the Arbours Crisis Centre and before that three months in a psychiatric hospital.

PART 1: FROM AUTUMN 1989 TO SPRING 1990

This piece is about my stay at the Crisis Centre and the transition to one of the long-stay communities; but I find I am unable to write about that in isolation. I need to put it in context of my life now and of my life prior to breaking down and going to hospital. I seem to need to see my life as a continuum and not just as a series of separate episodes.

Shortly after leaving the Crisis Centre I had a follow-up team meeting. 'What's it like at Crouch End?', asked Joe. 'Pretty lonely and pretty painful', I replied. 'We never promised you a rose garden', said Joe.

About 18 months before my breakdown (which precipitated my going to hospital) my marriage broke up as a result of an affair with one of the staff in the voluntary agency in which I had been working becoming public. The affair caused me to lose my job too. I worked and lived in the same place so I lost my rich local community of friends and my home as well. The woman I loved wanted to try and sort things out with her husband, and that meant that I lost her for the time being as well.

About most of this loss there was no discussion: my wife simply would not talk to me and locked me out of our home; my employers took advantage of my shocked and guilt-ridden state to coerce me out of my job. I was too stunned to know that there was no legal reason for me to leave. I worked for a caring agency who showed no caring for me after many years' service. It also hurt that one of those who got rid of me was one of my best friends and also the local vicar; but he sat on the management committee of the agency. I suppose he squared his conscience by convincing himself that he had done it for my own good!

I was reeling from shock, feeling totally uprooted with almost none of my sources of security intact. For 18 months, living in a number of rooms with relations and friends, my feet did not touch the ground: I worked crazily in a freelance capacity. I would start my day with a three-mile run at 6.30 am and then work at all sorts of different locations all over London. Every evening I spent with friends, normally over a meal out.

I would see my children – I have three – fairly regularly but often feel very guilty. Slowly we got to know each other better than we had when we lived together and we learned to be open with each other. We had some good holidays. Gradually, my youngest daughter and I found it more and more difficult to be with each other in a civil manner. Finally, after about a year she said she did not want to see me again and we have not met since.

I spent most weekends with my brother and sister-in-law but I could not relax there either. I ran, talked or worked. On very rare occasions my lover and I would meet secretly and for a few hours life would be bliss.

Very often during this period, unbelievably bad feelings welled up in me. Whenever they did I would go for a run. I seldom cried but often wanted to; but I felt that crying would mean that I was cracking up. I was seeing a counsellor at the time and somehow it seemed more OK to cry when I was with him. I came to rely on him very much. I also spent a lot of time talking with friends about myself and my problems.

The bad feelings in my body became worse and more frequent. It was as if my flesh was creeping all over my body and there seemed to be a distance between me and the rest of the world. The only way to ease these feelings was to be busy or to have hot baths. I pushed myself even harder in my running but I began to notice that I had less and less energy.

When driving to London one day from my home in Surrey the feelings got worse and worse. I simply could not contain the agitation and I felt more and more panicky. I started to think about killing myself. When I got to London I asked a friend to take me to hospital. I saw the duty psychiatrist who listened to me and convinced me that it would be best if I tried to keep going. He gave me some valium and told me to go and see my GP. The incredible agitation was eased a bit by the pills, but two days later on the way to London exactly the same thing happened and again I had myself taken to hospital and pleaded to be taken in. Eventually

I was told I would be admitted, not in London, but to Netherne Hospital which was nearer to where I was then living. I felt terrible. I was completely agitated and needing to move and yet completely without energy.

As I walked into the hospital I had two thoughts going through my head: 'Have I really come to this – am I really mad?', on the one hand, and 'All I need is a good rest and I'll be back to work, right as rain', on the other. In fact, neither of them bore much relation to reality.

Netherne is a typical late-Victorian mental hospital set in open country isolated from everything and everyone around it. I was admitted to an acute ward, was allocated a room of my own. After 24 hours I started to feel much better. I thought I was in the right place and that the doctors and nurses would cure me. I now think it was that misguided belief that gave me a respite from the unbearable feelings. Experience was soon to show that those feelings would not stay away for long.

They didn't and because of the returning suicidal thoughts I was put under constant one-to-one observation: everywhere I went I was followed by a nurse. I was prescribed anti-depressants and tranquillizers. My thoughts and feelings were desperate for a lot of the time. Although I was on an acute ward I inevitably came into contact with patients who had been there for years and years, and as I began to give up hope of ever getting out, the intensity of my depression increased and I could hardly summon up the energy to speak.

I had regular visitors – family and friends, and I felt so guilty at not being well. I felt guilty about being in hospital. Sometimes I would talk about me non-stop but nearly always negatively, and sometimes I could hardly talk with them at all. I felt guilty at talking about myself so much but somehow knew that I needed to.

Many of the nursing staff were very nice people but there seemed to be a gulf between them and us. I often perceived them as being superior to us patients, knowing better, telling us how to get better rather than being understanding. Very seldom did I feel or was I allowed to feel myself their equal. I remember late one night two or three of us were sitting talking in the dayroom. A night nurse came in and told us it was about time we went to bed. I was furious. We were adults, disturbing no one and what we did was our business!

The consultant psychiatrist was very aloof. Every time I saw her I didn't feel listened to – really listened to. As my depression got deeper she talked about putting me on lithium carbonate and giving me electric shock treatment. I knew very little about either and felt terrified, particularly about the ECT. Of course she told me that there was nothing to worry about with either.

The only person on the staff who really listened to me was the art therapist. Even when I was feeling at my worst he managed to convey the feeling to me that I mattered and that what I wanted was important; he never told me what to do in that 'It's for your own good' sort of way. Nearly everyone else did. I'm sure their intentions were good; the effect was not. Even as I write this I get a vague feeling of guilt for being ungrateful and I know if I went back to see them I'd feel subordinate. If I saw the art therapist I think I'd feel an equal.

The people who helped me most in hospital were other patients. We talked about most things and perhaps most important of all, we talked about our suicidal feelings without getting 'tut-tutted'. That seemed so very important.

It was by talking to my patient friends that I heard that lithium carbonate could have serious physical side effects and also that it was a means of holding you 'in balance' and, therefore, would need to be taken forever. In so far as I was capable of wanting anything at all, I wanted to get better, not to be on drugs for the rest of my life. Even in my gloomiest times that's what I wanted. No, I definitely did not want them to put me on lithium, but could I stop them?

As for ECT, well I was completely terrified. I had no experience or knowledge of it other than having seen *One Flew Over The Cuckoo's Nest*. I feared that my brains would be addled and that I would be turned into a cabbage. I was in a state of constant panic.

But I sank lower and lower and eventually signed the paper. I was convinced that I could get no worse. Life was already hell on earth. I had nothing to lose. I had three treatments. Did it do any good? I don't know but I don't believe so. I regularly felt as bad after as before. Anyway, how can anyone know? I did gradually feel a bit better but it could have been the pills, it could have been my own inner workings or, yes, it could have been the ECT.

Most likely what made me begin to feel a little better was the straw that I clutched at when my lover suggested a place called Arbours. They had places to help you through crises and my brother and sister-in-law arranged a visit. Here was the possibility of getting out of hospital, of getting on a road that eventually could lead me to creating a new life for myself with some inner peace and fulfilment again.

With hindsight, I am convinced that it was that ray of hope that lifted me enough to drive with my brother Jonathan and my sister-in-law Penny to my consultation in Crouch End. The pills and ECT may have held some of the worst feelings at bay but it was the inner hope for a future that brought me up out of the depths of despair.

And so it was that a few days before Christmas I entered the Arbours Crisis Centre as one of six guests. I didn't have too much hope for the future but something must have been stirring within me.

The environment was so different from hospital. The first difference, and maybe one of the most important for me, was that the Crisis Centre is set in an ordinary house close to the centre of a small but busy shopping centre. Even though I may have been scared of them I was close to 'real' people and had the opportunity to do 'real' everyday things like shopping.

I was shown to a small room of my own and I unpacked my few things. I had done some paintings at hospital and pinned them on the wall: this was now 'my' room. I was shown the kitchen and told to help myself to anything and that everyone ate supper together at seven o'clock, but that lunch was an individual thing. I was introduced to other guests who were in the living room watching TV.

All these introductions were made by John, who was one of the three resident therapists, and one of the people who had been present when I had come for my initial consultation – he was to be my resident therapist. I soon learnt that I would have three team meetings (therapy sessions) a week and that there would be two therapists. John would be one and the team leader would be a non-resident therapist. In my case it was Joe.

I also learnt that there would be three house meetings a week – two of which were for residents only and the third attended by regularly visiting therapy students as well. These meetings seemed to provide the basic structure of the house. I didn't know what to expect from the place but looking back I recognize that I did expect 'them' to help me, to make me better. I saw 'them' – everyone other than the guests, as staff. In some ways they were above me. Again looking back I now see that there was really very little external cause for this feeling in me, as by and large the house was run as any other collective household. There were very few stated rules other than the rules of human concern one for another. I could and did share the cooking, but was not pushed to; likewise with the washing-up. Gradually, I realized that all decisions affecting my life were left to me to take – my life there in the house as well as in the future. In the state I was in this realization was pretty daunting. How I wanted some magic person to make me feel better and solve my problems for me – odd, really, as this had been the pervading atmosphere of hospital and it hadn't worked!

But something did begin to work for me. Once again with the benefit of hindsight I think the key was the underlying atmosphere that here were constant opportunities to feel my feelings and to explore them. It was OK to feel. I had held in my feelings for so long, held them in and run away from them and felt guilty about them. Now, not only was it OK as far as the other people were concerned to let go of my feelings, I was positively encouraged to.

I remember one occasion. I had been out with a friend and had had a particularly bad time. I came back for supper and took my place at the table rather gloomily. 'How was it?', someone asked. 'Not very good', I replied, with a controlled but wobbly voice. 'You seem to be holding back your feelings', said someone else. That was the permission I needed to break down and sob. It was a desperate cry of loss and the pain was almost unbearable. I cried many more times at the Crisis Centre, sometimes with others and sometimes alone. In so far as I consciously knew what I was crying about it seemed to be loss. The amount of grief that I felt was phenomenal: not surprising of course, as I had lost just about everything that had made my life worth living, but surprising or not, my whole background and training had done nothing to prepare me for the pain that I felt, much less to know that it was all right to feel it and express it.

Much of my time at the Crisis Centre was taken up with talking about my feelings. Thus in addition to team meetings and house meetings I talked to my fellow guests and also listened to them. There were also a lot of student therapists and these too were more than ready to listen to me and help me to let out my feelings and perhaps begin to understand them.

I don't think I did understand much of what was happening, though. Mainly I thought that all of what was happening to me was grief and that once I had cried enough I would be my old self and be able to pick up the threads of my life again. It is certainly true that I was suffering from great loss and grief, but from what I have begun to learn since that is not the whole story. So when in a team meeting Joe would say something like: 'I don't doubt that you are partly crying for the loss of your children, but also I would suggest that you are very angry at me for going away for a week', I simply could not understand what he was saying, even less feel angry with him.

Enough has happened in therapy since for me to know that I have a well of painful feelings like anger, hurt, desperation, rage and a sense of real loneliness that have been buried for years and years and are coming to the surface again, triggered off but not caused by the recent traumatic events of my life. I think that a part of me was also buried along with those feelings.

My stay at the Crisis Centre was only booked for four weeks. As this time came towards an end I began to panic. I feared I would be on the streets, homeless. I asked for an extension for two weeks and the friend who had funded the first four weeks kindly funded the extension. I knew I could not live on my own. I applied to an Arbours long-term residential community and was immensely relieved when I was accepted. Six weeks after I left hospital I moved into the Crouch End community.

When I first when to the Crisis Centre I had just a flicker of hope for the future. As I moved into Church Lane my hopes were risen a little. In regular therapy and with the other residents I am continuing to explore my feelings, slowly getting into that well of feeling buried long ago. I guess it was buried then because it was too painful to face. It's certainly painful now but my hope and growing belief is that in uncovering that buried pain I will also uncover that part of me that was buried with it.

Maybe my search for myself will give me some inner peace and the ability to build a new life and plant a rose garden of my own.

What you have just read was written after a great deal of pain. Rereading it makes me realize just what a lot of emotional water has flowed under the bridge since then and how much more there is probably still to come.

Publishing books and papers seems to be a lengthy process with the result in this case that I have the opportunity to write more about my life both here in Crouch End and in general in my wider world of relations, friends and colleagues.

PART 2: SPRING 1990 ONWARDS

The transition to my new dwelling place was fraught with difficulty and pain. For quite some time I found it very difficult to go out on my own unless I had a clear destination in mind with a person at the other end. I have never really understood why that was but it was very scary indeed.

One thing that I am beginning to understand, though, is that understanding what's behind my fears and desperate feelings is itself an absolutely vital part of getting rid of the fears and sense of desperation; but it's a funny sort of understanding, quite different from how I used to understand things. What I mean by this is that I need to understand in my guts and not just in my head. I need to understand with my whole being.

It's a very new sort of understanding for me, an understanding you feel and don't just think. Most of the feeling part of it is painful but when it really happens the feeling afterwards is one of well-being, peace and often an increase in energy and an ability to face what was unfaceable.

In my early days here at Crouch End I found it almost impossible to be still and alone. So I busied myself around the house doing my share of the chores and cooking and also developing an earlier interest I'd had in baking. While I felt bad about the fact that I didn't have paid work, a job, a career, I was pleased to have the opportunity to occupy myself with some sort of creative activity.

Just as at the Crisis Centre the whole ethos of the Crouch End community is geared towards facilitating the feeling, expressing and understanding of feelings. The level of outside support for this is significantly less than at the Crisis Centre. Although there is a room here for a live-in therapy student it has been empty for most of the time I have lived here. There are visiting students, though, and one of them used to stay every other weekend. We have two house co-ordinators who take it in turns to come to house meetings which are twice a week and last one-and-a-half hours.

The format of the house meetings is similar to that at the Crisis Centre. Thus anyone is free to say anything. It's an opportunity to talk about practical matters with regard to the running of the house – like who's cleaning the loos this week, and an opportunity to talk about our feelings with each other about living in the house – like what I would do to the bastard who's pissing on the loo floors if only I knew who it was! It's also an opportunity to talk about our feelings about ourselves, our pain, our fears and our anger, our sadness and our deep hurt; our hopes and our plans. It's another opportunity to dig into that well of feeling that was buried long ago and in so doing discover ourselves and a way of living that is worthwhile and with a measure of satisfaction and fulfilment.

As I write those words they seem very trite, describing a very simple and indeed simplistic process. It is not simple at all. It is one of the most difficult things I have ever done and at times it seems impossible to believe in it; but at this point in time I believe in it more and more and I am beginning to understand why. I once heard Joe say that mental illness was all to do with relationships – past and present. It seems to me that all the manifestations of so-called mental illness, the symptoms, are brought on by the pain caused by difficulties in relationships: rather than face the pain of those difficulties the body manufactures symptoms. At Crouch End we try to face our feelings about each other and about others and about ourselves, and in so doing rob them of their sting.

In the first few months that I was here I spent most of my time thinking about how I could get away. I made plans centring on finding a job and a place of my own. Looking back I wonder why I did that so soon after coming. I realize now that in some ways it is no different from how I've been all my life. In one way and another I've always been getting away from home. I rarely had friends round to my house as a kid. I certainly spent time with my friends but most of it was at their house or in the park or in the woods. In my marital home I spent much more time out of it than in it, most of it at work.

One day last autumn I had an incredibly bad time as far as my feelings were concerned. I seemed to be crying or wanting to cry nearly all day. I got to therapy somehow and let out howls of anguish and despair. I was beside myself with pain and for most of the hour could do nothing but writhe in agony, crying in a lost and desperate way. I was calmer at the end of it and managed to get back to Crouch End. In the kitchen it all started again and my distress felt endless. I repeated it all with 'Gill' and 'Max', disjointed words interspersing the sobs in an effort to try and convey what I was feeling, what it was about. They sat there holding me and listening to me. Gradually it eased and I was able to talk a bit more coherently. Later after a rest I realized that never before in my life had anyone given me such concern and support in a place in which I lived. For the first time in my life I really felt at home.

Feeling really at home brought about the realization that I did not have to gear everything in my life towards getting out of Crouch End as soon as I possibly could. Strangely, that realization in turn seemed to give me the strength and self-confidence that I needed to begin considering in very practical ways all the things that had to be considered in order to rebuild a life for myself along the lines that I wanted, which of course would one day, sooner rather than later I hoped, lead me to leaving Crouch End in a positive way. It now feels like a process that I'm in charge of rather than one that's in charge of me.

A major difference between my life now and when I first joined the Arbours network is that I've been in therapy three times a week for just over a year. How the hell to describe therapy? In some ways I don't think it's possible. In other ways I know I want to try because it's clearly an absolutely vital part in what's going on for me, in getting rid of the 'symptoms' and equally important in helping me begin to change in what

I hope is a quite radical way in my relationships with all sorts of people. I really do believe that that is slowly beginning to happen.

What do I do in therapy? What does my therapist do? Well, I sit or lie for 50 minutes and talk about whatever comes into my head. Quite often what comes into my head is how I feel about close friends and relatives, people at the house and sometimes about my therapist. Sometimes the things I say about current relationships trigger off thoughts and feelings about relationships from bygone days with my parents and brothers and other members of my wider family. From time to time I seem to become aware that feelings that I experience now about people are actually a repeat of long-lost feeings. Most of them are very painful. The most painful ones seem to be to do with feeling abandoned and alone. My therapist seems to let me do most of the talking. At times that can be infurating but most of the time it's just what I seem to need. Her comments seem to be a mixture of letting me know that she's heard and I hope understood and of helping me to discover patterns in my feelings and thoughts. The most important thing for me when I was really going through my worst time was simply to know that she was there and that she wouldn't go away. My head seemed to know that she wouldn't go away, but my heart and guts found that very difficult to believe.

It's a very strange sort of thing, therapy. I talk and talk and Sally listens and listens and occasionally comments; and that's it! And somehow I get 'better'. Maybe one day I'll understand that too. For now I'm simply grateful that it seems (more often than not) to work.

I say that I believe that being at Crouch End is helping me to change in some pretty radical ways. So what are they? So far I am aware of three. Max pointed out the first: when I came here I was a victim. My whole attitude showed that I viewed the world as if things happened to me about which I could do very little. Now I am becoming more and more in charge of my own life. Second, I am more able to be open both with myself and with others about how I am feeling. Third, I feel much more relaxed for more of the time. Radical? Well perhaps not but it feels like a big step for me.

So what's become of the rose garden they never promised me? Difficult to say really, other than it's still a very important symbol for me. One of these days . . .

12   PSYCHOTIC INTERVENTIONS

JOSEPH H. BERKE

'Psychotic interventions' is an ambiguous term. But I use it deliberately. It can refer to therapeutic interventions done on behalf of individuals who are suffering or have previously suffered psychotic breakdowns. And it can refer to the actions of people, often designated as 'patients', who are going through the process of breaking down. Equally relevant, the term can point out the reaction of a human environment, the family or milieu that was supposed to be of help, but couldn't and didn't. This is a container which can no longer contain terrible pain, confused thinking or angry outbursts. In other words I am considering the situation when the therapist or institution has collapsed, even if only for a temporary period. So this paper is about breakdowns on the part of both parties, those needing help and those giving it. And it is about the means by which these same two sides are able to reconstitute themselves.

I shall focus on events at the Arbours Crisis Centre. As I mentioned in Chapter 7, there are three separate but interrelated and interrelating therapeutic systems at the Centre. These are the team, the group and the milieu. The milieu is the Centre as an active therapeutic environment. Perhaps active interpersonal environment is more correct as the milieu can also be non-therapeutic or even anti-therapeutic, depending on, as we shall see, who is at the Centre and what is going on.

In order to illustrate the various implications of 'psychotic interventions', I will focus on the role of the milieu as the healing or damaging agent. Specifically, I want to tell the story of 'Hamid', a large man in his early twenties, whose family originally came from the Middle East. Hamid had a good intellect and did well at school. But as he approached university age, he began to bully his parents and younger sister, and make rude sexual overtures to women both inside and outside his home.

Hamid was first admitted to hospital in his late teens because of severe aggressive outbursts. He seemed to seek out weak and vulnerable women and terrorize them. At his worst he appeared to be totally out of touch with reality and his behaviour was nearly uncontainable. He was referred to the Centre because hospitalization did not help. After the usual medications and restraint, he remained the same incorrigible human being, but with the added burden of being diagnosed as schizophrenic.

Hamid came to the Centre for a three-month period, what we call a medium-length stay. At first he was very demanding and wildly abusive. He soaked up huge amounts of food, especially milk and sugar, while refusing to sit for any meals. His great delight was to make a huge mess in the kitchen. In the house he took on the role of overbearing potentate. All the women were his playthings or prey. In return they hated him. But when confronted he would deny what he had done and shout abuse. Generally he was extremely negative about the Centre, and usually refused to go to house meetings. But he did attend his team meetings fairly regularly.

As his stay progressed he gradually calmed down and became more sociable. He surprised everyone with a keen sense of humour and a capacity for clear thinking. People began to see him as a bad boy, rather than a mad boy. Certainly he tried everyone's patience to the limit, so much so that on a few occasions he was asked to go home for a day or two so the house could cool down.

Towards the end of his stay, Hamid showed sustained periods of sadness and could be intellectually impressive, engaging residents in long discussions about politics or philosophy. But these reflective periods were often interrupted by angry, impulsive, demanding outbursts. Hamid's accomplishments seemed in danger of being lost. He had reverted back to being chaotic and unbearable. Both the resident therapists and other guests were at their wits' end, in outrage and despair. This was a turning point. Hamid had begun his 'leaving crisis'.

What do I mean by the expression 'leaving crisis'? In my previous chapter (see above, p. 65), I have explained that all guests pass through five distinct crises or stages while they are at the Centre, regardless of their reasons for coming. As I said, these stages can be compared to five states of mind and greatly influence the feelings and actions of the guests while they are at the Centre. They are *Arriving, Settling-In, Settling-Down, Leaving* and *Following-Up*.

The fourth stage, *Leaving*, invariably precipitates a fresh crisis because leaving necessarily arouses uncertainty and sadness which may seem too strong to bear. To avoid the experience, many guests try to repeat their original breakdown. This was certainly the case with Hamid.

Everything seemed to blow up before his leaving date. Over the previous week he had become increasingly angry and abusive, and tempers were at boiling point among the therapists and other guests. Then, in mid-week, the house itself seemed to respond in kind because the sinks suddenly blocked up with a black, foul-smelling liquid. The same morning we had our semi-annual medical inspection. There was a frantic rush to get the sinks unblocked, which RTs accomplished just before the inspector, a very pleasant, elderly doctor arrived. She had been to the Centre many times before and always enjoyed a quiet relaxed visit. As she had entered the kitchen for a cup of tea, Hamid suddenly brushed past her, screaming: 'Get out of the way you fucking old bag'. Everyone was appalled and one of the guests, 'Anna', started to cry. Even the RTs were shaking. But the doctor was not the least phased. She calmly commented, 'You know, it really is exciting to have a taste of real life!'

The inspection being over, the RTs began to prepare for a reception in the evening. Every other month the Arbours sponsors a public lecture. Afterwards the lecturer and invited guests and therapists return to the Centre for refreshments and further discussion. So, having set out the food and drink in the front room, they specifically asked Hamid not to touch the stuff. Well, this was like a red rag to a bull. Upon getting back to the Centre after the lecture, they found that he had not only eaten a lot of the food, but had been bullying the female guests.

Hamid saw the RTs and tried to be jolly: 'George, George, did you have a nice evening?' But they were furious. For them gobbling the food was the straw that broke the camel's back. Once again Hamid had broken all boundaries, and they were left in complete chaos. All they wanted was for him to go, immediately. They called his team leader and told him what had happened, that Hamid had been warned and had to go. The RTs feared that if they backed down and he didn't leave, they would lose face and appear like Hamid's father, waffling and indecisive. Without further ado, the team leader concurred and suggested they call the father to come and collect him.

While they were about to carry this out, the RTs saw that I had just come back from the lecture and was about to sit down and talk with our visitors. Before I could do so, they literally pounced on me and insisted that I retreat with them to the rear consulting room to discuss him. So I excused myself and joined a group of very angry therapists. At this point

I myself felt quite menaced, for I could see that they would not take no for an answer:

'Hamid's been on the rampage. He's eaten the food and hit another guest. He's been warned several times. He has to go.'

Nervously, 'Umm, I can see that you have tried and sentenced him. It seems that I'm to act as your executioner.'

In the meantime I realized no one was able to think. The situation was crazy. Hamid had become their 'dreaded object'. And as far as they were concerned, their sanity, or at least peace of mind, depended on my getting rid of him.

While all this was happening, I remembered a similar incident that had happened several years before. The Norwegian government had referred a young woman to the Centre with a long history of, I would say reputation for, autism and schizophrenia. She was a huge person and very aggressive. If she had lived a thousand years previously, she could easily have been a Viking raping and pillaging the north of England. In fact the referral was so unusual that we decided that a main point was to simply get her out of Norway. Anyway, 'Ingrid' had been at the Centre for several months and had just begun to form ties with the residents and settle down. One late afternoon I was called to the Centre by a nearly incoherent RT. 'Ingrid has thrown a chair at me for the last time. Either she goes or I go.'

In fact Ingrid had also been upset by someone's leaving. So she responded with violence, the one way she knew that would destroy her nascent feelings of sadness and depression. Really, what she did was not much different from previous episodes and I thought that once I came over and spoke with people, it would blow over. But it didn't. The RT was adamant. Either Ingrid left, or he did. In desperation I called my colleague, Dr Morty Schatzman, a co-founder of the Arbours, to come over and help me out. He too argued with the RT, while Ingrid was storming around in the garden. All to no avail.

Several hours passed. The atmosphere remained explosive. Morty and I realized that neither gentle persuasion nor harsh facts would work. So we told the RT to stay and said we would take Ingrid to the Casualty department of a nearby hospital, the Royal Free, for a shot of Largactil and, hopefully, a bed for the night. We didn't know and couldn't think about what else to do. By then we were tired and desperate and Ingrid was still storming. Off we went to the Royal Free. By the time we arrived, Ingrid had begun to calm down, but we were extremely anxious, so much so that I was prepared to do something that is totally against the grain, revert to tranquillizers and hospitalization.

In Casualty Ingrid insisted that I buy her endless cups of coffee and cigarettes. 'Anything to shut her up', I mused. 'This whole thing is nuts.' Finally the duty psychiatrist, a tiny, young Asian lady, came out for Ingrid. Quick as a wink I pounced on her, yelled a potted history and insisted on what I wanted her to do. She looked up and curtly reminded me that she was the doctor in charge and wouldn't decide anything till she had seen the patient.

Another half-hour passed. Morty and I felt our agitation level rise to new heights. Then the doctor came out. I was just beginning to feel relieved that we could go home when I heard the hideous news. 'This person can go home. She doesn't need any medication.' 'What!', I roared. 'You can't do that. Look how upset and violent she is.'

While this was going on Ingrid came out and calmly sat on a chair smoking a cigarette. The doctor pointed out that she was perfectly calm and didn't need treatment. I was dumbfounded. Suddenly a smile crossed my lips. The doctor and I had exchanged roles. I had called Ingrid a dangerous schizophrenic. The doctor saw her as a tired if slightly confused young woman. I was arguing for drugs, she was arguing against drugs. I wanted hospitalization. She said it wasn't necessary. And not only had I changed roles with the doctor, I had exchanged roles with Ingrid. She was calm and quiet. I was raging like a maniac. The irony was not lost on Morty or myself. With that we began to calm down. Morty volunteered, 'Listen, it's 2.30. I'll take Ingrid back to my house for the night. A good night's sleep will do us all good.' I readily concurred and that's how the crisis ended. In fact Ingrid did not go back to the Centre. She stayed as Morty's guest for a few days and then we found her a small flat of her own. She had never lived in her own flat before.

This whole episode flashed through my mind while I was trying to think how to handle Hamid and the RTs. One decision came quickly. Whatever was going to happen, I did not intend to become the knight in shining armour, the all-powerful father who provided omnipotent solutions for his regressed children. But I also realized that far from playing the omnipotent father, the RTs had allowed me little room to manoeuvre. They clearly wanted me to become the impotent father who had to do their bidding. Surely, this was their sadistic revenge for my having inflicted 'Him' on them in the first place, and for having caused them so much psychic pain.

Angrily, one of the group said: 'Well, what are you going to do? We can't spend another night with Hamid in the state he's in.'

Again, I was taken aback by the extreme hostility, but now I wanted to avoid appearing omnipotent or getting sucked in further.

'Well', hanging my head for effect, 'I don't know. I don't know what to do.'

Really I was trying to buy time so that we could all begin to think.

'Let me see, you know we do have other options. I know we can get rid of him. Indeed that's one option. Let's see if there are any others. Right now I recall my friend Ross Speck.[1] He used to work with large families with one or more very disturbed members. He'd call them the designated patients. Could it be that is the case with Hamid? Could he be our designated patient, the carrier of all our craziness?'

Murmurs of annoyance.

'What Ross used to do when the large family group threatened to fragment, and expel a member, was to expand the group. Bring in more members, distant relatives, neighbours, even relative strangers. The point was to get people who could think to join the group. Maybe we can do that by carrying the discussion to the reception. Let's ask our visitors what they would do. Let's ask everyone else in the house too.'

More murmurs, but at least the proposal wasn't rejected out of hand.

'You know, we could also ask Hamid to join us. Perhaps he might come up with something himself.'

At that moment, as if on cue, Hamid came into the back room and looked at me somewhat plaintively.

I said, 'Hamid, I feel very sad and upset about the situation.' (I actually did feel this way, but I was also being deliberately vague.)

Hamid, who knew everyone in the house wanted him out, began to shake. He shot off to the kitchen for some milk. Then back in the room, and before anyone could comment he went up to me and exclaimed, 'Don't worry. I'll go to bed'.

With that, he started up the stairs towards his room.

It was now 10.30, Hamid had been quite disarming and I thought it safe to suggest that we rejoin the reception. I said it would help to think. The RTs agreed.

There were about 20 people there, our speaker, a few of his friends and colleagues, a few Arbours therapists, and the rest from the Crisis Centre. Everyone seemed to want to talk at once. 'What's happening, why weren't you here, where's Hamid?'

I explained what was going on, that we had a big problem, and asked everyone for their suggestions.

A few of the guests at the Centre went on the attack. Hamid had to go! 'Look, he hit me today.' 'Why should we put up with that?'

Our lecturer, Dr 'T', gently enquired, 'Is he on drugs?'

Somewhat flippantly I retorted, 'Maybe we should all take some drugs, it could help us to calm down.'

The lecturer let a few guffaws pass and continued, 'You say you want him to leave. This is an unusual problem. Where I work we usually try to get patients to stay, not to leave'.

He was quickly accosted by Anna, a thin young woman who liked to cut her arms and face in order to reduce the tensions in herself. 'How can you say that. Don't you know what I've been through?' Another resident interjected that she hasn't been able to sleep for days because of Hamid. And the RTs, still angry, joined in.

Dr T continued. 'You know, we could all leave. Leave him alone in the house. But then, where would the RTs go?'

An animated discussion ensued. After a few more minutes I encouraged Dr T to add to his earlier remarks.

First, he asked a few questions. Why did Hamid come to the Centre? How long for? Then Dr T presented his views about schizophrenia and schizophrenics as well as the treatments available, especially medication. People weren't too interested and I could see they were shocked by all the medical psychiatric terms he deployed. Then he decided to tell a story. This was a story prefaced by the quip, 'You know, it's often easier to start again than to clean up a big mess'.

The story went: 'In Ireland there was a mother and two boys. The boys went out one day to play by a bog. One fell in and was quickly pulled under. The other boy ran home to get his mother. She ran back to the bog and saw that her son was about to go under the quicksand. She rushed over and pushed his head under. Her other son was horrified. "Mam, why did you do that?" The mother replied, "Well, since I couldn't save him, I thought I might as well get it over with quick. Then I could start again."'

A stunned silence prevailed. Then Dr T added, 'In putting the boy back into the MUD, she was really putting him back into the MAD, into madness. Perhaps there was nothing more she could do. After all, she didn't have any drugs.'

This seemed to break the mood. I took a glass of wine and both guests and residents started to tuck into the food and drink. Everyone seemed to be talking at once. There was a jolly, almost hypomanic atmosphere.

Midnight came. Dr T and his friends said they had to go. While I escorted them to the door, another complete change of mood took place.

The residents seemed to forget Hamid and focused on Dr T. He had become the whipping boy. Kate got angry with him for advocating drugs. Another accused him of being a tool of the establishment. And so on.

Midnight went. I had to struggle with myself to return to the meeting. I was dead tired and wanted to go home, especially since the Hamid issue was no longer pressing. But it had not been settled and I decided to stay as long as necessary to resolve things. In his talk, Dr T had spoken about guilt and forgiveness. I hoped that the anger and guilt that previously had pervaded the house might be replaced by a mellowing of mood and feeling of forgiveness. Back at the meeting, I sniffed the atmosphere. The frenzied pressure to oust Hamid had gone. People were more uncertain about what to do.

Kate spoke about him, how he had called her a whore and slag. I queried whether this image might be connected to how he saw himself? An animated discussion about Hamid and sex ensued. How perverted his ideas all seemed. Was he really angry with his sister because she was good-looking? Somehow the phrase 'condom soup' slipped in. Condom soup?

'Sue', a shy black girl who usually tried not to be noticed, piped up: 'At last some of the shit is out in the open. Anyway there were times when Hamid was OK with me.' Another guest at the Centre, 'Will', seemed to be falling asleep on a big pillow. But he was awake enough to remark that Hamid reminded him how nervous he felt at times. In fact, he was usually extremely depressed.

Suddenly, I realized that no one was angry with Hamid. People were chatting away about other things. However, in order not to lose the opportunity to conclude 'the problem', the point of the evening, I focused on Hamid again by asking, 'What do you think it feels like to be Hamid? What is it like to be so full of despair and fear and terror?' More talk. The meeting turned back to Hamid.

By now it was 1.15. I said, 'I think our feelings about Hamid have softened a bit. But I don't think we should just let things hang. You know, when I came over tonight after the lecture, you seemed ready to throw him out. This doesn't seem to be the issue now, but let's go over what we can do, what the options are.'

Almost as if I were reading from a prepared list of possibilities, I started, one, two, three . . .

1. We can get rid of him, immediately, forever.

2. We can get rid of him in the morning after allowing him to stay overnight.

3. We can ask him to leave for the night and come back tomorrow, as we have done before.

4. We can let him stay, but set up a rota for people to stay up with him during the night.

5. We can all stay up and cancel meetings for the next day.

6. We can bring him back into the group, into the meeting right now.

7. We can follow Dr T's advice and use medication. But who should take it and how much? Should Hamid take 100 mgm Largactil, or the whole group?

8. We can all have a double Scotch.

At this point I interjected that when patients get agitated their drug is Largactil, but when therapists get upset their drug is alcohol.

Many lively exchanges ensued.

Kate exclaimed: 'I'm against the use of all drugs.'

'OK, then I suggest we all take a glass of milk and honey. Let's give one to Hamid too. Then we can all go up and express our love for Hamid and hug him. I think Hamid's biggest problem is expressing and receiving affection. So, let's all give him some affection.'

Kate shouted as if speaking for the whole group, 'Joe, you give it to him first.'

I replied, 'OK, no problem, but before I do, let's all hold hands.'

In this way I tried to open a delicate subject, the open expression of affection in and by members of the group as a whole. After all, how could we direct it to Hamid if affection remained blocked among everyone else?

A bit reluctantly, everyone stood up and shuffled around in order to form a circle and hold hands.

Suddenly Sonia, the RT, said, 'Let's all hug, holding hands is not enough.'

She then proceeded to hug everyone near her. I was amazed. Sonia is an affectionate, but not a very huggy, woman.

Sue found all this very difficult and half started to run away. Sensing that she was frightened, and because she was near me, I stopped her and gave her a mild hug. At the same time I could see that the whole group had begun to exchange hugs.

Meanwhile Will had left for the kitchen. Like someone green with envy, he started to complain, 'Why is Hamid getting so much attention?'

George had gone to the kitchen to prepare the warm milk and honey. I might add that this is a brew which guests often take at night in place of sleeping pills. At my suggestion, and when not inappropriate, we may also add a tablespoon of fine brandy. A very important part of this ritual is that the guests see that a very special brandy has been added. In this way they feel special too. The ensuing drink has been goodheartedly called the 'Joe Berke special'.

Anyway, George made a point of giving Ron the milk and honey.

Back in the front room Kate volunteered to take a drink to Hamid.

But I proposed that we should ask Hamid to join the meeting. After all, all the hugs and warmth began after we had focused on helping Hamid to receive and express affection. He had sort of got lost, Ron's complaint notwithstanding, during all the recent exchanges of goodwill.

So Kate went to invite him down. A few minutes later she returned to the meeting to let us know that he had gone to bed.

It appeared that while we were all very very agitated, Hamid had calmed down and gone to sleep. Once again I was reminded of the story of Ingrid. While Morty and I had become increasingly agitated in Casualty at the Royal Free, she had calmed down.

The group again asked me to take some milk and honey to Hamid. I agreed and went upstairs. In fact Hamid was not asleep, just lying quietly on his bed. Hamid took the drink and thanked me in a pleasant, respectful way. He wasn't agitated. He wasn't psychotic.

By now it was 2.30 in the morning and it seemed that the immediate crisis had passed. No one was suggesting that Hamid had to leave that night, in fact no one was talking about his having to leave at all.

I was very tired and said good night to everyone.

In turn they thanked me and allowed me to leave without feeling anxious.

But as I was later told, the evening continued.

After I left, Hamid came downstairs and joined the group of his own accord.

Sonia, who previously couldn't bear to touch him, suggested that they all hug. Hamid demurred, but agreed to hold hands.

Ron shook Hamid's hands. Then the rest of the group greeted him and made a place for him.

All, including Hamid, helped to clean up. They continued to be huggy.

Hamid sported a huge smile. He was amused by the group's affection for him and said playfully: 'You lot are all mad and gay.'

This statement was not a challenge. Rather, it was the harbinger of a calm and pleasant mood which pervaded the house. By the early morning everyone drifted off to bed.

It had been a good night. The group had reconstituted itself. The mad behaviour of Hamid as well as that of the therapists and other guests had ceased. Clearly, their psychotic anxieties, and thoughts, or rather lack of thinking, had receded too. All of the residents seemed much more able to regain and contain their own feelings.

A couple of days later Hamid had his leaving meal. This is a big event for the guest who is finishing his stay as well as the whole house. Extra food is prepared, wine is served. Candles are lit. It is a real occasion. The celebration reflects work well done, on everyone's part. But completion leads to departure, so that there is usually an air of sadness too. Notably, the Centre may feel flat and empty for days afterwards.

Hamid's leaving meal was by no means certain. He had never previously stayed for dinner at any time during his stay. Yet, on the day after the lecture, when asked whether he wanted to forget the meal and leave early, he replied, 'No way. I can't leave. It's my leaving meal tomorrow.' And indeed he helped plan the dinner and stayed almost to the end.

When he did leave, it was uneventful.

Now let's try to consider what all this was about. Both with Hamid and Ingrid, as with other guests at the Centre, psychotic regressions in thinking and behaviour can brew up very quickly. This particularly happens when individuals who are unable to cope with sadness and depression are threatened by loss. Or to put it another way, catastrophic reactions occur when these same people are threatened by attachment, whether by making friends, or losing friends. Their capacity to hold depressive tensions is very poor and primitive defences against these tensions quickly unfold. I have used the word 'tensions' rather than anxieties. Really we are talking about a particular state of mind, one touched by sadness, loss and frustration and so on, but unable to contain these experiences. The ensuing chaos, or regressive madness, can not only engulf the person concerned, but also everyone else in their immediate social field.

The result of our intervention with Hamid was that he formed an intense attachment to the Centre, both the guests and therapists. The actual process whereby this happened was painful and difficult. In retrospect many of his angry outbursts had to do with his trying to reject the relationships which he was trying to establish or had already established. His final blow-up, the fury and reversion to a prior state of extremely provocative behaviour, occurred when his stay at the Centre was coming to an end and he was devastated by feelings of loss.

The situation with Ingrid was different. She was tormented by the nascent process of forming friendships. This was something she had never previously been able to accomplish. Her prior attachments were to caregivers in institutionalized care. But I think we underestimated the attachments she did form at the Centre, for, as I previously mentioned, she was clearly upset by another guest's leaving. And, as with Hamid, her ongoing tumult was an indication that little friendships were being established.

The massive outbursts of Hamid and Ingrid initially provoked similar responses on the part of the Centre. The resident therapists closest to them were overwhelmed by panic, rage and despair. These feelings were so powerful that they could no longer think or act as therapists. Like Hamid and Ingrid they just wanted to get rid of the threat, that is, the presence of Hamid and Ingrid, experienced as frightening monsters. These concrete experiences were the counterpart of the 'dreaded objects' which Hamid and Ingrid faced, 'sadness and depression'. When the therapists called for help, it was not to resolve the problem, but to execute the demons.

It would appear that we acted differently in these two instances. With Hamid we were able to keep him at the Centre and I was able to 'keep my cool'. But with Ingrid we could not manage this and Schatzman and I had to take her out of the Centre. Subsequently I felt overwhelmed by panic too, and could not think.

But on closer consideration, the reaction of the Centre, and by that I include myself, was similar. In both interventions we acted to expand the group. For Ingrid this included Morty and the duty psychiatrist at the Royal Free Hospital. For Hamid this included Dr T, all the guests at the Centre and all the visitors who accompanied Dr T to the reception. Then we played for time, hoping that it would have an ameliorative effect, which it did. Perhaps most significantly in both interventions we were able to shift the focus of 'bad object' from the designated patient to another person.

The duty psychiatrist certainly became, for a brief period at least, my 'bad object', the person who refused to take my instructions and frustrated my needs. Dr T served the same function for Hamid by becoming a focus of anger for people at the Centre. They then neglected to be upset with their primary 'bad boy'.

In fact, Dr T is a highly skilled and very experienced dynamic practitioner who is very sympathetic towards the work of the Centre. He also favours psychotherapy as a basic treatment modality for psychotic patients. Certainly it was unfair to embroil him in an emotional maelstrom. He had just come back for a quiet drink. Nonetheless, when the episode blew up, it was very important for us to involve him and for him to become part of the treatment milieu. Dr T, as did the duty psychiatrist, served commendably in the role of surrogate ego, as well as surrogate demon, and in so doing, helped us all to think again.

Essentially both disturbances were ameliorated by a therapeutic milieu that initially had been overwhelmed by chaotic currents, and was later able to reconstitute itself. The result was a strictly limited breakdown, contained by the willingness of the therapists involved to suffer, and by their capacity to ask for help and regain their thinking processes. This enabled the therapists as well as Hamid, Ingrid and all the guests at the Centre to discover and rediscover their sanity and humanity.

NOTE

1. Ross Speck and his wife, Joan Speck, worked for many years as family and network therapists in Philadelphia. See Speck and Attneave, 1973.

PART III
TRAINING

13   The Arbours Training Programme: a Subjective Account

ANDREA SABBADINI

I would like to present a brief history of the Arbours Training Programme in Psychotherapy from a personal perspective. Having been a student myself in this programme, and later its director (from 1977 to 1992), I have in the course of nearly 20 years been involved – actively or as a simple spectator – with many of its vicissitudes. I have seen it grow and develop and change, as well as having played some part in shaping it.

At its beginning, in the early Seventies, the Training Programme did not have a director. The whole programme started, and then crystallized around, the clinical seminars which Joe Berke and Morty Schatzman, the Arbours 'founding fathers', had enthusiastically set up: a forum, *the* forum for people connected with Arbours, including themselves and us and the many visitors from abroad, to get together and discuss our ideas and clinical work – in our young practices, in the newly opened Crisis Centre, in the Norbury therapeutic community. The programme was inspired by the same ideal principles that had underlain the work of Arbours in general from its inception: the provision of a valid alternative to traditional psychiatric ideologies and institutions, an awareness of the social implications of the stigma of mental illness, a reference to the humanistic values expressed by contemporary philosophies such as existentialism and phenomenology, a belief in the meaningfulness of all experiences and behaviours, the adoption of a complex theoretical framework combining the psychoanalytical model with those of therapeutic communities and of crisis intervention.

The co-ordinator of training activities for Arbours in the course of the first couple of years was Gregorio Kohon, who was involved in such responsibilities as inviting colleagues to present seminars, interviewing those who expressed an interest in learning about our work, writing a few letters and paying some meagre cheques. The quality of seminars and lectures was often excellent, and the choice of topics and teachers was adventurous and original (for instance, alongside more traditional seminars on Freud or Klein, there were courses on philosophy, on the history of institutions or on social anthropology). However, everything was still mostly quite informal and unstructured.

Around the mid-1970s teaching and learning activities got going in a more regular way. A small core of first students had formed: six of us who eventually qualified, plus two or three more who did not stick with it. My recollection of those years is that we had to struggle – not, like today, against some Authority, some bossy Director, some anonymous and mysteriously operating Training Committee – but in order to find enough energy and discipline to decide what courses we needed, what teachers might be available to give them, and where we could get hold of their telephone numbers and of our courage to contact them. Morty and Joe helped considerably, with their experience, acquaintances and advice, but in fact many training activities were arranged by us students. Although there were no formal assessment procedures (which in some respects was a good thing), Joe and Morty agreed that after about three years of training we had successfully completed all the requirements and were qualified to work as psychotherapists: something that by then most of us had already been doing, under supervision, for a long time.

Having then qualified as an Arbours psychotherapist, and been made more confident in myself by two-and-a-half years as resident therapist at the Crisis Centre, I proposed to take charge of the Arbours programme. My intention was to turn it into a programme with a more solid and formalized structure (while not depriving it of the positive aspects of its informality), to advertise it, to provide it with a sensible administration and to recruit good teachers and students. I must confess, however, that I did not have a clear idea of what I was doing. It was more a trial-and-error process, for which I was using aspects of my own experience as a student, what I was learning from other training programmes, the ideas of a number of Arbours therapists and, most important of all, the feedback – sometimes accepted rather uncritically – from our trainees. Such a feedback, by the way, has led through the years to gradual but major changes in most aspects of the training; unsatisfactory courses have been scrapped, new ones have been introduced, certain requirements have been tightened up, some teachers have not been reinvited, and so on. Even the seats in the students' room have at one time been changed, after we received a semi-serious letter from a group of students complaining of 'the damage caused to their brains, *via* their bums' by the old, uncomfortable chairs on which they were forced to sit, seminar after seminar!

Of course, it's pleasing to know that we do listen to our trainees and follow, whenever appropriate, their suggestions. However, it's also somewhat perplexing when one realizes that analytically oriented psychotherapy training programmes, including our own, are tending to become more and more alike: similar expectations, same courses with similar reading lists, same entry and qualification requirements – what does all this indicate? That we are running the risk of losing the idealism – rooted both in humanistic principles and in an awareness of the social dimension of personal problems – that has always characterized the spirit of our therapeutic work? That we are all moving, through different roads, towards the same 'perfect' format for training psychotherapists? Or, rather, that various pressures, both internal and external, are eroding those margins of originality that until a few years ago characterized different organizations, their ideologies, values and techniques? It is a question over which I think it is worth pondering, even if raising it may lead to lacerating conflicts within the already brittle world of psychotherapy. What will *not* be in the best interests of our profession is an artificial flattening of its form and contents, a castration of new initiatives and of healthy experimentation with fresh ideas, in the name of abstract conformity or political expediency. In all this, as is well known, the issues concerning training are of central importance.

In the course of the years, my colleagues and I gradually came to realize that a good training institution, such as we wanted the Arbours Training Programme to be, should aim at providing a least five interrelated components to its students: (1) intensive and long-term personal psychotherapy with an experienced therapist who should know of, and be sympathetic to, the demands placed on our students; (2) a solid body of theory – that strikes the right balance between the excesses of dogmatism on the one hand, and the confusion of eclecticism on the other – and an open forum where views can be shared, discussed, questioned and changed; (3) sound, and possibly varied, clinical work – both with individual patients and through the placements in our communities and Crisis Centre – under close supervision; (4) the living example of practising therapists sharing their experiences, their problems, their ethical and technical dilemmas, their enthusiasm and their doubts with the trainees; and (5) the creation of a group within and from which to learn and grow as therapists – a group to offer support and to advise; to test and challenge new ideas in relative safety; to help relieve at least some of the inevitable, and always painful, anxiety that stems from the loneliness of therapeutic work with patients; and to reinforce the trainee's, and later the therapist's, sense of professional identity.

As soon as I took over the co-ordination of training activities, I realized that a growing programme needed a committee, rather than a single individual, to run it. I also felt that it would have been helpful for that committee to have one member who was not otherwise involved with Arbours, but was sympathetic to our work and could contribute from the outside to the dynamics in our group, forcing us to spell things out more explicitly and to clarify our assumptions. The first such external committee member, who played a crucial part for years, was Dr Nina Coltart, a prominent member of the British Psycho-Analytical Society. I was impressed by her enthusiastic approach to our work and by her feeling deeply committed to it. 'When is *our* next meeting going to be?' was the first question she asked me when I invited her to join the Arbours Training Committee. She was to remain closely involved with our activities between 1978 and 1984. Nina's main functions in the Committee were to help us find suitable lecturers and teachers for the programme and to interview our new trainees in order to refer them to suitable training therapists, and, later, to supervisors – often, but not always, psychoanalysts.

The Committee makes general policy decisions about the programme, reviews administrative matters, changes training requirements and formally qualifies students at the end of the course. It also listens to tutors' reports about each student – based on tutorials and feedback from teachers and supervisors – through which their progress (or lack of it) is constantly monitored and assessed.

Decisions are normally made, often after lively and occasionally acrimonious discussion, by consensus. Conflict among us can often reflect personality differences, as well as private jealousies, envies, rivalries and vendettas (which we have all tried to restrain ourselves from interpreting to one another – interpreting such things being an ignoble, but unfortunately widespread custom among therapists). More often, though, they have expressed wider, and often unresolved, problems within our profession, and are thereby a useful barometer of the theoretical, clinical and political themes affecting psychotherapy, well beyond the boundaries of Arbours. We might argue over the difference between psychoanalytically oriented therapy and psychoanalysis: is the former a more liberal, less dogmatic version of the latter? Or a watered-down imitation of it? Or is there, indeed, a substantial difference between the two? Another (often not explicitly mentioned) conflict in the committee is between those, suspicious of other psychotherapy organizations, who would like our programme to be self-sufficient, independent, and proud of its achievements; and those who constantly seek contact, debates and fresh blood from other institutions, in the belief that cross-fertilization is possible and desirable, for scientific and diplomatic reasons. Rigidity *versus* flexibility is another meaty bone of contention, often leading to unsatisfactory compromises that leave both parties frustrated, as in the end no one likes to be seen as being a semi-unprofessional anarchist or an old-fashioned dogmatist. Yet another source of discord in the Committee is over our views about the very nature of psychotherapy: an essentially private, closely observed, one-to-one relationship taking place in the therapist's consulting room, or else a form of social activity, more concerned with the 'real' events of interpersonal relationships than with the intrapersonal world of artificially isolated individuals? This also affects our attitude towards the relative importance of our work in the communities and Crisis Centre: is it just one source of clinical experience for our trainees, or is it the most central feature of our programme? It is a fact that, in our Committee, in Arbours, and indeed in the psychotherapeutic world at large, these views are not clearly defined, easily recognizable, or free of internal contradictions.

Our introductory course, which we called the Associates' Programme, was started in 1978,[1] with the purpose of allowing applicants to find out more about us before they committed themselves to training. The Associates' Programme has in later years been enriched by a new series of seminars on the work of Arbours and on psychotherapy as a profession, by ongoing group work and by an optional programme of infant observation. People who apply to train with us often come from related professions, such as social work, psychology or nursing. For some, though, the main contact with psychotherapy has been through their own therapy, and sometimes becoming a therapist can result from an identification – not always entirely healthy – with their therapist. In the course of the years we received many hundreds of applications, some of which were truly remarkable for their inappropriateness. I remember, for instance, one by a young woman announcing that, if accepted, she did not intend to fulfil our requirement of getting into therapy, as she had already been in self-analysis since the previous September! Assessing prospective students is a delicate task, for which we rely not only on a Curriculum Vitae, reference letters and separate interviews with two members of the Training Committee, but also on the Associates'

Programme itself, which then serves the purpose of an ongoing assessment, allowing us to get to know our potential trainees in some depth
before deciding to train them as psychotherapists in the full programme,
thus reducing the drop-out rate.

I shall sketch here the structure of the Training Programme: its requirements, its function, its ideology. The two supervised placements – one in
a long-stay therapeutic community, the other at the Crisis Centre – are an
original aspect of the Arbours programme. Our students have an
opportunity to gain invaluable experience as part of their training, within
our group, rather than being required to have previously had such
experience as a prerequisite for acceptance. We have noticed that many
of our applicants have chosen Arbours over other similar training
organizations *because* of these requirements, and are particularly keen to
get involved with the activities of the communities as soon and as intensely
as possible. Other applicants, though, indicate that they have applied
despite our requirement for placements. To them, it is an enormous, not
entirely justified expenditure of time and energy, which they may find
difficult to fit in with other work and family commitments; in these cases,
we make flexible arrangements, in terms of format of placements, times
for visiting the houses and supervision. But, ultimately, placements have
to be done; they should be enriching experiences, both for the trainees
and for the residents in the houses; and the programme rejects applicants
whose external or internal conditions are too unfavourable in this respect.

In our opinion, therapeutic work should all along complement the
academic and theoretical aspects of training; the programme is structured
in such a way as to guarantee a constant interaction between theory and
closely supervised practice. Some of the seminars themselves are led by
senior Arbours therapists, some by invited teachers. Increased experience
and self-confidence among ourselves has progressively led to a higher
proportion of courses being taught by us. A few years ago we introduced
a series of Saturday workshops, from the second year onwards, replacing
some evening seminars: partly to bring more variety into the programme
and partly because we believe certain subjects are best taught in this new
format. The curriculum includes, among other subjects, courses on
psychopathology, crisis intervention, psychoanalytical literature (with
reading seminars on Freud, Klein, Winnicott and Jung), group dynamics,
child development, sexuality and psychotherapeutic techniques. I consider it a positive sign that trainees – while objecting to any suggestions

that their training might be extended in time – often complain that the courses we offer them are too short!

The general orientation of the training is psychodynamic and psycho-analytical. While members of the Training Committee themselves come from different theoretical and professional backgrounds and have different personalities, intellectual interests and political orientations, I believe that we all share some basic principles: a need for clear boundaries, as well as for considerable flexibility and tolerance within those boundaries; a non-directive style of intervention; a respect for our patients' experiences, however different from our own, in particular for their suffering; the need to see patients as whole persons, and not just as collections of symptoms; a belief that the therapist has the role of active (and therefore responsible) participant in the therapeutic situation, and not just of passive spectator; and a critical attitude towards traditional psychiatric ways of diagnosing and treating mental patients. Our views over these and other matters, however, have developed as we have acquired fresh experience ourselves and refined our conceptual and technical tools. Certainly, working in contact with our students – as teachers, tutors and supervisors – has greatly helped all of us to grow and change, and I am convinced that we have all become better therapists to our patients as a result of our training work.

Tutors had a more marginal function in the initial years of the Arbours programme. I do not recall having had one myself, though I do remember both Joe and Morty being available for advice when I needed it. But today tutors have a crucial part to play in helping students go through their training as smoothly as possible. They are the formal link between individual trainees and the Training Committee, and their task is to make sure that obstacles of any sort are overcome in the best way. Tutors clarify training requirements, and if decisions have to be reached – about an Associate joining the full programme, about a trainee getting a grant or doing a placement or seeing a first patient or qualifying – these are made in a friendly atmosphere, giving the students opportunities to explain their position and wishes, and ensuring that their interests are formally represented at the Training Committee.

We have often observed the tendency on the part of tutors to 'take sides', through a process of 'protective' identification, with their students, at times in quite irrational ways. This may indicate a tendency, which exists in most training institutions, towards an infantilization of the trainee – an apparently absurd situation, as most psychotherapy students are fully mature, grown-up men and women, often with years of professional experience behind them, major responsibilities in their families and respectable positions in society.

The last year of training involves intensive individual therapeutic work with patients. These are referred to our trainees by the Arbours Psychotherapy Service. The function of the Psychotherapy Service is to centralize all referrals to Arbours (except those in acute crises, to be interviewed directly by the Crisis Centre), so that anybody coming to us for therapeutic help can be promptly met, assessed and, if appropriate, referred. We are faced with the unresolved problem of what kind of patients would be most suitable for trainees, given that the criteria for 'difficult' (as opposed to 'easy') patients are hard to demarcate. Quite arbitrary considerations come into play here: the 'feeling' that a certain patient would be suited to a certain trainee; the 'impression' that they could well understand one another; the 'certainty' that they will develop a fruitful therapeutic relationship, that the patient will benefit from the therapy and the trainee learn from the patient. On top of this, practical factors also have to be taken into account, including logistics (how long it would take the patient to reach the therapists' consulting room) and financial ones (trainees are only allowed to charge low fees).

Another later introduction into the structure of the programme was the trainee's 'final presentation', a clinical paper on work carried out under supervision with the first of two training cases in individual therapy and presented on a Tuesday evening to all the Arbours trainees and to some therapists. The final presentation is supposed to conclude the formal part of training with us. After it, the tutor normally recommends the student for qualification to the Training Committee, we send a letter of congratulations and, later, a rather impressive Certificate in Psychotherapy, with the red seal of the Association and the signatures of the Director of the Arbours Association and of the Director of the Arbours Training Programme.

But training in psychotherapy does not end on a Tuesday evening with a final presentation, a congratulatory letter, or a red-sealed certificate. Training in psychotherapy, like psychotherapy itself, is an intrinsically interminable process. The day a therapist – however well trained, however senior a position he holds in the institution where he belongs, however experienced in his clinical practice – stops learning about his work while doing it; the day he stops being curious about, and stimulated by, the variety and richness of human experiences as he has a chance of observing them in his consulting room (and outside of it); the day this therapist believes he is just a professional doing his job – that day, he is ready for retirement.

NOTE

1. Another history of the Arbours Training Programme can be found in Jan Abram's *Individual Psychotherapy Trainings: A Guide* (Abram, 1992).

14   Psychic Muscles

ALEXANDRA FANNING

I look up *placement* in the dictionary and I read: 'placing or setting: assigning to places: assigning to a job' and I feel disappointed and frustrated. This short, dry definition in no way relates to my experience of a placement and in no way conveys the centrality of it in my training or in the training of others as psychotherapists.

All analytic psychotherapists take their personal therapy as a crucial component of their training. In Arbours we rank the placements as of equal importance in the training of our psychotherapists. We feel them to be so important and so fundamental that we will not consider training anyone who isn't prepared to undertake two placements. One, ideally residential, in one of our communities for a minimum of six months, and the other, non-residential, in the Crisis Centre. The whole of the students' progress and development is then monitored through these two placements.

Clearly this requirement, bordering on the vocational, rules out many otherwise suitable applicants. Those who do feel able to make this daunting commitment are already expressing their willingness to enter into the unknown, an essential quality for any psychotherapist. Having this requirement enables us to take risks with our students; it gives us the luxury to be able to take on some students who may be lacking in related experience but who display qualities that might make them creative therapists. We know that our trainees are going to grow and develop but in which direction? It is a very exciting time for the trainers to be party to these changes and growth. To witness the new, emerging therapist.

Once the students have started their training the placement takes on a 'mystical' quality. There are those who have done their placements and those who are still waiting and preparing themselves for the experience. These two groups are divided by an invisible line. The placement has the sense of a rite of passage, an initiation ceremony. It is something that is prepared for in excitement and in fear. During the preparation period the only thing certain and known is that the student will emerge from the experience forever changed. There will be no going back. In working with students I have often been struck by the joking sadism expressed by the 'after' group to the 'before' group; the experience gets dressed up as a horror story as they are told, ' . . . *and you'll be lucky if you survive!*' It is striking how often the word survive is used in relationship to the placements.

The first placement always takes place in the communities and is far less structured than the later placement in the Crisis Centre. Students anticipate the placement in many different ways. There are those who want to throw themselves into it while others, more cautious, want to feel ready, to know more. One thing that they all have in common is that however worried and anxious they are, they all assume certain things about themselves. They all enter with some sense of how they imagine they will cope and manage; they are always surprised. This then is an essential feature of the placement, the surprise at having your own assumptions about yourself and about others, questioned; in finding strengths when you believed there were none and in finding weaknesses in safe and solid areas.

I was very fortunate in my training in that the community I joined was new and still very fragmented and lost, not having developed its own identity; this gave me the space to find a place for myself. Nowadays, it is much more difficult for students since they are, realistically, often seen as the outsiders. They have a much more difficult time in order to 'prove' themselves. We often joke about the residents being more experienced and knowledgeable than the students and this is completely true. The residents will have lived through the comings and goings of many students as well as sharing their lives with many other residents in varying degrees of distress. I have often heard students express with gratitude the expertise with which residents interviewed them for their forthcoming placement, their relief being that the residents knew what was needed and required from the meeting even when they didn't know themselves.

One main function of the placement is to find out about oneself in the face of the distress of the other. This is something that is impossible to communicate or to teach, and however thorough the training therapy it cannot deal adequately with this particular highly charged and demanding area. One student has written of this:

From my personal point of view, the first month of my placement was about setting up my boundaries in the community. Was my role that of a friend or that of a 'baby-therapist'? What was the definition of the Arbours student in relation to the therapeutic community? My anxiety about the lack of clear-cut answers was the manifestation of a much deeper anxiety about the lack of structure in the house and therefore the potential for destruction, my own unconscious fear of breaking down or losing control. As soon as I was able to explore these issues in my own therapy, I was able to accept the lack of rigid definition and tolerate my own role and boundaries. I could test and examine my thoughts and actions in a space that was mine but that was also different from my therapy.

All students approach the placements with ideas of wanting to help or with ideas of wanting to learn about others. They believe this to be the purpose of the placement, while they believe that their own therapy is where they learn about themselves. Once in the placement this artificial split is impossible to maintain. If it were to be maintained we would question the student's suitability to become a therapist. Another student wrote of this experience:

My expectations were that this experience would teach me something about becoming a therapist. I thought I was going to learn about the people in the community, who they were, what shaped their internal world and how they responded to their emotional difficulties. What I came to realize was that I too was living there and while I have learnt something of the facts of the residents' lives, and something of the pattern of their struggles, the person I learnt the most about was me.

Students who come to us with a great deal of relevant experience in psychiatric care still find the placement a unique and a once-in-a-lifetime experience. The lack of structure and the minimizing of roles forces the students back on themselves in a way that confronts them and questions their attitudes and expectations for the first time. What is constantly being explored is not the patients' crazy behaviour, but the interaction between resident and student, thereby acknowledging each other as equals with equal rights to be listened to and to be heard.

The most vulnerable students are those who have entered personal therapy as a training requirement. Those who have entered therapy prior to training for acknowledged personal reasons can feel more easy in recognizing their sameness to the residents, while the 'training' ones have to undergo a seachange in order to recognize that chaos and disturbance do indeed lie within themselves. This then is where the sense of 'survival' comes in for the student. In this context the term means the survival of the student's own inner turmoil and confusion. A second-year student wrote in the conclusion to his placement report:

> My six-month placement in the community was far the hardest part of my training, but also the most valuable one. It was a kind of 'breaking in' and I was aware that survival was my main purpose. But this survival did not just mean the actual avoidance of my own breakdown or leaving or giving up the training altogether. That kind of survival is fairly easy: by setting rigid boundaries and a distance from the emotional upheaval of others; by being very 'helpful' and 'popular' and 'much loved'; by being an observer instead of a participant – all these defensive measures can help us through the placement without ever getting into conflict with the residents, ever feeling distressed and helpless. Instead, surviving by growth, by learning to cope with the fear of destruction, investigating my fantasies of madness, engaging in real relationships without ever losing sight of my role as 'helper' or avoiding submergence in crisis or identification: that is helping by not reinforcing others' false self; these proved to be far more difficult. I failed each and every one of these aims many times: I withdrew when tension became unbearable; I did not challenge at times, fearing retaliation; I used interpretations revengefully; I acted out others' fantasies, and so on. I cannot judge how useful or 'therapeutic' my presence was – I can only be sure of how useful it was for me.

When trainees can no longer dismiss the other with neat labels and categories, then they have to allow the feelings that rise up inside themselves. Very often these feelings are experienced as foreign and disturbing. While responding to and being with the other, they also have to listen to their own inner dialogue, checking, watching and listening to their own responses.

It is through the continual observance of this inner dialogue that the student starts the process of what I think of as the development of *psychic muscles*. This dialogue takes place within that internal space which is the reservoir of one's own emotional experience and history – all the different nuances that go into the making of the individual. Within this internal space, that is psychic space, there is an interaction between responses, reactions, memories, prejudices, feelings, past experiences and future expectations. These diverse elements are held together in psychic space. Through a mental process of observation they can be used actively to further the understanding of what is currently taking place. It is this conscious gathering up of and holding together of all these different elements that I think of as the function of the psychic muscles. These muscles can only be developed when utilized in responding to and being

with another. For this development to take place the individual has to
leave him/herself open to all these diverse elements; to tolerate them
entering the psychic space.

It is human nature to avoid upsetting, disturbing and unknown
situations and to seek out those which, if not comfortable, are at least
familiar. The arena in which all good psychotherapy takes place is just
this area of disturbance and upset. The capacity to experience the
unknown repeatedly is a prerequisite of therapeutic practice and, in my
view, depends largely on the ability to use the psychic muscles. Just as
the athlete has to train to face all the limits of physical demands so the
therapist has to train the psychic muscles to be aware of every fleeting,
shadowy nuance so that they can be called upon to meet all extremes and
facets of human experience and feeling. First the trainee has to become
aware of these muscles, often with trepidation, pain and exhaustion; then
they have to utilize and develop them until later, when they are in their
own consulting rooms, they can take pleasure in these muscles, knowing
that they have been truly tested. Knowing that they can be relied on to
sustain them through the daily demands of therapeutic work, where they
will meet again those elements of human conflict and suffering in which
the psychic muscles were first recognized and developed.

The student entering a placement carries very similar feelings that our
patients bring to the beginning of their therapy. The mixture of fears and
hopes, fantasies and expectations, terror and excitement. Just as we watch
how our patients navigate this 'traumatic' situation so we watch our
students. Are they going to become paralysed by fear or will they become
manic in their defence against anxiety? From here on in the student has
to learn to walk the tightrope between their personal experience and
emotional response on the one side, while thinking and trying to
understand on the other. We know that they will frequently fall down one
side or the other of this tightrope but we also anticipate that once in their
consulting rooms, their aim will be to mostly maintain the balance. More
importantly, when they do indeed fall down one side or the other this will
not be experienced as a 'mistake' but rather as evidence of further
material that needs to be explored about the nature of the relationship in
which they are engaged. When they do fall down from the tightrope are
they able to get up again? Indeed, are they able to know that they have
fallen down? One of the most difficult responses to deal with is the student
who is convinced of the rightness of whatever it is they are doing and so
cannot tolerate the possibility of not knowing or not understanding. The

student who can say 'I don't understand' is already on the road to understanding.

Just as the residents bring their past history, their complete families, with them into the community, so does the student. Of course, this is no different in essence from all our daily experiences except that the relatively unstructured environment of the community acts as a catalyst for all the conflicts from earlier times to come bursting forth. The communities invite regression in both resident and student. It is not within the scope of this chapter for me to tackle the issue of symbolic regression as distinct from actual physical regression. Here I am referring to symbolic regression although, naturally, there is an overlap. The absence of formal rules invites the regressive tendencies that are within all of us. Although the trainees will be faced with this in their own personal therapy we expect that their transference manifestations will not be met head on by their therapists' transference manifestations. This is different from the situation in the placement and it is just that hotbed of unresolved conflicts that the trainee has to face.

The student constantly has to face the dilemma that they are just another person in the house, participating and sharing and yet they have to live with and acknowledge the paradox that they are also different. They are not in the house because, for whatever reason, they are unable to cope in the outside world. They are in the house as a requirement of their training to become psychotherapists.

We always have to bear in mind that for everybody, the communities are hard places in which to live. Although people come with fantasies and expectations of a safe haven, the reality is very different. Students and residents alike have to face their fantasies in the context of that reality. When there is a denial of reality you can get a house in which every individual has the expectation that the house and its occupants are there to provide perfect care and understanding of that individual. This caring is meant to be magical in that the house should intuit what the individual needs without that individual holding any responsibility in the process. The intuition should take place in much the same way that an ideal mother is supposed to know exactly what her baby wants from moment to moment. At such times you have a community full of depressed residents feeling isolated and resentful, full of hurt and angry feelings towards others who are not caring for them in the ideal way. At these times the house gets dirtier and meals skimpier and skimpier; the rationale being that the individual should not have to do these things, that the others should be understanding and caring. In these phases it is as though there is a competition of suffering: 'What you have to put up with is nothing compared to what I have to put up with.'

Entering a house during this sort of phase the unwary student can get pulled more and more into the belief that it is up to them to make things all right. If only they spent another five minutes talking to one person it might make all the difference. As a student has written of this experience: 'My internal struggle was about working through my omnipotent defence structure of feeling I had to "provide everything" to just being myself.' Another has written: 'So being there became the issue I had to work through and my attempt to escape into "doing things" there was a strong pull towards a defensive flight.'

Students can very quickly become totally exhausted as they run from one person to another, answering one demand after another in an unrealistic belief that they should be and can be 'fair'. They divide up their time on this basis in order to try and deal with their guilt feelings that wait around ready to pounce. Of course what happens in these situations is that the residents also feel guilty for their demandingness and the whole thing can spiral. For the student this can be a very shattering and humiliating process as they painfully discover that their well-intentioned contributions do not magically change things. As we know from our consulting rooms we can do our best and yet this does not necessarily mean that changes are forthcoming or, even more disturbing, our patients may get worse.

It is in the placement that the student first meets the negative therapeutic response. What they have to survive at this point is not just the attack from the other but their own overwhelming feelings of not being allowed to help or to make a difference. Their own feelings of outrage, hurt and dismay in response to being so badly treated, misunderstood and unappreciated – at having their need to be therapeutic so cruelly frustrated. This circle has to be broken into through the help of the student's supervision and through the house meetings. Here the sibling rivalry can be articulated and understood as well as the student's omnipotent need to appease and to be appreciated. These omnipotent needs match the residents' omnipotent demands for an all-giving, perfect environment. This shattering of omnipotent fantasies is the same in both student and resident and is also an integral part of more formal therapeutic relationships. A first-year student wrote of this painful yet essential experience:

I felt totally deskilled, inadequate and a failure. Any attempt I made at verbal understanding was derided by X until I fell into my own brooding silence. I was devoid of speech or the capacity to think. I was awash with feelings of helplessness and inadequacy. I had some awareness that something was happening but no understanding of what it was. I felt out of my depth, unable to contribute anything helpful or constructive and very far from the helpful figure I had been told to be. I sank deeper and deeper into the pit of confusion, despair and depression. How could I *ever* be a therapist if I could allow a situation to get so out of hand and be powerless to intervene? What was I doing here when I was clearly failing so miserably in my brief? What would my supervisor, my tutor, Arbours think of me if they knew just how profoundly I was failing? I needed time to digest my experiences and the opportunity to talk through my feelings in supervision in order for me to understand that those very feelings were perhaps an important indicator as to X's own inner turmoil. How was I to understand the feelings she evoked in me? At the time concepts such as projection and projective identification were simply words without real meaning and did not have a place in my understanding. My task was simply to survive the placement with all that it entailed.

The constant dilemma in the placement facing the student is the question of how much to do? How little? The placement poses the same questions that are constantly being juggled within the consulting room – how much – how little structure is required for a sense of safety and containment without infringement and interference? They have to learn to know when to let be and when to intervene. Before they can begin to think about these questions they have to learn about their own tolerances. They may find that they intervene because they cannot bear not to. Once this has occurred we can look with them at the meaning for them and so start the never-ending process of sorting out what belongs to them and what belongs to others. It is through this process that they learn to move backwards and forwards from group to individual, from themselves to individual and group, so that when they are working as individual therapists they have a model inside themselves of individuals in relationship to other individuals within a group/family. With this model the future therapist can avoid the bad practice of only seeing the individual in isolation, in a void, as it were.

The Arbours trainee has to maintain an intricate network of relationships and confidentialities which at times can feel unbearable and overwhelming. Having been borne, these experiences can help develop a respect and understanding of the intricacies of group/family living. The placement is a constant juggling/balancing act between the inner and outer needs of individuals. The psychic experience and understanding has to take place within the day-to-day needs of shopping, cooking and cleaning. Having undertaken a placement the future therapist should be well grounded. After all, psychotherapy can only take place when certain basic human needs are being met.

When I approached my own placement in my training many years ago in 1975 I was one of the more cautious students in that I took my time in order to find out more about what was expected of me. Also, I had to make all the necessary arrangements that were involved with moving into a community with my husband and 4-year-old son. For me the experience of having sat through endless meetings and discussions about the communities prior to my placement proved invaluable. It meant that frequently during my placement I would suddenly recognize something that I had heard others discussing; what had previously been someone else's struggle or a complicated bit of theory became vividly alive in the here and now. I would have the sense of 'so that's what that means!'

I still remember walking through the front door of the community and the strong sense I had of leaving one world and entering another. In crossing that threshold I left behind me theories and ideas and entered the world of 'being'. It is the crossing of this threshold that makes the Arbours training unique. For me the development of my own psychic muscles started the moment that I crossed that threshold and the residents slowly emerged from their rooms and gathered around me, using me as a focus and putting all kinds of expectations onto me of being a provider and a nurturer. From those first few moments I had to wrestle with the ongoing conflict of my needs versus their needs and of trying to understand and make sense of the interaction between us.

I was constantly faced with issues of when to intervene and when not to and of how much to tolerate. The following two incidents illustrate this dilemma and also were typical of the sort of daily experiences that helped me to develop my own psychic muscles. My wish to be 'helpful', 'understanding' and 'therapeutic' was quickly put under considerable strain when I was nightly kept awake by the resident above me hoovering throughout the night. I went through stages of trying to discuss it with him, discussing it with the rest of the house, interpreting it to him and eventually telling him it had to stop. None of these things changed the situation one iota! I finally resorted to hammering on his door when he started the hoovering and when he complained bitterly about the noise that I was making I informed him that I would keep it up as long as he went on with the hoovering. It worked! After that incident we were able to have a reasonable, although difficult, 'therapeutic' relationship – therapeutic because we had struggled with something together, not because I had sat making interpretations.

The other incident was when I returned to my room one day to find one of the residents standing in front of my mirror putting on my jewellery and telling me that she was 'Alex' and asking me what was I doing in her room? Although it was extremely disturbing to be suddenly faced with this without warning, I knew enough about this woman and what was happening for her to be able to sit and talk to her and help her make sense of her actions until she was able, in her own time, to take off my jewellery and reclaim her own identity. For me the experience of being faced with someone who had taken over my physical space and my identity was very shocking. By being able to acknowledge my feelings to myself I was able to tolerate a bizarre and disturbing situation and so help this very confused woman.

All through my placements and training I had a worry, an anxiety, as to how I would respond if I was ever physically threatened. My worry was just the sense of unknownness, that this was something that I did not and could not know about myself. When once it did happen I was totally surprised and taken aback at my own response. It was some years after I had completed my training and I was working at the Crisis Centre as a team leader. I was involved with a young, very violent adolescent girl. On one occasion we were having a meeting at the Centre with all the people involved. We were discussing her attacks on the resident therapists. She was roaming around the room while we were talking, and suddenly, without warning, she lunged at me from behind, pulling hard at my hair. Without thinking I stood up in a quiet fury and ordered everyone except her from the room. After they had all scuttled out I turned on her and told her with absolute certainty that she would never, ever, attack me again (which she didn't, although she continued to attack others). My surprise was that I had no idea that I would react so quickly and without fear but with a white fury that certainly communicated itself to her! It was only after my spontaneous response to her that together we were able to look at the meaning of her attack on me. I found it a very reassuring experience as my fear has always been that in the face of that sort of attack I would turn into a gibbering jellyfish! Following this experience I felt much more certain about my ability to take care of myself and to take appropriate action when necessary, and so I knew that I could be relied on to take care of the other.

In looking back at my first placement many of my fond memories come from the times when we were united in the house and the differences between resident and student were bridged – such as the times of humour in the very midst of a desperate crisis: looking out of the window of our Kensington ambassadorial house to collapse in disbelief and merriment at the tree in the front of the house in that elegant residential area 'dressed' with all the clothes of one of the residents, right down to the cowboy boots that he had bought the previous day.

The humour of these times was heightened just because everything was so difficult, and there was a sense of us all hanging on together in order to get through. At these times there was a strong sense of a close, enclosed family pulling together against all the odds. This was the same family that would watch with amusement as visitors would try to sort out who were the students and who were the residents. They usually got it wrong and we would get sadistic pleasure from watching their discomfort when they realized that the person they had been talking to on the assumption of their 'sanity' was in fact a resident. This was a time when we hadn't learnt to say no to requests from visitors and we were running an 'open' house. This quickly became intolerable and houses now are much more selective in their visitors.

My experience of the house coming together in the face of the outside world is one frequently referred to by trainees and is in itself a crucial learning experience for the future therapist. At times it can be irresistible to collude in a cosy 'us' against 'them' state of affairs which prevents questions and confrontation. It is this collusion which is constantly being offered to us in our consulting rooms, albeit in very disguised and subtle ways. One student, in describing a highly charged situation during her placement, has written:

> I felt my logic and sanity were sorely stretched as I sat with them in the dining room that night. There was such a strong pressure to collude with the fears and paranoid anxieties and to add my own internal fears and anxieties into the group's cauldron, bubbling with persecutory projections.

As therapists we have only ourselves to work with. We can't learn a skill which we can then utilize, we can only learn about ourselves in conjunction with learning different theories. The skill comes from the finding and developing of the psychic muscles, as I have described. Often in supervision the trainee therapist struggling with their first patients will ask, 'But how do you know when to say it, how to put it?' This is an unanswerable question – how do you describe how the many different levels of awareness that are taking place will help you, the therapist, to make a decision as to when to respond or when to make a mental note for future reference? I am not talking about the image of the therapist as the cold and clinical scientist regarding an insect. I am talking about the experience of allowing oneself to follow the tide, the turns, the eddies and of allowing oneself to get caught up in it while simultaneously being able to acknowledge the feelings in the self, secure in the knowledge that all subtleties of feelings can be tolerated and utilized in order to make an informed decision as to how and when to respond. Frequently this response will come spontaneously based on subliminal awareness while sometimes it will be more considered and consciously thought through. In spite of parody, jokes and criticism the good therapist is not a cut-off mask but is him/herself working in highly demanding and challenging psychic areas – the good therapist does not protect him/herself by switching off or by intellectualizing but rather observes these tendencies and so simultaneously strives to make sense of their appearance. What is being communicated – why – how – what does it mean? It is just these psychic areas that get explored and challenged in the unique setting of the placement; a setting in which it is extremely difficult to hide from oneself.

As I write this I am surprised at my reluctance to think in too much detail of my own placement. Although the sense of it lives on within me it is as though in some imperceptible way I feel threatened in having to think too clearly about it. I am reminded of the feeling I had when I left the community, accompanied by my family, where we had lived for one year – a year in which I had been totally caught up with and enmeshed in the life of the community. I found it difficult to say goodbye and left while a house meeting was in progress. As I stepped out on to the pavement, a warm, still, sunny evening, I knew with absolute certainty that I would never again be able to undertake such an experience. Perhaps it is one of those undertakings that, however important, leave one with the feeling that if you had known what you were entering you wouldn't have taken it on in the first place. Isn't that just what our patients say to us even when acknowledging the positive elements of their therapy? In the same way an experienced therapist might feel weary as well as pleased at taking on a new patient. The previous experiences alert us to what we are letting ourselves in for and yet it is just those very experiences that enable us to be able to continue to meet the needs and demands of our patients. A young student wrote:

Being in the community was an overwhelming and utterly exhausting experience. It is not one I would ever wish to repeat. Yet it is one I would not have missed.

My placement experience taught me how and when to utilize theoretical concepts as an aid to further understanding and exploration. Any 'list' that I might make of what I learnt from my placement would do sorry justice to the experience but it would contain the following. It taught me to be able to sit with whatever and not be surprised either by myself or the other; it taught me that internal processes have their own time plan and should be respected; it taught me not to be alarmed in the face of drama or crisis; it taught me not to remedy by doing; it taught me when to take appropriate action. Most importantly, it taught me that my security lies in taking into account and making use of all the material that is brought into the consulting room in *whatever* form and not to view some things as acceptable and some as unacceptable; that this 'material' also includes my own second-to-second shadowy responses. In order to avoid any confusion I must state here that I am in no way talking about encouraging what is often referred to as 'acting-out'. In my experience it is often just those therapists who have not had the opportunity to develop their 'psychic muscles' in the ways which I have described who get into management difficulties with their patients and have to resort to talking about 'acting-out', the danger being that if their own psychic muscles have not been developed they can miss nuances and subtleties until things get out of hand.

The placement gave me internal security. I knew that having survived the unknown, the bizarre, the mundane, the pain, the grief, the boredom, the fear, the humour, the excitement, the confusion and the love of community life I could face and meet the daily challenges of therapeutic work.

You cannot teach a student when to respond – when to intervene or when it is more important to just be with the other – they have to learn it by being there themselves and by allowing themselves to be muddled, confused, frightened, insecure and unknowing. Understanding can only be arrived at when chaos and confusion have not been avoided. In Arbours we have therapists working within widely different theoretical models; what unites us and enables us to encompass our differences is that we have all been there. We all developed our psychic muscles in our early placement experiences and it is those experiences that are the making of an Arbours psychotherapist.

Now, many years after my first placement, I carry fond and grateful memories of those of you who 'trained' me by allowing me the unique privilege of being and sharing with you and who now sit inside me in my consulting room joining me on each new exploration into the unknown which is my daily work.

PART IV

PHILOSOPHY, CONTEXT AND OTHER CONSIDERATIONS

15 STILL PIONEERING AFTER ALL THESE YEARS

RON LACEY

> We are so fond of one another, because our ailments are the same.
>
> Jonathan Swift, *Journal to Stella*, 1 February 1711

Those of us who were involved in or entertained by 'anti-psychiatry' in the Sixties will find it salutary to realize that the Arbours Association is now a quarter of a century old. Joe Berke's brief to me in this chapter was to 'put the work of the Arbours in a historical and ideological perspective'. As an old friend of Arbours I was honoured to be asked to contribute a chapter to this book. When I began I had intended to write a scholarly review of the life and times of the Arbours Association. I have patently failed in this self-imposed task and have written a polemical tribute. I make no apology for this. The work of the Arbours is worthy of a tribute not because it has reached an important chronological landmark, but because it has shone like a beacon of optimistic endeavour throughout the 25 years of its existence.

My own career in and with mental health services began 25 years ago as a social worker in London. I later joined Mind, where I had the privilege to share with Tony Smythe, Larry Gostin and other colleagues the work of campaigning for the rights of patients. These campaigns were strongly influenced by the turbulent 'anti-psychiatrists' of the Sixties, from among whom emerged the founders of the Arbours. 'Anti-psychiatry' set many of the agendas for the debates about the rights of patients almost 10 years before they were taken up by Mind in the mid-Seventies. It is almost a contradiction in terms to describe a service which has been in existence in a more or less similar way for 25 years. But, seen in the context of the rather depressing milieu of contemporary mainstream psychiatric services in Britain, the work of the Arbours is as pioneering now as it was all those long years ago. Mainstream psychiatry in this country has been influenced more by the introduction of chlorpromazine in 1951 than it has by anything which might be described as an idea or principle. The Arbours Association was founded, in part as an expression of a rejection of the mechanistic approach of organic psychiatry, but more importantly to provide mentally distressed people with an alternative to becoming psychiatric patients. That such an alternative should exist remains for all practical purposes as innovative now as it did in 1970 when the Arbours Association began.

In these days when nostalgia for traditional family values is cited as the guiding principle of public policy, the Sixties seem almost as remote as the days of the Empire. The 'permissive society' of the Sixties has become the Sodom and Gomorrah of the 'back to basics' consciousness of the Nineties. The Arbours was born in the cradle of the turbulent optimism of the Sixties and has survived and prospered as a respected provider of mental health services. As I have said, the founders of Arbours were among the leading figures of that loose alliance of people who were at the core of the British 'anti-psychiatry' movement. 'Anti-psychiatry', in so far as it could be described as a movement, was very much shaped by the prevailing forces of radical opinion of the Sixties. If there was a single theme that characterized those times, it was a rejection by the young of the old world values and authorities. This rejection took many forms – protests against the war in Vietnam, student sit-ins, the 1968 revolt by students and workers in Paris, sex, drugs and rock'n'roll (Neville, 1971). The revolt of the Sixties was swept along on a tide of optimism in which the possibility of changing things for the better seemed very real indeed. Optimism was an important thread in anti-psychiatry that has survived through the work of the Arbours. The services provided by the Arbours and the Philadelphia Associations remain as those parts of the legacy of anti-psychiatry which transcended mere protest.

David Cooper first coined the term anti-psychiatry drawing an analogy with the anti-art of the Dada movement. Dadaism originated in Zurich in the wake of World War One as an expression of revolt against the bourgeois artistic and social institutions of the time. The term anti-psychiatry movement is used here as a form of shorthand. Anti-psychiatry was most certainly not a movement. It embraced far too many different ideologies and perspectives to be described as a movement. It is more accurate to describe anti-psychiatry as a set of libertarian ideas and ideologies which informed a critique of psychiatry shared by a loose alliance of people on the broad left. Even among anti-psychiatry's inner circle of the gurus and activists, differences were as much hallmarks of the 'movement' as were shared ideas and principles. Some of these differences were rooted in personal animosities, while others were ideological.

In using the term anti-psychiatry Cooper meant to convey more than a simple hostility to beliefs and practices of mainstream organic psychiatry. However, the rejection of mainstream psychiatric theory and practice was probably the most important single thread that attracted people to the movement. Later in his life Cooper adopted the term 'the critical movement of and in psychiatry' (quoted in Lacey, 1983) to encompass the diversity of ideological and theoretical approaches which shaped radical alternatives to psychiatry in different parts of the world. Cooper had conducted his own 'experiment in anti-psychiatry' (Cooper, 1967) in Villa 21 of Shenley Hospital in Hertfordshire between 1962 and 1966. In reporting that experiment Cooper (Cooper, 1967) was at pains to point out that although he was describing work in a ward for young 'schizophrenics' he fundamentally rejected the validity of that label. This rejection of the medical model of mental illness was another of the principal tenets of anti-psychiatry. Laing saw the experiences which psychiatrists described as symptoms as being potentially transcendental, as the means by which an individual attempts to make sense of a mad situation (Laing, 1970). Joe Berke (Berke, 1977) describes schizophrenia as 'an expertise in producing disquiet in others, when the altered state of reality is culturally unacceptable and inadvertently upsetting. In other words, it is often against the social rules to have certain experiences or manifest certain behaviour' (p. 21). This social or phenomenological view of schizophrenia was shared by others who had no direct relationship with anti-psychiatry. The double bind theory (Bateson et al., 1956) posits that schizophrenia is the consequence of a child being constantly exposed to incompatible and contradictory emotional demands by a parent, in particular, the mother.

The critique of organic psychiatry went beyond rejecting the scientific basis of its diagnostic labels. It argued that psychiatric labels were little more than the means by which people whose ideas or behaviour are disturbing to others are marginalized and invalidated. Once labelled such people are segregated and abused with crude physical treatments that alienated them from their own experience and damaged their physical and psychological well-being. Luminaries of anti-psychiatry like Cooper, Laing and others pointed to potential and real abuses of people by organic psychiatry. Joe Berke (Berke, 1977) was probably the most specific in pointing to the dangers of treatments with anti-psychotic drugs, electroshock and psychosurgery. In discussing the use of chlorpromazine (Largactil or Thorazine) Joe draws a parallel between its earlier use as an insecticide and its current use as a means of managing 'schizophrenics', two different forms of 'pest control' using the same basic substance!

Perhaps the least contentious aspect of anti-psychiatry's critique of mainstream psychiatric treatment concerned its base in the old Victorian asylums. The seeds of the concept of the 'toxic institution' are almost as old as the asylums themselves. Andrew Scull in *Museums of Madness* (1979) relates how, as long ago as 1870, Friern Barnet hospital (then called the Middlesex County Asylum at Colney Hatch) was described in the *Lancet* as 'a colossal mistake' by a certain Mortimer Granville. By the 1930s the momentum of the flow of opinion against the asylum was growing. The negative effects of institutionalism were increasingly being recognized as a major iatrogenic consequence of treating people in the large old asylums. At the end of World War Two the old asylums were further discredited as being unsuitable places in which to treat returning war heroes' psychological problems. By the late 1940s the in-patient population of mental hospitals had begun to decline substantially. This was some years before the advent of chlorpromazine in psychiatry in 1951. (It has been claimed that the decline in in-patient populations of mental hospitals can be directly attributed to chlorpromazine, but this claim does not stand up to even the most cursory examinations of the statistical evidence.)

In 1961 Erving Goffman published his seminal work *Asylums*, in which he described the disabling effects of total institutions. In 1961 Enoch Powell, the then Minister of Health, predicted the closure of the last of 'these imperious institutions' (mental hospitals) within a 15-year period (Powell, 1961). In the United States the Kennedy Act was passed in 1963 and gave momentum to the policy of 'decarceration' of psychiatric patients. What was unique, at least in Britain at that time, was the establishment by Laing, Cooper and others of the Philadelphia Association of Kingsley Hall.

Morton Schatzman (Schatzman, 1972) described the community at Kingsley Hall as one in which 'lost souls [could] be cured by going mad among people who see madness as a chance to die and be reborn'. Joe Berke, with Schatzman one of the co-founders of the Arbours Association, was a member of the community at Kingsley Hall. Life in that community was by a number of accounts far from dull. One of the best-known descriptions of life in the community was that of Mary Barnes who, with Joe Berke, wrote an account of her journey through madness at Kingsley Hall (Barnes and Berke, 1991). The Philadelphia Association was a link in a chain of 'counterculture' centres whose other links included experimental drama groups, social scientists of the New Left, leaders of the commune movement, people involved in the broad avant-garde arts and, it must be said, the psychedelic drug culture. Hallucinogenic drugs, notably LSD, were used experimentally and recreationally by members of the community. At that time LSD and cannabis were very much part of the contemporary cultural scene as a means by which inner space could be explored. Timothy Leary was urging people to 'tune in, turn on and drop out'.

In 1970, as earlier chapters in this book have described, Morton Schatzman and his wife Vivian opened their home to a group of people 'who might otherwise have been in mental hospitals'. This initiative led to the setting up of the Arbours Association. In the light of the Arbours founders' well-publicized central role in anti-psychiatry it is perhaps surprising that the association has survived and grown as it has through the past 25 years. The opening sentence of an early Arbours brochure explicitly sets out Arbours' rejection of the all-pervading medical model in British psychiatry. 'We feel it is more helpful and humane to give persons who have been or could become mental patients a chance not to be seen as mentally ill, called mentally ill or treated as mentally ill' (see also above, p. xviii).

Had the Arbours been set up as a private nursing home for well-off distressed people its survival and growth would be attributed simply to market forces. There always has been and always will be a market for places which for a price will accommodate the disturbed and disturbing at their own or relatives' expense. However, although Arbours has provided and continues to provide accommodation and care to private 'guests', its growth has to a large extent been dependent on its ability to attract referrals from the statutory mental health services.

Arbours' therapeutic method uses a great deal of psychoanalytic theory and practice. But in the canons of organic psychiatry, it is an article of faith that psychoanalytic therapy has no role in the treatment of schizophrenia. This is stated as a matter of principle in *Clinical Psychiatry* (Slater and Roth, 1969), a classic reference text of British psychiatry. The authors underline this point of principle by quoting comments made by Freud to Binswanger that the use of psychoanalysis in schizophrenia is a professional error ('*ein Kunstfehler*'). However, Freud's pessimism was not shared by his contemporaries or later psychoanalysts. Karl Abraham among others reported successes in treating schizophrenia using modified psychoanalytic techniques. Hanna Segal, the Kleinian analyst, also published positive accounts of her own work with psychotic individuals. The Arbours is not alone in this country in using psychoanalytic approaches in helping people who might be diagnosed as being schizophrenic or psychotic. Psychoanalytic theory also underpins the therapeutic approach of the Philadelphia Association. Moreover, Bertram Karon and Gary Vandenbos, two American psychoanalytic practitioners involved in the treatment of schizophrenia, have published the results of their work in a book confidently entitled *Psychotherapy of Schizophrenia: The Treatment of Choice* (1981). Their work demonstrates that psycho-analytically-based work can be both helpful and cost-effective.

In Trieste, where the reforms based on the work of Franco Basaglia have been more successfully implemented than most other places in Italy, psychoanalysis is anathema, as are all forms of individual therapy. This hostility is more overtly ideological in Trieste than it is in mainstream British psychiatry. In Italy there is a tradition of mental health workers identifying their work with their politics. Organic psychiatry, on the other hand, masks its ideology in pseudo-science and does so with considerable success. The high professional prestige and salaries enjoyed by psychia-trists bear no real relationship to the reality of their actual knowledge of the causes of the conditions they treat, or to the complexity of the tasks they undertake in mental health services. Behind all the professional dressing up and posturing psychiatrists actually know little more than the geography of the brain. Their main role in services is to write prescriptions for drugs. Most of the drugs they prescribe were discovered by serendipity, that is to say, by giving them to patients on a suck it and see basis. They know little about the specific actions of these drugs and less about the 'illnesses' whose symptoms may or may not respond to them. The prescription pad is the magical fetish object which maintains organic psychiatry's lofty position as the final arbiter on the needs of the 'mentally ill'.

Even at its best, psychiatric prescription-writing can only be pragmatic. There is no formula by which the optimum dose required to achieve a specific effect in a particular individual can be known. All the current mainstream psychotropic drugs have serious and often severe adverse effects. The common iatrogenic hazards of the anti-psychotic drugs (see, for example, the restrained discussion of these hazards in Warner, 1985) seem to be all but ignored in mainstream psychiatric practice. A study based on the experiences of 515 patients in mainstream psychiatric services (Rogers et al., 1993, p. 121) concluded that 'most patients appear to have received most of the available treatments (in particular drugs) for most of the time'. Thus regardless of diagnosis, people receiving treatment from psychiatrists are likely to receive anti-psychotic, anti-depressant and hypnotic medications concurrently. These findings echo repeated similar findings of polypharmacy and cocktail-prescribing reported in many formal studies and clinical audits published over the years in the medical press. I have long held the view that without the mystification of the prescription pad it is probable that any moderate literate person could do the average consultant psychiatrist's job. All that would be required, it seems to me, is a copy of the *British National Formulary* and a home medical dictionary. It is a matter of continuing surprise to me that the busier, less well-paid and more accessible members of so-called multi-disciplinary mental health teams seem to continue to maintain an appearance of admiring the emperor's very old and shabby clothes.

The Arbours Association offers a real alternative to the mental illness services developed and ruled over by the barons of organic psychiatry. The biological determinism of mainstream psychiatry requires nothing more of its patients than that they become the passive objects of the treatments prescribed for them. At the risk of overdrawing the caricature, the most lasting image that I have of most (but not all) of the mainstream psychiatric services that I have worked with and described during the past 25 years has been of universities of helplessness presided over by enforcers of applied passivity. Guests in the Arbours are required to be active participants in seeking more effective means of confronting and negotiating their own ways through their own individual circumstances.

A number of reasons can be adduced as to why Arbours has survived as a mental health service provider despite its apparent incompatibility with the ideology and ethos of mainstream psychiatric services. The British tradition of having services provided by a strong and often radical voluntary sector must have been helpful (although the signs are that the climate is changing). Voluntary sector service provision fits well with the current government policy of introducing market forces into health and social care, but the prospects for new radical voluntary organization initiatives in service provision look more uncertain. I believe that the two most significant factors in Arbours' survival and growth are first, the fact that its services are identified as a radical alternative to mainstream services, and second, the high quality of those services. To deal with the quality issue first, as it is simple to explain. As a number of contributors to this book have stressed the Arbours houses are comfortable, well maintained and have a warm and homely feel about them. Most telling of all to the casual visitor is the fact that the staff are invisible. This invisibility is a measure of the sensitivity, effort and care that the workers put into their jobs. It is possible to feel profoundly uncomfortable in the most luxurious of surroundings if human ambience does not work. The human ambience in the Arbours works because of the effort that has been put into making it work.

The explanation as to why Arbours should survive in what looks on the surface as a hostile climate is also relatively straightforward. It is not psychiatrists who place or arrange funding for people with mental health problems in community services. It is local authority social workers who do this. Social workers in the main are more likely to be sympathetic to the ideology and therapeutic approach of Arbours. Psychodynamic theory has traditionally occupied a significant place in social work training although its influence has waned rapidly. Most social workers will have been exposed to the work of Laing, and probably that of Cooper, and will find some sympathy with it. Another strong element in social work training and consciousness is the notion that advocacy for and with 'clients' is an intrinsic part of the job. The anti-psychiatry traditions of Arbours are thus perceived by social workers as being pro the 'users', 'recipients' or 'survivors' of psychiatric services. Added to these factors, and perhaps most telling of all, is the fact that the medical barony in mainstream psychiatric services offers little or nothing in terms of professional prestige to the social worker. In the so-called multi-disciplinary mental health team the psychiatrist is always the leader, regardless of whether his knowledge or experience is relevant to the tasks in hand. For all these reasons social workers are likely to feel sympathetic to the work of the Arbours and thus feel disposed to make referrals to them.

Earlier I mentioned in passing Cooper's adoption of the term 'the critical movement of and in psychiatry'. David explained the term to me when I interviewed him in his noisy little flat in rue des Entrepreneurs in Paris shortly before he died. During that interview he was completely candid about his own madness, which had alienated him from many of his erstwhile colleagues and comrades. The anti-psychiatry which he had fathered in Villa 21 had died before him leaving him an exile in Paris surrounded by a small but devoted group of followers. He told me of the work he was doing in North Africa and of his enthusiasm for the Italian psychiatric reforms. As our conversation continued it became increasingly clear to me that the anti-psychiatry of Cooper's heyday had simply ceased to be relevant to the Europe of the Eighties. Cooper and his colleagues had lit a torch of enthusiasm in the Sixties which was carried around Europe and beyond. In California Loren Mosher, who had spent a year working with the Philadelphia Association, set up the Soteria project based partly on the notion of 'nontreatment communal care' (Mosher, quoted in Mosher and Berti, 1989) that he had participated in at Kingsley Hall. The

Soteria project continued for 12 years before its funding was withdrawn. Subsequently Mosher went on to establish new communities in Washington DC based on these same principles. Mosher also spent time in Italy studying the reforms and there he met Franco Basaglia.

Basaglia shared many of the concerns and interests of the loose alliance of activists who made up the British anti-psychiatry movement. His writings were influenced by many of the same philosophers and thinkers. Basaglia and his colleagues also rejected the medicalization of madness and described mental hospitals as 'institutions of violence' (Basaglia, 1965, quoted in Scheper-Hughes and Lovell, 1987), setting out to destroy them from within. But Basaglia rejected therapies and therapists in favour of political actions and politically committed volunteer activists. The reforms achieved in Italy were patchy. In some parts of northern Italy mental health services were literally revolutionized but in others they remained and continue to remain as gruesome as they ever were. Basaglia saw madness as being primarily a socio-political issue and focused his efforts on the macrocosmic issues. Basaglia was essentially a political leader, the founding father of the Italian Democratic Psychiatry movement. For Basaglia the plight of the weak, the impaired and the sick 'always had an explicit class meaning' (quoted in Scheper-Hughes and Lovell, 1987, p. xix). The British anti- or critical psychiatry movement was also on the political broad left. However, its political activism was essentially limited to polemics rather than being explicit in the work of its protagonists. There was no single leader of anti-psychiatry, although Laing and Cooper often seemed to have adopted or had thrust upon them the role of gurus. Laing's interests in things mystical made him an ideal candidate for gurudom. Towards the end of his life Cooper increasingly resembled an old testament prophet while preaching 'Orgasmic politics' (Cooper, 1978) to his dwindled band of followers. Both are now gone, leaving behind them enormous legacies of ideas, personal influences and ambivalent feelings. However, had they not embarked on setting up the Kingsley Hall community, the Arbours Association would not subsequently have come into being.

Here we are, a quarter of a century into the history of Arbours at a time which only a madman or a politician would describe as being optimistic. Optimism was the keynote of the Sixties, and inspired the best and worst which emerged from those turbulent times. Anti-psychiatry was founded on optimistic views of human experience that challenged the mechanistic determinism of organic psychiatry. Kingsley Hall was an optimistic and brave (some said foolhardy) exploration of the nature and meaning of madness. Organic psychiatry appears even more secure now in the Nineties than it was in the Sixties. Those among us who are labelled as 'schizophrenics' can now be 'maintained in the community' on monthly depot injections of anti-psychotic drugs courtesy of 'Modecate® clinics'. Those unable or unprepared to attend such clinics can receive their monthly injection in their own homes, lodging houses, prison cells or cardboard boxes. The concerns for the rights of patients pioneered by anti-psychiatry in the Sixties and campaigned for by Mind in the Seventies and Eighties are now perceived as being irreconcilable with their 'needs'. Needs that are defined and met in services shaped and controlled by the ideology of organic psychiatry. As I write this the forces of neo-conservatism in the shape of Sane are in the ascendant. Sane's chief executive Marjorie Wallace has publicly attacked misguided libertarians as being responsible for what she seems to perceive as the crimes of community care. It is within this bleak climate that the Arbours continues to offer a service that can still be described as innovative, a quarter of a century after its inception. A service, for those able or prepared to take it, which offers a real alternative to embarking on a lifetime career as a psychiatric patient. The Arbours Association is still fired by the spirit of optimism of the times in which it was born. Long may it prosper.

16 SCHIZOPHRENIA AND THE FREEDOM TO BE IRRESPONSIBLE

RUTH CIGMAN

A small number of residents in the Arbours communities behave in ways which psychiatrists associate with schizophrenia: they report hallucinations, speak incoherently, and so on. Occasionally one of them has got into some sort of 'trouble', by physically harming either him/herself or another person. Then the police or psychiatric establishment has become involved, often accusing Arbours of negligence and ideological naivety. The view of outsiders tends to be that so-called schizophrenics are not responsible for their actions, and should be constrained from harming themselves or others.

This view includes a theory of mental illness; a popular image, or myth; and (I suggest) a legitimate concern. We are all familiar with the idea that schizophrenia is a chemical imbalance, depriving people of the capacity to take responsibility for their own lives. We are familiar too with horror-story images of madmen on the loose with pick-axes and the like. The horror-story image still holds sway with much of the public and press, although comparable clichés about miserly Jews or mentally defective Negroes are unacceptable in our society. I think this discrepancy is due in part to ignorance, in part to the fact that very disturbed people do occasionally harm themselves or others, raising difficult questions about the limits of freedom. One guest at the Crisis Centre threw a bowl at a therapist in a fit of anger, just missing his eye. Another became pregnant (attracting considerable publicity), though she was obviously far too disturbed to care for a child. Very rarely there is a suicide at Arbours. The cliché about madness and physical danger cannot be summarily dismissed; Arbours has sometimes been accused of doing this, though in reality the problem receives frequent and at times urgent attention.

I should like to discuss the Arbours approach to the problem of responsibility with disturbed people. I also want to comment on the theory of mental illness mentioned above. Personally I have always been puzzled by the debate about whether schizophrenia is a biochemical condition. Premenstrual tension is a biochemical condition. Excitement, happiness, not to mention the great variety of thoughts, feelings, moods, etc., which make up our mental lives doubtless have a biochemical aspect. What does this have to do with responsibility? The question is not whether biochemistry comes into the picture, or whether schizophrenia exists, but whether the people who are known as schizophrenics *may reasonably be treated as responsible for their lives.* You cannot treat newborn infants as responsible for their lives. Nor can you treat a comatose or severely mentally retarded adult this way. You can – this was one of the insights of R.D. Laing – treat deeply disturbed human beings as 'in some respect' responsible for their lives; indeed there is usually so much evidence of understanding and insight that it is absurd not to. The work at Arbours involves a continuing, clinical preoccupation with what this means.

The concept of responsibility attracts a fair amount of muddle. The father of 'Megan', the pregnant woman mentioned above, beautifully articulated this muddle on a television film when he expressed amazement that Arbours considered Megan 'responsible' for her actions. On the contrary, he said, she was so obviously irresponsible. Two concepts of responsibility are being confused here. The first is liberal, and has its main intellectual source in the nineteenth-century work *On Liberty,* by J.S. Mill (1887). Very simply, this concept is expressed in the idea that people should be free to do as they please – to act responsibly or irresponsibly. A minimal qualification to this, as I shall discuss below, is that we should not be free to harm others. The second concept is psychoanalytic, and has its main intellectual source in Freud. Here responsibility is related to the idea that behind our conscious thoughts and actions lie unconscious motives, intentions, phantasies, etc. In this context the aim is to discover the real significance of our motives, etc., and the notion of irresponsibility has no place.

The Arbours approach is to try to reach the 'unconsciously responsible', choosing, intending, etc., part of the person, by interfering as little as possible with the freedom to make responsible *and* irresponsible choices. In other words, a relatively liberal approach to individual behaviour is considered essential if people are to gain insight into their own motives, etc., through communal living. From a theoretical point of view, this may be seen as an application of the free association principle to a residential context. But the approach is not, as so often assumed, essentially a theoretical one. It is based on the fact that many people become more in touch with themselves, less violent and so on, through such means. This happens not because people are psychiatrically undiagnosed, and allowed to do pretty much as they please; it happens because their freedom is balanced by hour upon hour of skilled, sympathetic attention, in which they grow to understand their own behaviour and its effects on others. Freedom and sustained therapeutic attention are the complementary axes with which Arbours works. Through repeated therapeutic and everyday encounters, someone who has been referred as a vaguely threatening, babbling schizophrenic becomes known in the community as a relatively coherent individual, with strengths and weaknesses, likable and dislikable qualities, and so on. The likelihood of irresponsible behaviour then falls into much sharper focus.

I have spoken of the 'relatively liberal' approach of Arbours. Clearly the liberal concept of responsibility, unlike the psychoanalytic one, is one of degree, and the idea that guests at the Crisis Centre are allowed to do exactly as they please (expressed on more than one occasion by the press) distorts the Arbours position. As in any other professional organization, there are differences of opinion. Everyone agrees that a line must be drawn at harming other people, and rather as the social significance of this line has long been debated by philosophers and political scientists, so is its clinical and practical significance a recurrent theme at Arbours. How far should one go, when a guest seems to be gaining insight into his or her own behaviour, to protect other guests and residents from the possible (but extremely unlikely) dangers of an occasional outburst? To what extent should a line be drawn at possible *self*-harm as well as the harming of others, especially when this might conceivably be irreversible?

Such questions arise for every parent who seeks a balance between strict authority and negligence. They arise, as I have said, for social theorists, and naturally they arise at Arbours. In the context of a therapeutic community, they require careful, case-by-case attention, since the weight of risk varies according to individual circumstances, and is always a matter for judgement. It seems sad that discussions in this area are so frequently overshadowed by theory and polemics. R.D. Laing was often accused of excessive theorizing, although he deplored the tendency to regard schizophrenics as types rather than individuals, particularly as types of biochemical disorder. Whether or not there is a biochemical correlate to the disturbance known as schizophrenia, it is undeniable that each patient or guest is different, raising different questions about danger and risk. Laing once said, comparing the understanding of a schizophrenic to an investigation of murder, that each investigation was an original project.

An organization which places so much emphasis on the individual is bound, with the passing of time, to have individual casualties as well as individual successes. Inevitably, given the controversy which exists around mental issues, these casualties are seized upon by the public from time to time. In fact they are exceedingly rare. As a former trainee therapist at the Crisis Centre, my impression was that most of the destructive behaviour arises out of an understandable rage about having to leave. Many guests experience leaving as a cruel eviction from their own homes. In a sense this is precisely the situation they face, at a time when their dependency on the place and the people may be great. They are becoming used to communicating with others, and although individual therapy will continue, they will very likely return to an environment in which medication is a substitute for talking and listening.

It has often been said, against the feminist repudiation of Freud, that Freud was the first person to listen to women. It seems clear that Arbours is the only context in which many of the guests have been enduringly, genuinely listened to. Whether or not their disturbances arise from a biochemical source is irrelevant here. So long as they are regarded as human beings who think, feel and suffer, it is appropriate to attend to their inner worlds in a therapeutic way.

17 ATTENTION

NINA COLTART

It was very pleasing to me to be asked to contribute a chapter to this book. It is a talk I gave in celebration of the Twentieth Anniversary of the Arbours Association. I have been one of their supporters from the beginning, and for six years I had the privilege of being on their Training Committee. During that time I had a special function which meant that I came to know a large number of them in a very special way. It linked up directly with one of my other interests which had been the building up and running of a consultation practice at home: nearly 30 years ago now, it struck me that there was a gap in the London scene where it seemed that a sort of broker was needed. There were not as many good psychotherapists around then as there are now, but even so there were quite a few, and quite a few analysts who too often were short of patients. On the other hand, when I was still working in the NHS, I not only discovered that it is almost impossible to do good, detailed, long therapy there, but also that there were plenty of potential patients for such therapists and analysts and that many of these patients could get together the price of a couple of sessions a week, simply by deciding that having some therapy might be more important than two or three nights in the pub or a visit to the movies. So I started the consultation practice to try to bring the two together and 'match' them if possible, a process I became more interested in as time went by. When I worked for Arbours, all the students to be trained were of course carefully selected by members of the Training Committee; then they would come and see me for a single long discussion, after which I would place them with an analyst for what is the central feature of their three-year training as therapists, the training analysis, which they committed themselves to, three times a week or possibly more, for anything up to eight years. Analysts in training have to do this, too, but have to attend five times a week. In fact, the frequency of sessions is one

of the few things that distinguishes full analysis from analytical psychotherapy. From that meeting I took an interest in the various individuals I
had met that way, during their trainings, and of course this paid off over
the years as they would qualify and start their own practices and I gained
a growing pool of good Arbours therapists to whom to refer new patients
from the consultation service, who did not need or want full analyses.
And I also came to know the senior, pioneering members of Arbours, who
were mostly on the Training Committee, very well over a long period and
continued to observe the growth of Arbours with great admiration. They
built a thorough analytic training for their students, created a low-fee clinic
for patients, established and nurtured their community houses, ran the
Crisis Centre, and earned themselves a unique and respected place on the
London therapy scene.

The capacity for taking for granted what is *there*, which I will speak
about more later in a somewhat different context, is so developed in
human nature that we are in danger of forgetting that the successful
maintenance of community houses for disturbed patients, with resident
therapists, and of the Crisis Centre for short-term acute admissions, was a
new phenomenon in our world 20 years ago. It had certainly been
attempted but on a smaller scale and with less forethought and less skill.
Some individual communities had foundered, run down or fragmented
from lack of good, professional administration and of consistent discipline
among the staff. This lacuna Arbours filled and continues to do so, and I
would like it to be known more widely how hard they struggled, this
handful of dedicated and well-trained pioneer therapists, and against what
odds, not least desperate shortages of funds and also the suspicious, almost
paranoid attitudes to a new development which I am sad to say often
characterizes the outlook of older established professionals such as the
psychoanalysts.

Arbours arose originally, like the phoenix, from the ashes of the first
Kingsley Hall, Ronnie Laing's own early attempt at a therapeutic
community, where Joe Berke and Morty Schatzman – who together we
might say *were* that phoenix – had originally worked. The people who
worked with Laing brought a stunningly (almost shamingly) original idea
to their project, and it was this simple, fundamental idea which was carried
forward into the new embryonic organization, the Arbours, and which has
continued to infuse it with its own power ever since. It may seem
surprising that the revolutionary notion of paying attention to a person
who is labelled Mad, and trying to understand him or her, is not much
more than 30 years old. When I was taught psychiatry in the early 1950s

as a medical student, we were taken in small groups to big psychiatric hospitals, even then commonly known as 'bins' or 'the asylum', and a series of patients was wheeled on before us, sometimes literally, strapped into chairs or straitjackets or both. A consultant would then proudly take them through their paces, demonstrating the signs by which we were meant to learn the nature of madness: one sign I have never forgotten was called *flexibilitas cerea* or waxy passive immobility. A catatonic schizophrenic man was wheeled on, and our consultant pushed and pulled bits of his body into strange unnatural positions where they stayed – eerily – until they were put back. Then another schizophrenic man, who spoke in a cheerful, stream-of-consciousness babble, demonstrated 'word salad', thought disorder and neologisms. A mute woman with a hysterical psychosis displayed the stigmata, clearly oozing blood from her hands and feet. And so on and so forth. We gaped for a while and went away. No attempt was made to give close attention to a patient as a whole person, to engage in any sort of dialogue, however mad-sounding, not even to establish eye contact. The patients were unfortunate objects and likely to stay that way, since, when I started psychiatry, few of the psychotropic drugs had appeared.

Although Arbours has always tried not to use major drugs, as far as is concomitant with relative stability in the communities, I would like to insert a note here about their value, speaking as one who did psychiatry before their advent. They started to come in while I was working as the admitting doctor for the acute wards at the North Middlesex Hospital, and I don't think any psychiatrist who witnessed what a huge difference they made could sincerely argue with their value, *if used judiciously.* It was they which eliminated the hitherto frequent use of the padded cells and the excessive, random use of ECT, and they produced a reduction in severe anxiety states, violent schizophrenic disorders, melancholia and mania which really did provide a good basis to work from. But having put in my plea not to throw out the baby with the bath water, I must add that I would not like you to think the new era of care, understanding and enlightenment has even yet fully dawned: indeed, American psychiatry recently has shown a regressive tendency to revert to complex classification of signs and elaborate use of drugs, as its major diagnostic tools.

What was revolutionary about the early work of R.D. Laing, and people like our Joe Berke and Morty Schatzman, was that prolonged, careful and humane attention was paid to trying to make sense, in context, of what was happening to a mad patient. I am not implying that psychoanalysis did not do this. It was Freud's greatest contribution to the twentieth century that in 1895 he started doing just that; but, with very rare exceptions, psychoanalysts have worked with neurotic patients. Psychotic disturbance has usually been considered to be beyond its scope. The distinctive innovation which Laing, himself a psychoanalyst by training, brought to analytical therapy was to direct the attention of the technique of psychoanalysis to psychotically disordered people, on a holistic basis. It is to this ideal that Arbours dedicated itself, its structure and its trainings and treatments, and does to this day. One of the great strengths of Arbours has always been that it attracts, most often, and from many walks of life, potentially gifted therapists who have a strong sense of vocation. The Arbours policy of not stipulating that applicants must have certain bits of paper registering them as doctors or psychologists, but of relying on skilful selection from a wide spectrum of people who *want to do* therapy, means that they continue to attract gifted people. You can teach a lot of people a lot of things but a first-rate therapist is born, not made, and many of them train and work at Arbours. I believe being a good therapist is a vocation; it did not surprise me to discover that some resident therapists in the communities, who offer holistic care and treatment for extremely disturbed patients, have been nicknamed 'psychiatric monks'.

In order that this great resource should be used to its maximum advantage, certain supportive features have grown and been maintained in the structure of Arbours. One is that there is a definite hierarchy of authority for purposes of administration, consultation, supervision, regulation, treatment and support. It is no good baulking psychological truth, and one truth is that human beings in groups form hierarchies and need authority. Another source of strength is that many of their therapists, trained in the ordinary, psychodynamic programme which has been constructed for their students, move laterally into the communities or the Crisis Centre to work while they are training and also when they qualify, as well as starting to build up their own part-time private therapy practices. And another is the continued source of inspiration represented by the dedication and hard work of the few at the top, and their ceaseless attention to detail and to the maintenance of professional standards and of the Arbours ethos.

These keys to their success over 20 years bring us to the subject I selected for the Arbours Anniversary celebration: *attention* – a subject extraordinarily neglected or overlooked. In all our vast literature, very little attention has been paid to attention. In clinical discussion, public or private, one finds the same neglect. I think this may be to do with its being so taken for granted – it *must* be there as the invisible, essential ingredient – this seems to be a sort of given. Or perhaps we have not developed any kind of language to speak about it. Or perhaps it verges on the religious. Certainly some of those who do attend to it and write about it with clarity are found in religious fields. And there is little more calculated to stir up anxiety and defensiveness in your average analyst than any hint of religion.

In a paper I first published in 1986 called 'Slouching towards Bethlehem', I tried to say something about the faith with a small f that learning to be a therapist requires, and discussed some of the dark passages we have to negotiate, or just plain sit through, when 'not knowing' is a daily experience (Coltart, 1986). Usually not, I am glad to say, with all our patients at once, though there can be days in the early years of running a practice when that is what it feels like. Winnicott used to say that there is a sort of self-regulating ladder among the patients in your practice, and in some extraordinary way they seem to sort themselves out and take it in turns to clamber to the top to be Number 1 mind-blowing problem for a while: to the therapist, that is! This is usually the patient whom you feel you know least about, will never understand and with whom your faith is most severely tested. Then, by dint not so much of thinking – though that certainly has its place in a phase of bafflement – but of perpetual bare attention, light of a sort does eventually dawn, something is unravelled, that patient slides down the ladder and usually, before long, someone else clambers to the top to take that place.

During these extremely testing passages in a treatment when bewilderment and maybe anxiety predominate in the therapist, and despairing feelings, frustration and anxiety in the patient, one's attention is focused sharply with little effort. And it is as a result of this (and we can notice and store away for future reference the sense of inevitability, of cause and effect here) that we begin to understand what is going on. Many of you must know the state directly from within, from times when you have been sitting in a session, with all your skills and experience gathered preconsciously at your sensory and psychological nerve endings, when everything comes together, light begins to shine through the darkness, and you have a brief phase of enlightenment about what is happening between you and your patient; and the gift of communicating an insight in *appropriate language* often suddenly occurs as part of this phenomenon.

So here I am, ten years on from writing 'Slouching towards Bethlehem', still virtually saying the same thing, or returning to aspects of the subject which I obviously feel can never be stressed too much. It is in the early

stages of learning to be analysts and therapists when we are developing
our technique, our confidence and our clinical acumen generally that the
use of 'bare attention' absolutely has to be the scaffolding of everything
else we do. Even when we are doing nothing (or appear to be), sitting in
silence, testing our faith in the process – our constant, perhaps I should
say *only*, attitude is one of 'bare attention'. In this we try to teach ourselves
so continuously to observe, and watch, and listen, and feel, in silence,
that this kind of attention becomes – in the end – second nature. It is the
bedrock of our day's work. And it is as this bedrock that it becomes
forgotten or overlooked.

You will note that I have added an adjective, that I am now calling it
'bare attention'. This is a phrase lifted from Buddhist teaching where it is
also the main feature of the meditation practice, which in turn is the
essential basis of the whole philosophy. I have been involved in both
practices for a long time now and have always found that Buddhism melds
harmoniously with the practice of psychoanalysis in every aspect; I want
to make use of their concept – 'bare attention' – as I think it says even
more clearly something about this skilful capacity which we need to learn
than does the single word 'attention'. That after all can become at worst
an order – Attention! *Achtung*! – or a reminder, a threat or a warning. And
in so doing it becomes a terse command and loses the quality of profound
and self-forgetful opening of oneself to another person. A few months ago
I happened to hear someone talking about the last novel that Aldous
Huxley wrote, which was called *Island* (1962), in which it was said there
were birds whose cry was 'Attention!' Thinking my troubles were over
and that I could plagiarize Huxley, I managed to get hold of the book and
read it eagerly. It does indeed have birds in it which cry out 'Attention',
and they also cry 'Here and now, here and now' – with what I must say
I came to feel was a deadly monotony. The book as a whole I found
dreadfully boring and rather priggish: having only hitherto read some of
the wonderful early novels, among them *Brave New World* (1932) to which
this was supposed to be a kind of long footnote. I had not fully realized
that Huxley's life folded over, as on a hinge, in the late 1930s; at that point
he ran away to America to escape the war and embraced Vedanta which,
although contaminated by a certain amount of loose occult and theistic
embroidery, also contains some of the same philosophy of life as does
austere and atheistic Buddhism. Years of drug experimentation mixed with
this ill-digested Eastern religious diet ruined Huxley's elegant and witty
style. *Island*, his last book, is an attempt to put a great philosophy, which
had taken thousands of years to evolve, into a fanciful modern-day fiction.

I think it is a failure. Those birds, however, do stick in the mind; they are trained to issue continual reminders to the islanders about focusing their attention on the immediate present. As a religious practice, this is fundamental to Buddhism and has a strongly therapeutic effect. This is not surprising since the teaching of Buddhism is what is called *bhavana* or the cultivation of the mind with the direct aim of the relief of suffering in all its forms, however small; the method and the aim are regarded as indissolubly interconnected; so it seems to me logical that neutral attention to the immediate present, which includes first and foremost the study of our own minds, should turn out to be our sharpest and most reliable therapeutic tool in psychoanalytic technique since there, too, we aim to study the workings of the mind, our own and others, with a view to relieving suffering.

Freud said, in a paper in 1912 discussing the technique of psychoanalysis, that the essential constant attitude is one of 'evenly-suspended attention without which the physician is in danger of never finding anything but what he already knows' (pp. 111–12). I quote the founder of psychoanalysis here because, although substantial developments in theory and technique have taken place since his time, it is a salutary experience to return to him occasionally and, on rereading, to come to realize how much of what he said is still true of psychoanalytic therapeutic practice today: I quote also to allay any stirrings of anxiety in those who can receive gratefully what Freud has to offer, but who begin to quail if I draw on sources which not only long pre-date him but which are avowedly religious. When analysts become anxious and defensive at the mention of religious teaching or meditation practice, I have to say that this most often represents prejudice, an ugly characteristic which besets psychoanalysts quite extensively, and which itself, wherever it crops up, deserves attentive study. Perhaps I should add here that I certainly do *not* consider that analytical therapists, doing their daily work in the most professional way possible, have any need or right to introduce religious teachings into that practice; but occasionally, for all our sustained attempts to preserve our anonymity – in order to provide blank screens on which the patients' fantasies may play – patients do tend to discover odd things about us and weave them into their own communications. And then it is very instructive to observe which patients, with what psychopathology, exhibit fury, sarcasm and denigration towards any hint of religious interest in their analysts, and which are respectful, careful or interested. I need hardly say that it is invariably those who are ignorant about religion in any form and whose own upbringing was deprived of any religious or philosophical input, who are the most vociferous in their criticism. This goes for attacks made by analysts, too. Many analysts come from secular backgrounds and are still inclined to hold Freud's own view – that all religion is neurosis – which betrays their discomfort and anxiety in the face of what they may regard as competing systems which threaten them.

In fact the aims and practice of bare attention are exactly the same whether taught by a Buddhist meditation master or by an experienced analyst such as Freud, Searles or Bion. One can summarize these aims by saying they are to calm the mind, reduce anxiety and misery, deepen our knowledge and produce a sustained increase in a sense of well-being, peace and happiness. If I were to present you with a medley of quotations from such teachings, I would be willing to bet that you would find it hard to distinguish one set, the religious, from another, the psychoanalytic. For example:

> The practice of attention is rooted in pure listening, a listening that becomes deepened by trust. We allow ourselves to be aware of our own pain, or that of others, of darkness, upset, unfulfilled yearnings; an awareness is allowed to grow and should not be unthinkingly forged through idealism. This trust then allows direct experience of ourself and others to grow in silence; we strive for being at ease with all workings of the mind, reached through being silently attentive to its endless wanderings, and non-judgemental about them. The silence that embraces rather than resists has a healing touch. Using the silence as a container for anxiety and sorrow brings its own serenity.

This was said by a western Buddhist monk (Sucitto, 1989, p. 3) but, especially in its use of the idea of the container, the concepts of becoming more at ease with silence and being non-judgemental, it could as well be any of a dozen good analytic teachers. In my Bethlehem paper, I was concerned to stress the importance of this capacity to sit in darkness, not knowing. Here I am more concerned to identify some aspects of our professional life and work which require continuous attention in order to sharpen our particular skills and also aspects which may, without our conscious awareness, interfere with the development of our capacity to attend.

One of the most important of these is the subtle effect on all we do of our own basic personality – its type, colouring and biases. In our field, of course, the essential background of our training is our own personal analysis and it is hoped that, as a result of this, the worst of our own neurotic excesses is ironed out. I would like to erase the erroneous idea that a training analysis is in any important way different from an ordinary analytic treatment; it most certainly is not. Anyone who trains to be an analyst is, anyway, probably quite disturbed and is as much in need of their own personal analysis as anyone else who is labelled 'patient'. But there is no such thing as a fully analysed person or a fully treated patient, as Freud rather sadly came to admit in his last great paper 'Analysis terminable and interminable' (1937). We have undertaken to live by what has been called 'the impossible profession'. We emerge from our training analyses, struggle through our lives as analytical therapists with all our own secret inclinations, fantasies, emotions, likes and dislikes, defence systems and residual neurotic tendencies, and it is only by ceaseless attention to ourselves operating *with* ourselves as our only resource that we can more or less make the best of the package.

You *feel* a lot as a therapist – it comes with the job. It is all very well to start off with an idealistic view of oneself as a reflecting mirror or a purveyor of neutral compassionate interest. The every essence of long treatments, which depend entirely on the transference and the counter-transference as their main vehicles, is that the coolness of the theory is soon lost in the thicket of day-to-day work where we have to use our own skills, our personalities and all the patients' communications, including their unconscious projections into us – in fact everything that comes to hand in any one session. Only by the most continuous endeavour to focus an evenly hovering attention on all that is going on can we hope to maintain an equilibrium so that we can continue to *work*, to be of therapeutic value to the patient, and not to disintegrate ourselves. It is within the remit of our job not to act out ill-observed feelings, either deep old stuff of our own or projected into us as intolerable by the patient. Learning about the countertransference and projection in student seminars is only part of it. We used to have rather nervous discussions about such papers as Donald Winnicott's 'Hate in the counter-transference' (1947), and tried to think about it all coolly – at that point – although the very idea that *hate* could feature as part of the countertransference was thoroughly alarming to us. We were still struggling to achieve equanimity and benevolence. All that was necessary, of course, as forewarned is forearmed. But in the day-to-day struggles in the consulting room, it is pretty disturbing actually to *experience* violent emotions, although that is the only genuine way to know what your countertransference is; perhaps, for a while, you may not even know rightly to whom the emotions belong, you or the patient. The hallmark of a true projection is that the patient's buried feelings do somehow get into your own system, and you do learn about them primarily by *feeling* them first and foremost.

Then you have to sort them from your own. Hence the enormous importance of knowing yourself well. Sometimes a willed and heroic attempt to maintain an island of attention in ourselves will keep the treatment going. I like to think of the capacity for bare attention as a sort of observatory in our own minds – and I find an image like this can be a help in times of trouble; even to visualize it briefly when struggling can send a salutary breath of cool breeze over one's heated judgement. At times, all we can hang on to is a recollection of what we know, a sort of flash of memory about the capacity to be attentive or detached.

While on the subject of the constant attention we need ourselves, here is an illustration of its necessity – and its difficulty – taken not from analytic literature, nor from the religious traditions, but from a novelist. I often think that we are all novelists *manqués*; we live through life stories of extraordinary intricacy and suffering, and by participating, change them. For us to pay attention to skilful novelists also can be a rich source of insights we might never have gained elsewhere. Occasionally, one encounters people who say loftily that they 'never read novels', somehow implying that those of us who do have not got much beyond the stage of *Beano* and *Dandy*. Most analytical therapists, however, do read novels as one of their great relaxations and know just how valuable they can be. Anna Freud was a mine of information about Agatha Christie – she could have done a Mastermind appearance on her. The quotation I'm about to give you is from *The Black Prince*, one of Iris Murdoch's dense, packed and psychologically complicated novels. I have rarely come across a passage, anywhere, which tackles so vividly the very subject we are most concerned with: human consciousness and the attention we need to try to give it. Incidentally, she is always deeply concerned with the morality inherent in our task, an aspect I have not even touched on here. Certainly, no analyst has written so vividly and succinctly about it. Here, in doing one of her elaborate digressions on human wickedness, she writes:

> I daresay human wickedness is sometimes the product of a sort of conscious leeringly evil intent . . . But more usually it is the product of a semi-deliberate inattention, a sort of swooning relationship to time . . . the space between the stage where the work is too unformed to have committed itself and the stage where it is too late to improve it can be as thin as a needle . . . most artists, through sheer idleness, weariness, *inability to attend*, drift again and again and again from the one stage straight into the other, in spite of good resolutions and the hope with which each new work begins. This is of course a moral problem, since all art [and I must insert here that I consider the practice of psychoanalysis to be more an art than a science] is the struggle to be, in a

particular sort of way, virtuous . . . We ignore what we are doing until it is too late to alter it. We never allow ourselves quite to focus upon moments of decision; and these are often in fact hard to find even if we are searching for them . . . There is thus an eternal discrepancy between the self-knowledge which we gain by observing ourselves objectively and the self-awareness which we have of ourselves subjectively: a discrepancy which probably makes it impossible for us ever to arrive at the truth. Our self-knowledge is too abstract, our self-awareness is too intimate and swoony and dazed. Perhaps some kind of integrity of the imagination, a sort of moral genius, could verify the scene, producing minute sensibility and control of the moment . . . In fact, the problem remains unclarified because no philosopher and hardly any novelist [or analyst, I would insert here] has ever managed to explain what that weird stuff, human consciousness, is really made of. [Here she embarks on an amazing list of the contents of consciousness.] Body, external objects, darty memories, warm fantasies, other minds, guilt, fear, hesitation, lies, glees, doles, breathtaking pains, a thousand things which words can only fumble at, coexist, many fused together in a single unit of consciousness . . . How can such a thing be tinkered with and improved, how can one change the quality of consciousness? Around '*will*', it flows like water round a stone . . . There is so much grit in the bottom of the container, almost all our natural preoccupations are low ones, and in most cases the rag-bag of consciousness is only unified by the experience of great art or of intense love [and to these I would add 'single-minded attention'] . . . (1973, pp. 154–5; my italics)

I am sure I am speaking for all of us who work in the therapy world when I say that this extraordinary passage expresses better than we can what the daily experience of ourselves in our work is like. I am particularly struck by the image of the will – the continued effort required to keep the will-to-attend functioning, as the crowded waters of consciousness swirl and swirl around.

Tempting as it is to stay with the subject of morality, I think it is too demanding to be part of this chapter; the view that in our work we are morally neutral is quite widespread and needs a strong challenge. I think it is quite simply a wrong view; but it deserves a paper in its own right. I would only issue a signal here to say that I think we need to direct attention to the possibility that we are, whether we like it or not, conveying moral judgements in many of the things we say; they derive from our own views, whether thought out or deeply conditioned, and it seems to me that not, at least, to acknowledge this is to be imprisoned within a straitjacket of denial or to turn a blind eye to important aspects of ourselves, and to what we may be imposing on our patients.

I would, however, like to comment on the need to study our very use of language and ideas. Much of our hard-won theory and conceptualizing becomes gradually metabolized into our own being so that eventually we hardly know, when we think, decide and speak, from whence it comes. There is nothing wrong with this – indeed, I see it as an aim for young therapists still earnestly acquiring the wherewithal of their trade. The machinery should not be creaking; our aim should be to develop a technique marked by ease and spontaneity, drawing primarily on our own *un*conscious as we work and trusting it, not '*thinking*' about everything we do and say, with a visible effort. But this has its own dangers; we become very accustomed to our own ways of thinking, especially if we have the repeated experience, in practice, that they 'work', that is, effect response and change in the patient. The danger is that we may fall off our own tightropes, which represent the need for continually fresh judgements, down on to one of several rocky places: we may become inordinately self-satisfied with a piece of technique, or an idea, and come to use it almost automatically, perhaps even fail to notice when it misses the target, or produces a negative response. We may also become possessive about it, as if we have been original or clever and invented this manoeuvre, when all we have done is stamp with our own personal style an idea first broached by Freud or one of the other very few true innovators of all time, among whom we ourselves are unlikely to be numbered; and unless we rethink a tired old concept each time for each new use with each unique patient, we will certainly undermine its effectiveness. This is one of my major criticisms of the repetition of clichés when teaching such concepts as 'the patient's anxiety about separation' at holiday breaks; students are taught that this is part of a proper tool-kit; often they have had some experience of it in their own analyses, especially at a point where they were dependent or regressed, or working through some sad old trauma of their own; but to trot it out with mechanical regularity from the very beginning of every treatment seems to me to be a gross error and a neglect of the true state of each patient at that moment; in other words, a failure of attention.

This is linked with the tendency in our profession to overestimate our own importance in an unthinking way. Of course, an analytical therapy is important to a patient and of course, as its agent, we become an important figure in the life of that patient. But there are analysts who teach that the analyst is *always* overwhelmingly important, that the rest of external reality pales into insignificance beside the analysis, and at all costs the sort of 'you mean me' type of interpretation must be forced into every exchange in every session. I have no respect for this so-called technique which seems to me at best meaningless and at worst unreal and insulting to the patient's individual self.

Quite apart from this, there is also the tightrope of the transference to be considered. The transference is a huge feature of our sort of therapy; it takes a lot of learning about in all its complexity, and is ever-present. An experienced analyst teaching about transference interpretation may be so deeply familiar with its use that when he or she dissects a reported session, in supervision, with the subtle insertion of 'you mean me' interpretations, it really is transformed and we are thereby enlightened. Whereas an awkward, ill-digested use of this approach can make it sound as if practitioners really do feel themselves to be all-important and omnipotent. And indeed, one does sometimes hear inexperienced workers being a bit boastful or self-satisfied when a patient is passionately grateful or attached to them; the same therapists would be the first to invoke 'negative transference' as the explanation if patients hated them or were being critical. It does not do to forget that when our patients think that we are wonderful or lovable, this is *just as much transference* as is their hate and fear. Freud himself, that sceptical realist, was of the opinion that no particular credit was attributable to the personal charms of the physician (1914).

To return to the cliché about agonized separation anxiety at holiday times, I think, for example, it should always be attentively borne in mind that some patients may be glad to get away from us; that the defences *against* dependency may be far stronger than any true sense of need or closeness or fear of loss; and it is these which should be dealt with by the interpretation. We should avoid the danger of brainwashing our patients into submitting compliantly to a technique just because we happen to have learned how to handle it. There is a particular version of this which can be utterly maddening to lay people and which, if it does not bring the whole of analytic work into disrepute, at the very least renders it ludicrous. As a way of defending themselves against criticism of, say, an automatic interpretation about separation anxiety over a holiday, an analyst may say, 'Oh, but the patient is only resisting; *unconsciously* he is very upset, and is just putting up defences.' Thus the inattentive analyst takes refuge in the 'heads I win, tails you lose' argument; if the patient is overtly distressed, fine; if he is not, then the distress is unconscious. This can be not only infuriating but also shows a neglect of the importance of the defences in question. I must put in here another plea for special attention to those significant words 'only' and 'just' and issue a caveat; that if you hear yourself saying that *anything* about a patient's feelings or

behaviour is 'only' this or 'just' that, *that* requires instant attention: nothing
is *ever* only or just something.

Closely linked with the problem of making assumptions and taking
things for granted is a subject that connects with the question of morality.
It is one through which our profession overlaps with that of the sociologist,
the historian, the teacher of morality on whatever level. I refer to the
subject of manners. Some people's first reaction is that manners, good or
bad, have little to do with the practice of our impossible profession. I
would contend that they have everything to do with it. The study of
manners reveals that they convey subtle messages about the whole
life-philosophy of a person. Manners are not merely a matter of
remembering to say please and thank you; nor are they the fossilized
remnants of a few social lubricants learned in the nursery; nor are they a
thin, superficial coating of falsity. They are the very stuff of how we are
in our being-in-the-world. I would be very suspicious of any analyst or
therapist who maintained that his manners were irrelevant to his behaviour
in the consulting room. They are not a disposable piece of clothing to be
shed in the morning – what do you put on instead? Detached observation
is not a manners-substitute. Just after Ronnie Laing died, there was a
Channel 4 programme about him (1989) which had been made over a
series of visits to his home and consulting rooms. At one point he said:

> Most of the people we meet are very frightened; they are putting up all sorts
> of defences, consciously and unconsciously. They can, however inexperienced
> we are, be guaranteed to be more anxious than us. It is therefore required of
> us that we conduct ourselves with courtesy; the ordinary rules of politeness
> should be *our* rules; we are harmless, and our intentions are on the whole
> benevolent; but we have to show it. It is *not apparent* to a frightened person.
> Don't say 'Trust me', and expect them to. Why should they? It is in the very
> way we *treat* each other that *treatment* itself lies . . .

And speaking of the ways in which we treat each other, you may have
noticed that I have so far not mentioned what is called 'attention-seeking'.
The phrase is ubiquitous, pejorative, and is often the only context in which
my subject for tonight crops up at all. Children are said to be
attention-seeking if they show off or interrupt the grown-ups with
demands and complaints. Adolescents are attention-seeking, whether they
dress eccentrically and make a lot of uncouth noises, or sulk in their rooms
in speechless malaise. Patients, particularly in the 'bins' I was referring to,
are called attention-seekers if they ignore the ward-sister's rules, throw
their food about, pester other people's visitors, cut their wrists or hang

themselves. On the whole the behaviour identified as attention-seeking is unattractive, disruptive and aggravating. The label would be different if you sat down at the piano and played a Mozart sonata from memory; or told a really funny joke at the dinner table; or even with some confidence pointed to a picture you had just painted, or to how lovely your garden was looking. Attention-seekers in our culture are not only desperately and rather pathetically trying to get someone – anyone, really – to notice them at all, but are also infringing one of the most sacred rules of British society, which approximates to some version of being seen and not heard. Seeking attention is very natural, human behaviour. We all need attention and we all seek it; it is just that most of us are more subtle or more successful. The failures – the people described above – remind us uneasily of our secret selves. I suggest that we put the phrase in a rag-bag marked 'Words and phrases to be avoided if possible' along with 'hysterical', 'manipulative', 'selfish', 'greedy' and 'childish', all of which carry a strong negative moralistic flavour, and should have no place in psychotherapeutic clinical descriptions.

I would like to make, finally, a plea for enjoyment – that we should all attend to the very real and, as we go on, growing possibility that we enjoy what we do. Kit Bollas, in his excellent book *Forces of Destiny* (1989), has a chapter on what he calls celebration, the celebrating of good things in a patient's life, of ground gained and of increased happiness, and shows us how celebration may be permitted between analyst and patient. It is still, I note with regret, a subject which has some shreds of taboo hanging around it. I am not talking directly about humour, though the capacity to laugh and to use humour in our work does come with enjoyment and does grow with experience, and does occur in celebration. I am certainly not talking about making light of suffering, not at all; that would be some sort of manic defence and the sooner dismantled the better. I am talking about the fact that, although it may be easier to groan a bit and be grim about our heavy tasks, these tasks after all are self-chosen, and it was with our eyes open that we entered the impossible profession; and with any luck most of us have the sense, most of the time, that we are round pegs in round holes; or that, to use another notion from Bollas's book, we are creating our own destinies as we work through our lives, rather than being doomed to live helplessly, pushed about by Fate. This is one of the most rewarding things about this life, and I see every reason to be attentively conscious, from day to day, of our enjoyment. The late Dr Bion was a distinguished and in some ways rather awe-inspiring analyst. He was one of the first analysts to teach the use and value of silence, and he could be very intimidating in his way of doing it. He would come into a student seminar and sit down and stare at us in silence. He was a large man with a solemn appearance and penetrating dark brown eyes; he made me think that that was what a basilisk would look like. He tended to provoke anxiety and the seminar frequently turned into something rather more like a therapeutic group, and he would then interpret how we were handling the experience. It was unnerving but it was brilliant teaching and I, for one, have never forgotten what he taught us by this unorthodox method. He was teaching a seminar in Brazil in the 1970s, which fortunately for us was recorded and transcribed, and in it he was being more freely talkative than he often was with us, and he said:

> I wonder if it is within the rules of psycho-analysis to be able to laugh at ourselves? Is it according to the rules of psycho-analysis that we should be amused and find things funny? Is it permissible to enjoy a psycho-analytical meeting? I suggest that, having broken through in this revolutionary matter of being amused in the sacred progress of psycho-analysis, we might as well continue to see where that more joyous state of mind might take us. (1980, pp. 94–5)

And in the television programme I referred to, Ronnie Laing said, towards the end:

> Getting through a day is one of the most difficult things in life – and I have come to the conclusion that you can't be miserable for long if you notice that in some small way you are enjoying yourself. Let us try to celebrate and enjoy ourselves – I am really only interested now in trying to entice people with all the skills at my disposal to live in that sort of way if they possibly can.

And I would like to second that. So am I.

CONCLUSION

JOSEPH H. BERKE, CHANDRA MASOLIVER and THOMAS J. RYAN

When we established the Arbours in 1970, our aim was to help persons who were in great emotional turmoil and to do so without their having to be seen, called or treated as 'mentally ill'. Having presented many facets of the Arbours – the communities, the Crisis Centre and the Training Programme – we think that the gap between ideals and actuality is a good place to begin our review of our efforts over the years.

It was easier in the early days to be a 'purist'. Many of the people who sought us out had read *Mary Barnes*, the book Joe Berke and Mary Barnes wrote just after Kingsley Hall closed, and were wide-eyed with enthusiasm (see Barnes and Berke, 1991). We refer, of course, to both the young people seeking help and the young people wanting to be helpers. This is a point the importance of which we did not quite appreciate at the time. Really, the Arbours was established for healers seeking a new framework, a new home, just as much as for anyone else.

Perhaps our first accomplishment was a sense of community. The group was small. The idealism was strong. The 'enemy' was obvious, or so it appeared at the time. The whole paraphernalia of traditional psychiatry had to change.

Almost by magic a couple of dozen people who had been in hospital trickled by. How did they know where we were? Word of mouth, we think. But however they heard of us, they did come and, to use the psychological currency of the Eighties, some were 'well contained' by the residents in our first communities.

We recall one young woman who joined our south London community, Norbury, almost at its inception. At times, she was chaotic, seductive and deceptively aggressive. She had been 'hard done by', and only needed some space to 'hang out' and time to 'keep cool', before she would be able to 'get it together'. The actuality was more complicated and much more difficult. Within weeks the community split around her into two factions. One proposed to be with her and care for her night and day. The other queried the need for this and suggested that she think about her problems, as well as the impact she was having on the other residents. But she didn't want to do so. She only wanted to stay in her bed and play the Queen Bee.

At that time the house co-ordinator was Morty Schatzman. He spent many meetings trying to reach out to 'Ms Bee', and get the two factions to work together, but to no avail. Finally, after a lot of discussion all around, we decided to ask 'Ms Bee' to leave. Needless to say she got very upset. What kind of 'anti-psychiatry' group were we? Didn't we say we provided sanctuary? Didn't we know how much care she needed? And so on. Then she threw down the gauntlet. If she had to leave, all her friends would leave too. Still we held firm to what we thought was necessary, a willingness to explore personal hurts and relationships. So she moved out and took half of the group with her.

We were devastated with confusion and guilt. Maybe she was right. And what would happen to the girl and the community? Most of the residents had left with her. But the truth be told, we were also very relieved that she was out of sight, if not out of mind.

A couple of years passed. From time to time we heard that 'Ms Bee' was in a flat being looked after by former Norbury residents. Then we lost touch. One Sunday, about the Summer of 1976, the Arbours gathered for a 'network meeting' at Morty's home. This was a monthly occasion when Arbours therapists, residents and trainees got together to exchange information about various events and socialize. In the early days of the Arbours, before we could afford a secretary, this was our main administrative meeting as well. Suddenly, there was a knock as the door. In walked 'Ms Bee' accompanied by a young man who looked as if he were her boyfriend.

'I have come here today to thank you for all you have done for me. I'm feeling much better. So I've decided to return to America with my boyfriend. Thanks again for all your help.'

Perhaps we shouldn't have been so surprised. As Ruth Cigman has pointed out, some people need a lot of time and space to take responsibility for their lives. 'Illness' is the reaction when people give up responsibility or have it taken from them. Part of the Arbours ethos is to help people retain or regain such responsibility. The converse is diagnostic labelling, that is, the point when self-responsibility is lost.

When 'Ms Bee' left the community, we were not happy with her decision. But she had the freedom to choose what she wanted. Similarly, we retained our freedom to decide our boundaries, our focus, our points of intervention.

In the 25 years since Arbours was founded, we could cite many examples where a basic respect for people and their problems, as well as for their capacity for 'self-healing', has led them to overcome the diagnosis of, we would say, reputation for, madness and let them get on with the risk of living. This is our second accomplishment.

In this respect, it is worth reiterating that the Arbours is not just a particular household, rather it is a group, a network of like-minded people, wanting to work in a more humane, less restrictive way. This network, in turn, established sanctuaries, special places where people would feel safe, whether pursued by inner demons, or outer ones too.

Our third accomplishment, very much connected to creating an Arbours community and sanctuaries, is that we have sometimes been able to live up to our ideals. This leads to a further conclusion. Sanctuary is not simply a physical place of safety. It is a state of mind. Moreover, since this state of mind takes place in and between people, we can see that our very accomplishment, the Arbours community, was itself a sanctuary, an interpersonal sanctuary, both for the therapists who created it, the men and women who sought our help, and those who came to learn. So the place of safety, the Sanctuary, which we fought to establish is much more than a safe space. Really, it is a network of relationships and a continuity of thought. In this respect, it is noteworthy that almost all the original members of the Arbours, and subsequent generations of Arbours-trained therapists, have managed to continue to work together, rather than fissure and split, as happens in so many other groups. This is certainly no mean achievement, although whether this will continue to be the case, in the face of an ever increasing barrage of financial and bureaucratic pressures, it is hard to say.

But, if sanctuary has been our major accomplishment, what have been and are our difficulties, our failures? To begin, the answer is simple. All too often we have failed to maintain a tolerant state of mind and to treat each other kindly. We refer not only to what passes between therapists and residents, but also among the therapists themselves. So there have been many occasions when the Arbours has been less than a sanctuary.

There are many reasons for these lapses. Let's begin with the inner tensions we have had to withstand. The Arbours has always tried to intervene on behalf of the most disturbed, the most chaotic, the most self-destructive individuals. These are people often labelled borderline or psychotic whom other therapists and facilities would not approach personally or psychotherapeutically. These are the lost souls, the 'patients' most likely to be given physical treatments like extensive tranquillizers or electric shock and enforced hospitalization.

The more chaotic and destructive people are, the more they try to deal with this disturbance by evacuating it into others by physical and psychological means. In short, they are powerful projectors of emotional worlds which are oppressive, violent and extremely painful. Is it any wonder that caregivers may wish to keep their patients at arm's length? Yet we have tried to reach out to these people, rather than keep them away. If anything, we encourage them to share these experiences with us.

Not surprisingly it is very difficult to retain emotional openness to the terrible experiences we are expected to hold in ourselves. There is a high burnout rate. People get tired. They become less than containing. Instead of holding these projections, they project them back, towards the residents, or towards each other.

These problems also reflect the fact that we have often reacted to despair with omnipotence, surely another form of non-containment. In the early years of the group especially, we thought that no one was too wounded, too destructive to help. In fact this is not true, and there have been quite a few residents and guests (Ms Bee was a good example) who left us feeling helpless and hopeless. Basically these have been times when we refused to learn our limitations and boundaries.

Both at the Crisis Centre and the communities the Arbours therapists have tried to deal with these problems by being open with each other. Although I think we succeed more than most other groups, where senior therapists are rarely open to junior staff, we still have a long way to go. This is particularly true in the interfaces between Arbours facilities. By which we mean that although Crisis Centre therapists may be open with each other, they are not necessarily open to the community co-ordinators, or Training Programme teachers. And it is in these interfaces that a lot of tensions brew.

A second dilemma has to do with insight. For the 'sanctuary', and in particular we refer to the tolerant, accepting, holding state of mind, to be effective, it has to be able to be reflective, capable of insight. But insight is something that many of the people who come to us for help find exceedingly painful. So they attack, again by physical actions and projective processes, our capacity to think. Why? Because they don't want to think. A big aspect of our omnipotence was to believe that everyone wanted to think, or could be coaxed to do so. Again, many grey hairs showed us that this was not the case. Many people just want to shut off and shut down, even though they may have given out flickers of thought, of insight, of the wish to change. Too often we have been blinded by the flickers and haven't paid enough attention to the basic intention. So instead of therapy, there has been conflict.

It is very hard to maintain our ideals and idealism in the face of such pressures not to think and not to feel. How much easier it is to listen to the siren call of drugs in order to shut out feelings and shut people up. This reflects the tensions that impinge on us from within ourselves. Yet, it is also necessary to review the strains that come from without. In the early days of the Arbours this was the hostility of colleagues. But to a certain extent this hostility was also useful. It led to 'us' and 'them' tensions, always a potent force for group solidarity.

Nowadays the hostility of colleagues still exists, but it is not so obvious. Indifference is much more a problem. The kind of indifference that minimizes referrals of individuals we can most easily help. By this we mean individuals who may be acutely depressed or breaking down for the first time. Instead we tend to be referred people with the most intransigent problems, people about whom others have given up and don't want to engage.

Similarly, the Centre and the communities get a lot of calls about young men and women who mutilate themselves. Typically, a social worker will phone up. 'Will we admit a cutter?' Our response usually includes, 'You mean, would we consider helping a human being who cuts herself?' But in many respects our clients are the least of our worries. The worst is having to deal with the pervasive bureaucracy that envelops every intervention.

The 1992 government White Paper on mental health (*The Health of the Nation*, 1992) was supposedly designed to enable people to get help for mental problems. In practice, the opposite is the case. It has meant that individuals have to pass through a further layer of social workers, who often seemed to be charged with the task of obstructing support, rather than facilitating it.

Let us not be unjust. We have met and continue to meet social workers who act promptly and efficiently. Yet, in the main, the Crisis Centre has a long waiting list of people who would like to come in, but can't get grants, even though they are eligible for them. To a lesser extent the same holds true with the communities. The problem is most acute for people who need limited stays. One would think that short stays would be preferred as they are less costly. Our experience at the Crisis Centre is that it is practically impossible to get social service or local health authority funding for a client unless they have had a long career as a patient and would become a resident for months or years. Conversely, it is getting more difficult to get grants for residents of our communities, who need assured funding over longer periods.

But even when funding is agreed the contracts we are now asked to sign are so complicated and complex, that it is a wonder anyone could comply with them. The net effect is that more and more administration becomes necessary for every resident at the Crisis Centre and communities. So the relative proportion of monies spent for direct clinical help becomes less and for administrative hassle becomes more.

If this weren't bad enough, the social services and local health authorities try to dictate how we should practise. We are told how cold the fridge has to be, how hot the air has to be, the size of the rooms, the number of therapists, the size of the fire signs, the width of the doors, and so on. Most benignly this arises because the Arbours is so unique that no one can quite figure out how we should be. So the Centre and communities become lumped with the category of old people's homes. The regulators then regulate accordingly. What no one asked about, or no one seems to care about, are the intangible qualities that differentiate us from other facilities: about the willingness of the RTs to get up in the middle of the night to talk to a guest, about the help that residents and guests give to each other, about insight and respect and dignity.

Nonetheless, government regulations exert overt and covert coercion to institutionalize both the Centre and the communities. By institutionalize we mean that relationships are bound by external rules, rather than the direct needs of the guests and residents. Conformity replaces spontaneity. Administrative procedures supersede clinical judgement. There is little room for taking risks, that is, to live, rather than to batten down the hatches and behave.

Fundamentally we have aimed to help ourselves and those who seek our help, to become self-directed, rather than other-directed. Or, to put it another way, we have tried to break through the bounds of self-alienation, whereby 'others' take over control of one's life. This is commonly seen in what is called mental illness, when a person's entire life becomes directed by internalized others and the person or subject forgets who he or she is. Such a person lives in a world of falsifications whereby he may not even know that a 'true', 'real', 'authentic' self exists. In these instances the doctor, therapist, parents, whoever, simply serves as a representation of alienated and alienating internal figures and relationships.

Most insidiously, this means that we, as therapists, become more concerned with re-covering, than discovery; more preoccupied with playing safe, than enabling and empowering those people who may wish to do so, to descend into their darkness and to emerge renewed.

In the face of all these pressures, will it be possible to remember our vision and keep our integrity? Or will we become a somewhat offbeat, but basically conventional purveyor of therapy? We do have some major projects in the wings, to establish another long-stay community and expand our Consultation Service. But it may be better to lay low, or even become smaller and provide fewer services well, that is, to heed our ethos, rather than expand and succumb to outside pressures as well as the inner forces we have delineated.

Perhaps it is possible to phrase this dilemma in another way. Can the Arbours remain an alternative sanctuary, a place where, as one former guest at the Crisis Centre put it, 'I was able to emerge to find my dignity intact and my options still open'?

Will the Arbours succeed? Have we succeeded so far? This is a strange question. If we do not cure, we try to do no harm. We hope that people who come to us for help may find the selves they have lost, and the soul they never knew existed. Perhaps given time, given luck, they may hear the beat of their hearts and be able to elucidate the rhythm.

The task remains to comprehend the knots that bind the heart and soul, and to bring the 'treat', or joy, back into treatment. Then people can ascend from the abyss of self-torment and rediscover the inherent satisfaction of making bonds with each other and to life itself.

PUBLICATIONS ABOUT ARBOURS

BOOKS, PROFESSIONAL JOURNALS AND MAGAZINES

Berke, J. (1973) 'The Arbours Association', *Self and Society*.

Berke, J. (1979) 'I haven't had to go mad here', *Mind Out* no. 36.

Berke, J. (1979) *I Haven't Had To Go Mad Here*. Harmondsworth: Pelican.

Berke, J. (1981) 'The case of Peter and Susan: the psychotherapeutic treatment of an acute psychotic episode at the Arbours Crisis Centre', *Journal of Contemporary Psychotherapy* 12(2):75–87.

Berke, J. (1982) 'The Arbours Centre', *International Journal of Therapeutic Communities* 3(4):248–61.

Berke, J. (1983) 'An alternative sanctuary: the Arbours Crisis Centre', in U. Rueveni, J. Speck and R. Speck (eds) *Therapeutic Intervention: Healing Strategies for Human Relations*. New York: The Human Sciences Press.

Berke, J. (1987) 'Arriving, settling-in, settling-down, leaving and following-up: stages of stay at the Arbours Crisis Centre', *British Journal of Medical Psychology* 60:181–8.

Berke, J. (1987) 'El terapeuta residente: un estudio del sistema de terapia en residencia en el Centro de Crisis Arbours', in A. Espina and G. Sancho (eds) *Estructura Borderline, Psicosis y Feminidad*. Madrid: Editoria Fundamentos.

Berke, J. (1990) 'The Arbours, 20+ years', *British Journal of Psychotherapy* 7(2):204.

Berke, J. (1990) 'Conjoint therapy within a therapeutic milieu: the crisis team', *International Journal of Therapeutic Communities* 11(4). [This volume, Chapter 7.]

Berke, J. (1990) 'The network', *Keeping Abreast*, December.

Berke, J. (1990) 'Reflections of Arbours', *International Journal of Therapeutic Communities* 11(4).

Berke, J. (1990) 'The conjoint therapy of severely disturbed individuals within a therapeutic milieu', *International Journal of Therapeutic Communities* 11(4). (In Danish: 'Conjoint terapi i et terapeukisk miljo: Kriseteamet', *Agrippa: Psykiatriske Tekster* (1991) 13. argang, nr. 1–2. In Spanish: 'Co-terapia con individuos severamente perturbados', *Clinica y Analysis Grupal* (1992) 14(2).)

Berke, J. (1994) 'Confusional states at the Arbours Crisis Centre', *Therapeutic Communities* 15(1):39–48. (In Spanish: 'Estados confusionales en elcentro de crisis Arbours', *Clinica y Analysis Grupal* 15(2).)

Berke, J. (1994) 'Psychotic interventions at the Arbours Crisis Centre', *British Journal of Psychotherapy* 10(3):372–82. [This volume, Chapter 12.]

Berke, J. (1994) 'From psychiatry with love', *Metanoia* Spring: 23–30.

Berry, D. and Williams, M. (1983) 'First aid in mental health', *Open Mind*.

Coltart, N. (1990) 'Attention', *British Journal of Psychotherapy* 7(2):164–74. [This volume, Chapter 17.]

Elkaim, M. (1977) 'Interview de Laura Forti et Andrea Sabbadini', in M. Elkaim (ed.) *Reseau alternative a la psychiatrie.* Paris: 10–18.

Fanning, A. (1990) 'The placement: my training ground', *International Journal of Therapeutic Communities* 11(4). [This volume, Chapter 14.]

Forti, L. (1978) 'Il Crisis Centre di Londra: un esperimento di psichiatria alternativa', *Aut-Aut* 165/166:205–20.

General Practitioner (1973) 'Crisis Centre set up to combat stress'.

Hobson, J. (1974) 'Suppport for those in acute distress', *Doctor.*

Hudson, P. (1990) 'We never promised you a rose garden', *International Journal of Therapeutic Communities* 11(4). [This volume, Chapter 11.]

Jenkins, M. (1988) 'Fragmentation et reconstruction', in *Le Dedans et le dehors.* Lyon: Cesura.

Macario, M. (1990) 'Attarverso lo specchio'. Forte dei Marmi: Centro Studi Psichiatria e Territorio.

Masoliver, C. (1990) 'Learning co-ordination', *International Journal of Therapeutic Communities* 11(4). [This volume, Chapter 5.]

Melville, J. (1978) 'Helping people to survive a crisis', *New Society.*

Mind Out (1977) 'Crisis point'.

Navarro, T. (1990) 'A holding environment', *International Journal of Therapeutic Communities* 11(4). [This volume, Chapter 3.]

New Psychiatry (1975) 'Arbours as part of Mental Health Services Directory'.

Robinson, T.J. (1974) 'The Arbours way through madness', *Community Care.*

Ryan, T.J. (1990) 'Twenty years on', *International Journal of Therapeutic Communities* 11(4). [This volume, Chapter 1.]

Sabbadini, A. (1973) 'Le comunità antipsichiatriche Inglesi', *Aut-Aut* 135:59–73.

Sabbadini, A. (1975) 'Il Crisis Centre di Londra: un esperimento di psichiatria alternativa', *Avanti!.*

Sabbadini, A. (1990) 'The Arbours Association', *British Psycho-Analytical Society Bulletin* 26(6):43.

Sabbadini, A. (1992) 'Un alternativa psicoterapeutica alla psichiatria', *Inventario* 6:9–23.

Schlunke, J.M. and Garnett, M.H. (1984) 'Ideal structure and defence in a small therapeutic community', *International Journal of Therapeutic Communities* 5(1):38–46.

Seu, I.B. (1989) 'A year in the life of a therapeutic community: some considerations', *International Journal of Therapeutic Communities* 10(1):29–37. [This volume, Chapter 4.]

Stokeld, A. (1990) 'Building on metaphors', *International Journal of Therapeutic Communities* 11(4). [This volume, Chapter 10.]

NEWSPAPER AND MAGAZINE ARTICLES

The American (1977) 'Work of Arbours Crisis Centre'.

The American (1977) 'Arbours help distressed people'.

Bailey, A. (1982) 'The shock of self-awareness', *Harper's and Queen*.

Bailey, A. (1974) 'Haven at breaking point', *Daily Telegraph Magazine*.

Bell, B. (1973) 'A place for people in crisis', *International Herald Tribune*.

Descamps, C. (1983) 'Les libres espaces du Docteur Joseph Berke', *Le Monde Dimanche*.

Levine, S. (1973) 'Alternative to a mental hospital', *Jewish Chronicle*.

Levine, S. (1973) 'The widow's mite', *Jewish Chronicle*.

Lowe, S. (1973) 'Where to go for help: the story of a crisis centre', *Over 21*.

Miller, J. (1981) 'A sanctuary in time of crisis', *Jewish Chronicle*.

Read, S. (1974) 'Living to learn', *The Sunday Times*.

Reader's Digest (1983) 'Unique treatment'.

Rose, J. (1977) 'Mental illness: a growing communal problem', *Jewish Chronicle*.

Stacey, J. (1984) 'Havens for people in crisis!', *Hornsey Journal*.

Triunfo (1973) 'La antipsiquiatria'.

Winn, D. (1983) 'Full-time therapy', *The Observer*.

REFERENCES

Abram, Jan (1992) *Individual Psychotherapy Trainings: A Guide*. London: Free Association Books.

Barnes, Mary and Berke, Joseph (1991) *Mary Barnes: Two Accounts of a Journey through Madness*, 3rd edn. London: Free Association Books.

Basaglia, Franco (1965) 'Institutions of violence', in Nancy Scheper-Hughes and Anne M. Lovell (eds), *Psychiatry Inside Out: Selected Writings of Franco Basaglia*. New York: Columbia University Press, pp. 59–85.

Bateson, G., Jackson, D.D., Haley, J. and Weakland, J. (1956) 'Toward a theory of schizophrenia', *Behavioral Science* 1:251.

Berke, Joseph H. (1977) *Butterfly Man*. London: Hutchinson.

Berke, Joseph H. (1990) 'Reflections on Arbours', *International Journal of Therapeutic Communities* 11(4).

Berke, Joseph H. (1981) 'The case of Peter and Susan: the psychotherapeutic treatment of an acute psychotic episode at the Arbours Crisis Centre', *Journal of Contemporary Psychotherapy* 12:75–87.

Berke, Joseph H. (1987) 'Arriving, settling-in, settling-down, leaving and following-up: stages of stay at the Arbours Centre', *British Journal of Medical Psychology* 60:181–8.

Bollas, C. (1987) *The Shadow of the Object: Psychoanalysis of the Unthought Known*. London: Free Association Books.

Bollas, C. (1989) *Forces of Destiny: Psychoanalysis and Human Idiom*. London: Free Association Books.

Boyers, Robert and Orrill, Robert (eds) (1972) *Laing and Anti-Psychiatry*. London: Penguin.

Coltart, Nina (1986) 'Slouching towards Bethlehem . . . or thinking the unthinkable in psychoanalysis', in *Slouching Towards Bethlehem . . . And Further Psychoanalytic Explorations*. London: Free Association Books. 1992, pp. 1–14.

Cooper, David (1967) *Psychiatry and Anti-Psychiatry*. London: Tavistock Publications.

Cooper, David (ed.) (1968) *The Dialectics of Liberation*. London: Penguin.

Cooper, David (1978) *The Language of Madness*. London: Penguin.

Crick, Bernard and Robson, William (1970) *Protest and Discontent*. London: Penguin.

Fabietti, U. (1982) 'Rito' in G. Einaudi (ed.), *Enciclopedia Einaudi*. vol. XV: 542–51.

Fanning, Alexandra (1990) 'The placement: my training ground', *International Journal of Therapeutic Communities* 11(4):215–26. [This volume, pp. 126–39.]

Fenichel, Otto (1946) *The Psychoanalytical Theory of Neurosis*. London: Routledge & Kegan Paul.

Freud, S. (1912) 'Recommendations to physicians practising psycho-analysis', in James Strachey (ed). *The Standard Edition of the Complete Psychological Works of Sigmund Freud*, 25 vols. London: Hogarth, 1953–73, vol. 12, pp. 111–20.

Freud, S. (1914) 'Observations on transference love'. *S.E.* 12, pp. 159–71.

Freud, S. (1937) 'Analysis terminable and interminable'. *S.E.* 23, pp. 216–53.

Goffman, Erving (1961) *Asylums*. Harmondsworth: Penguin.

Haringey Social Services (1987) 'Guidelines for residential care homes'. London: London Borough of Haringey.

Hoffman, L. (1990–1991) 'How I changed my mind again', *Context: A News Magazine of Family Therapy*, no. 7, p. 30.

Huxley, A. (1932) *Brave New World*. London: Chatto & Windus.

Huxley, A. (1962) *Island*. London: Chatto & Windus.

Karon, Bertram P. and Vandenbos, Gary R. (1981) *Psychotherapy of Schizophrenia: The Treatment of Choice*. New York: Jason Aronson.

Kennard, David (1994) 'Editorial', *Therapeutic Communities: The International Journal for Therapeutic and Supportive Organizations* 15(2):75–6.

Lacey, Ron (1983) 'Interview with David Cooper', *Open Mind*, no. 3, p. 8.

Laing, R.D. (1970) *The Divided Self*. London: Pelican Books.

Malcolm, J. (1981) *Psychoanalysis: The Impossible Profession*. New York: Knopf. London: Karnac, 1988.

Mill, J.S. (1887) *On Liberty*. London: Longman, Green & Co.

Mosher, Loren and Berti, Lorenzo (1989) *Community Mental Health: Principles and Practice*. New York: W.W. Norton & Co.

Murdoch, Iris (1973) *The Black Prince*. London: Chatto & Windus.

Neville, Richard (1971) *Playpower*. London: Granada Publishing.

Powell, Enoch (1961) 'Emerging patterns for mental health services and the public', *Proceedings of a Conference, 9 and 10 March 1961*. London: National Association for Mental Health.

Rogers, Anne, Pilgrim, David and Lacey, Ron (1993) *Experiencing Psychiatry: Users' Views of Services*. Basingstoke: Macmillan.

Rose, M. (1986) 'The design of atmosphere: ego-nurture and psychic change in residential treatment', *J. Adolescence* 9:49–62.

Scull, Andrew (1979) *Museums of Madness*. Harmondsworth: Penguin.

Schatzman, M. (1972) 'Madness and morals', in Boyers and Orrill (eds), pp. 181–208.

Silver, D., Cardish, R. and Glassman, E. (1987) 'Intensive treatment of characterologically difficult patients', *Psychiatric Clinic of North America* 10:219–45.

Slater, Eliot and Roth, Martin (1969) *Clinical Psychiatry*. London: Bailliere, Tindall and Cassell.

Speck, R.V. and Attneave, C.L. (1973) *Family Networks*. New York: Pantheon.

Sucitto, The Ven. (1989) *The Forest Newsletter* (Journal of the Amaravati Buddhist Monastery) 3.

Szasz, Thomas (1961) *The Myth of Mental Illness*. New York: Harper.

The Health of the Nation (1992) *The Health of the Nation: A Strategy for Health in England.* London: HMSO, Cm 1986.

Warner, Richard (1985) 'Antipsychotic drugs: use, abuse and non-use', *Recovery from Schizophrenia: The Political Economy of Psychiatry.* London: Routledge & Kegan Paul, pp. 239–67.

Winnicott, D.W. (1947) 'Hate in the counter-transference', in *Collected Papers: Through Paediatrics to Psychoanalysis.* London: Tavistock.

Winnicott, D.W. (1965) *The Maturational Processes and the Facilitating Environment.* London: Hogarth.

Winnicott, D.W. (1975) *Playing and Reality.* London: Tavistock Publications.

INDEX